HISTORY OF DeKALB COUNTY TENNESSEE

By WILL T. HALE

*Author of "A History of Tennessee and Tennesseans,"
"The Indians and Tennessee Pioneers,"
"True Stories of Jamestown, Virginia," and Other Books*

Southern Historical Press, Inc.
Greenville, South Carolina

This volume was reproduced from
An 1915 edition located in the
Publisher's private Library

All rights reserved. No part of this publication may be reproduced,
stored in a retrieval system, transmitted in any form, posted
on to the web in any form or by any means without
the prior written permission of the publisher.

Please direct all correspondence and orders to:

www.southernhistoricalpress.com
or
SOUTHERN HISTORICAL PRESS, Inc.
PO Box 1267
375 West Broad Street
Greenville, SC   29601
southernhistoricalpress@gmail.com

Originally published: Nashville, TN. 1915
ISBN #0-89308-935-4
All rights Reserved.
Printed in the United States of America

Dedicated to
CHARLIE, HERBERT, HILDA
AND HOWELL

PREFACE AND ACKNOWLEDGMENT.

I HAVE thought the virtues and affairs of the people of my native county worthy of chronicling and trust there is a place among them for this little book. It is finished with the haze and hush of Indian summer about me and under the spell of the old hills. It is easy to see once-familiar faces, to hear remembered voices, to recall the little activities on farms and in villages, and I cherish the fact that I was once a part of all this. It should not be a matter for wonder, then, that I often feel what Burns felt when he gave expression to his perpetually quoted wish:

> That I for poor auld Scotland's sake
> Some useful plan or book could make,
> Or sing a sang at least.

The works which have been helpful are named where quoted. Very valuable, indeed, have been two musty account books referred to repeatedly herein; they have helped so much to illuminate a bygone time. The first is that of the Liberty physician and merchant, Ebenezer Wright, dated from April 22, 1832, to June 18, 1833. The second belonged to Dr. John W. Overall, of Alexandria, and dates from 1830 to 1834, but was afterwards used by his father, Col. Abraham Overall. While I never had much fondness for figures, these two documents, with all that they reveal in and between the lines, proved as interesting as romance. I must be pardoned for referring to them so often as well as for intruding my own recollections. Many individuals have offered data and suggestions, among them H. H. Jones, L. E. Simpson, Miss Effie Simpson, Mrs. Josie Davis, M. A. Stark, Rob Roy, Isaac Cooper, Dib Dinges, J. F. Roy, Alexandria; Mrs. Lizzie Hale, Mrs. Belle Overall, Mrs. C. L. Bright, W. L. Vick, T. G. Bratten, J. F. Caplinger, Liberty; Dr. R. M. Mason, Temperance Hall; Dr. T. W. Wood, Bellbuckle; Mrs. Rachel Payne, Watertown; Mrs. S. W. McClellan, Lieut. B. L. Ridley, Murfreesboro; Rev. J. H. Grime, Lebanon; Rev. J. W. Cullom, Triune; Hon. Norman Robinson, Allan Wright, Dowelltown; Ralph Robinson, Sparta; Rev. Van N. Smith, Laurel Hill; Horace McGuire, B. M. Cantrell, Smithville; Rev. G. L. Beale, Springfield; James H. Fite, Anthony, Kans.; John K. Bain, Shreveport, La.; Thomas J. Finley, Celina, Tex.; James H. Burton, Summers, Ark.; I. T. Rhea, M. L. Fletcher, Robert Quarles, Jr., H. Leo Boles, A. B. Hooper, Tal Allen, Isaiah White, Hon. J. W. Byrns, L. J. Watkins (a most competent proof reader for the Methodist Publishing House), and officials of the State and Carnegie Libraries, Nashville.

But for the following these annals could not have been written: My brother, H. L. Hale, Liberty, born about 1855, descendant of the pioneers Benjamin Hale and Abraham Overall; Ed Reece, Nashville, son of a hero of three wars, Capt. Jack Reece; Rev. Petway Banks, Dowelltown, born about 1857 and one of the purest citizens the county ever produced; James Givan, born in 1839, descendant of a first settler, a splendid type of citizen, and the best authority on local history around Liberty; Livingston Tubb, Alexandria, grandson of the patriot and pioneer Col. James Tubb; James Dearman, Smithville, born in 1851 of pioneer stock and the soul of helpful courtesy; Riley Dale, born in 1841 or 1842, grandson of pioneer William Dale and a man of correct walk; and Dr. J. B. Foster, born in Liberty in 1839, but now an honored physician of Meridian, Miss., a genius whose remarkable memory is as full and reliable as the famous diary of Samuel Pepys.

NASHVILLE, TENN.

TABLE OF CONTENTS.

CHAPTER. PAGE.

I. WHEN TENNESSEE WAS YOUNG.................... 1
   Once a County of North Carolina—Becomes a State—Memorials of a Vanished Race—Indian Tribes and Their Depredations—First Settler of DeKalb County—Indian Battle Near the Site of Liberty—Game.

II. DEKALB COUNTY ESTABLISHED—OFFICIALS.......... 9
   Bill to Erect the County—Sundry Changes in the Line—Organization of County, Circuit, and Chancery Courts—Topography—Resources and Leading Crops—Live Stock—Principal Streams—Early Mills—Politics—County Officers—Senators and Representatives.

III. THE OLDEST VILLAGE............................ 22
   First Settler Arrives at Liberty—Sketch of Adam Dale—First Merchants—Rise of the Dale Mill Settlement—Present Business Directory—Changes Since Early Times—Reminiscences of Mrs. Payne and Dr. Foster—Postal Affairs—Professional Men—Landmarks.

IV. PASTIMES OF THE FOREPARENTS.................... 39
   Social Matters—Primitive Music—Horse-Racing—Ariel, Noted Racer—Musters Great Occasions—The Chase—Hospitality—A Bibulous Generation—Cheapness of Intoxicants.

V. FARMING AND MERCHANDISING...................... 48
   Land Warrants—Hemp and Cotton Crops—Breeds of Stock—Prices for Produce—The Day of Homespun Clothes—The Village Stores and Long-Ago Prices—Men's and Women's Fashions.

History of DeKalb County

Chapter.	Page.

VI. RELATING TO EDUCATION.................................. 56

Old Field and Other Schools—Textbooks of Old Times — Punishments in School — Games — Earliest School in the County—Early and Latter-Day Tutors—Educational Institutions at Liberty, Alexandria, and Smithville.

VII. RELIGIOUS HISTORY.................................. 67

Salem Baptist Church—First Ministers, Deacons, and Clerks—Exhorters—Other Baptist Churches—Methodism and Its Two "Wings"—Interesting Personal Mention—Cumberland Presbyterians and Disciples—Memories of Rev. J. W. Cullom.

VIII. ANNALS OF ALEXANDRIA.................................. 88

The Pioneers—Incorporation—Business Men of Past and Present—Professional Men—Banks—Journalism—Milling Interests—A. and M. Association—Colored Fair—Personal References.

IX. CONCERNING SLAVES AND FREE NEGROES.................. 98

Negro Insurrections—Some Owners of Slaves—Locally Popular Types—A Colored Infidel—Three Notable "Runaways"—A Pathetic Story—Family of Free Negroes—Ante-Bellum Laws—Negroes in the War.

X. STAGECOACH AND TAVERN DAYS.......................... 106

The Turnpike Company Incorporated—The Route Surveyed—A Tragedy—Old Stage Road—Noted Taverns—General Jackson and Other Notables—Balls—Sligo—Scenery.

XI. THE COUNTY SEAT.................................. 119

"Macon" First Name Selected—Public Buildings—Incorporation—Names of Lawyers and Judges—Early and Late Business Men, Physicians, Postmas-

History of DeKalb County

CHAPTER. PAGE.

ters, and Others—Banking and Journalism—Hotels—Necrological.

XII. HISTORICAL JETSAM..................... 128

Physical Giants—Tall Men and Short—Two Erudite Physicians—Mysterious Disappearances—Story of a Monument—Study in Names—Noted Expatriates—Folk Stories.

XIII. SMALLER VILLAGES OF THE COUNTY.............. 139

Temperance Hall—The Stokeses and Other Families—Merchants, Physicians, and Others—Sketch of Dowelltown—The Gray Graveyard—Schools—Laurel Hill—Past and Present History—Forks-of-the-Pike and Keltonsburg.

XIV. IN THE EARLY WARS..................... 151

Revolutionary Soldiers—Veterans of 1812—Captains Tubb and Dale—Was There a Third Company?—Black Hawk War Veterans—DeKalb Troops in the War with Mexico.

XV. SECESSION—DEKALB CONFEDERATES............... 162

The Question of Secession—How DeKalb County Voted—Period of Intense Excitement—Call for Confederate Troops—Muster Rolls of DeKalb Confederates.

XVI. STOKES'S CAVALRY..................... 185

Companies from DeKalb County—Promotions, Resignations, and Deaths—Muster Rolls—In Many Engagements in Various Parts of the State—Sketch of General Stokes.

XVII. BLACKBURN'S AND GARRISON'S FEDERALS.......... 194

Sketches of Colonel Blackburn and Captain Garrison—Blackburn a Captain at Eighteen—Officers and Privates—Affair at Shelbyville—Casualty List.

History of DeKalb County

Chapter.	Page.

XVIII. Progress of the Big War................... 208

    Battles in the County Named—Morgan's Command—Camps at Liberty—Capt. Thomas Quirk—Battle of Milton—Scouting from Liberty—Exciting Days.

XIX. Personal Experiences........................ 218

    Noncombatants in War Times—Allison's Squadron—A Race and a Skirmish—Anecdote of Reece and Allison—Minor Tragedies—Skedaddling Stories—Boyish Memories.

XX. Regular and Guerrilla Warfare................ 229

    Battle of Snow's Hill—Wheeler Arrives at Alexandria—Scouting around That Town—Morgan Starts on His Northern Raid—Death of Morgan—Battle of the Calf Killer—Wheeler's Raid—Stockade Taken—Pomp Kersey's Men.

XXI. Peace and the Aftermath..................... 244

    Friction between Former Neighbors—The Freed Negroes—Loyal League and Ku-Klux Klan—Stokes's and Senter's Canvass—Makeshifts of the Citizens—Wonderful Latter-Day Progress.

HISTORY OF DeKALB COUNTY

CHAPTER I.

WHEN TENNESSEE WAS YOUNG.

As a definite district bearing its present name, DeKalb County is not old, since it was erected in 1837 and not organized until 1838. But the territory included within its boundaries has a history we need to know something about, along with that of the State, and this will be treated before taking up its organization.

The entire domain of Tennessee was once a part of the State of North Carolina. Between 1750 and 1775 the first settlements were made in that portion of the State now known as East Tennessee. When the colonies there numbered several hundred whites, North Carolina in 1777 asserted jurisdiction over the western part of her lands and formed it into Washington County. In other words, the whole of the State of Tennessee became Washington County, N. C.

In 1780, after Col. James Robertson with seven of his friends—William Overall (an uncle of Col. Abraham Overall), George Freeland, William Neely, Edward Swanson, James Hanley, Mark Robertson, and Zachariah White—had come over the mountains from East Tennessee and selected the site of Nashville for another settlement, a party of from two hundred to three hundred of his relatives and acquaintances ar-

HISTORY OF DEKALB COUNTY

rived on the Cumberland River and built homes and forts. In 1783 a new county was laid off by North Carolina. It was, of course, taken from Washington County, included a large scope of country west of the Cumberland Mountains (which were called the Wilderness), and became Davidson County. In 1786 Sumner County was laid off, its eastern boundary being the Wilderness; but in 1799 it was reduced by establishing Smith and Wilson Counties out of its eastern territory. Smith County at first included what later became Jackson, White, Warren, and Cannon Counties—or at least a great part of Cannon. Meanwhile, in 1790, North Carolina ceded all the Tennessee country to the United States, and it became, to use the short name, Southwest Territory, with William Blount appointed Governor by President Washington. In 1796 Southwest Territory was admitted into the Union as a State and was given the name of Tennessee.

DeKalb County was not erected until 1837, but of course settlers came and occupied the land while it was a part of some of the other counties. In what part of the country that was to become DeKalb County did the pioneers first make a settlement? It is believed by some of the older citizens that they reached the Alexandria neighborhood first, about 1795; others say the first settlement was made at Liberty by Adam Dale about 1797. Each contention has merits. There had been a settlement at Brush Creek, within two and a half miles of Alexandria, early enough for Rev. Cantrell Bethel, of Liberty, to constitute a Baptist

History of DeKalb County

Church May 2, 1802. Might there not have been some settler to locate two or three miles southward of Brush Creek some years earlier than the institution of the Church? On the other hand, the colony of forty souls who came from Maryland to Liberty about 1800 on hearing from Adam Dale had to cut a wagon road through the forest and canebrakes from a few miles out of Nashville to Liberty. All the traditions are to that effect, and no hint from the pioneers has come down to indicate that they passed any settlement in the vicinity of Alexandria. It is possible, however, that the road opened by the colony ran considerably south of the old stage road and turnpike upon which Alexandria is located. This point will probably never be settled and may well be left alone.

To go back many years, upon the arrival of the first whites in what is now East Tennessee, a vast portion of Middle Tennessee was unoccupied by Indians, though hunting parties camped here or passed back and forth in their tribal wars beyond the borders. It seems to have been agreed among the red men that it should be held as a common hunting ground. As a result it was a wilderness well stocked with buffaloes, bears, deer, and other wild animals. No one knows how long it had been uninhabited; the numerous burying grounds, mounds, and traces of forts prove that some race in the past had lived here. They had probably disappeared before stronger hostile tribes. For want of a better name, and because of their custom of building mounds and burying their dead in stone-walled graves, that vanished tribe were called the Mound

Builders, or Stone Grave race. Some ethnologists believe the Natchez Indians were a branch of this forgotten race.

The mounds and other remains indicate great age and a civilization more advanced than that of the tribes seen when the American explorers came. Judging from the location of the forts, mounds, and cemeteries, the Mound Builders selected the most fertile sections for habitation and near streams. These landmarks are numerous in Middle Tennessee, and the Smith Fork Valley, in DeKalb County, once echoed to the voices of the lost people. In the graves and some of the mounds have been discovered pipes, bowls, ornaments, weapons, and toys. In one place four miles south of Nashville three thousand graves were found and not far off one thousand more. From these were taken nearly seven hundred specimens of burned pottery—some of them semiglazed—representing animals, birds, fish, and the human figure. On the farm once owned by C. W. L. Hale, north of Liberty, is a very large Indian mound, which had perhaps been used for religious or observation purposes. Many graves adjacent have been plowed into. Graves have also been found on T. G. Bratten's farm, just west of Liberty, in the vicinity of the buffalo trail on which a battle was fought between Indians and whites in 1789. Mr. Leander Hayes, who had lived from boyhood four miles southwest of Liberty on Smith Fork, gave the writer in 1894 this description of the Mound Builders' graves on his farm: "A great number were rock-lined, square, and contained skeletons in a sitting posture. At our old home, which I own now, there are two of these graves which have not been molested since their discovery—one near the front gate and the other in the garden under an old apple tree."

The Cherokee and Chickasaw Indians lived in Tennessee when the first settlements were made—not in the "hunting grounds" proper, however. The former lived mainly along the mountains of the eastern border; while a portion, the banditti known as the Chickamaugas, had their villages near the present Chattanooga. The Chickasaws, who became friends of the whites after attacking the settlers on Cumberland River in 1781, claimed all West Tennessee. The bitterest enemies of the settlers were the Cherokees, assisted by the Creeks, who lived south of Tennessee.

When Adam Dale, James Alexander, Jesse Allen, and other pioneers came to what is now DeKalb County, the spirit of the Indians had been broken by the Nickajack expedition southward from Nashville in September, 1794; but there were still hostile tribes in the State. Adam Dale arrived on the site of Liberty in 1797, just three years after the Nickajack expedition. Until 1805 a part of the Cumberland Mountains was an Indian reserve known as the Wilderness. As late as 1791 Nettle Carrier, an Indian chief, lived there with his tribesmen. About 1800 a band of Cherokees, under the lead of Chief Calf Killer, had their homes in the present White County. These were called "friendly," but the savages were easily stirred to deeds of violence and readily took the warpath. Then, even after the Nickajack expedition, the Indians committed depredations. At noon November 11, 1794, an attack was made on Valentine Sevier's fort, near the present site of Clarksville, forty redskins being in the raid. Several whites were killed and scalped. With this state of affairs before us, shall we imagine that the Indians did not camp in or pass through some portion of DeKalb County after the first few settlers arrived?

For many years after Tennessee became a State roving families of vagabond Indians journeyed over the trails and highways. Subsequent to the War between the States the writer saw them go through Liberty. They were friendly and made a few cents target-shooting with bows. It was supposed that they came over the mountains from their old East Tennessee haunts. Prior to 1840 the Chickasaws, Cherokees, and Creeks relinquished all claims and were removed across the Mississippi River.

History records one Indian battle on DeKalb County soil. This was on the buffalo trail down Smith's Fork and up Clear Fork. Hon. Horace A. Overall assured the writer that, according to tradition, the battle field was near where the Bratten lane turns south a quarter of a mile west of Liberty. John Carr, a pioneer of Sumner County, says of the fight in his book, "Early Times in Middle Tennessee," published in 1857:

In 1789 General Winchester went out with a scouting party; and on Smith's Fork, a large tributary of the Caney Fork (I believe now in DeKalb Couny), he came upon a fresh trail of Indians. He pursued them down the creek on the buffalo path, and no doubt the Indians were apprised they were after them and accordingly selected their ground for battle. The path led through an open forest to the crossing of the creek, and immediately a heavy canebrake set in. The General's spies were a little in front. They were Maj. Joseph Muckelrath and Capt. John Hickerson, a couple of brave men.

Just after they entered the green cane a short distance the Indians, lying in ambush, fired upon them. They killed Hickerson at once, but missed Muckelrath. Winchester was close behind, rushing up. The action commenced, lasting some time. Frank Heany was wounded; and the Indians having greatly the advantage, General Winchester thought it proper to retreat, thinking to draw them out of the green cane. In this attempt he did not succeed.

There is no doubt but that Capt. James McKain, now [1857] eighty-five or eighty-six years old, killed a celebrated warrior and, I believe, chief called the Moon. He was a harelipped man, and it was said that there was but one harelipped Indian in the nation. No doubt the same Indian shot down and scalped Capt. Charles Morgan a year or two before (at Bledsoe's Lick).

One of my brothers was in this expedition. The Indians gave an account of the battle afterwards and said it was a drawn fight, that they had a man killed and that they had killed one of our men.

Carr says two of the whites were John and Martin Harpool, Dutchmen. Martin was foolhardy, and his brother suggested to him, after Winchester withdrew, to rush into the canebrake and drive the Indians out while he killed one. With a great whoop Martin entered the cane, making it crackle at a terrible rate, and the Indians fled.

On the first settlement of the county there may have been far inland a few bears and buffaloes left. We have no records. Just twenty years previously Tennessee was overrun with them. About 1781 twenty hunters went from Nashborough Fort up Cumberland River as far as the present Flynn's Lick and soon returned with one hundred and five bears, more than eighty deer, and seventy-five buffaloes. The late Elbert Robinson, of Temperance Hall, once said that when his grandfather came to that settlement bears were frequently seen. Dr. Foster says that when he was an infant (he was born in 1839) his parents removed to Dry Creek, but they were so disturbed by wolves howling at night that they moved back to Liberty within three days. John K. Bain writes that when he was a lad, about 1835, he ran three deer out of his father's cornfield in one day. That was in the eastern part of the county. He adds: "My uncle, Archibald Bain, killed a bear before I remember. Squirrels were so numerous as to destroy cornfields thirty feet from the fence. I killed forty in one day, and one fall (I kept tab) the number I killed was over three hundred." Doubtless game was sufficiently abundant to make hunting and the chase worth while to the first comers.

CHAPTER II.

DeKalb County Established—Officials.

In 1837 Hon. H. L. W. Hill, of Warren County, introduced in the Tennessee House of Representatives a bill to form a new county out of parts of Warren, Cannon, Jackson, and White Counties, to be named for Baron DeKalb, a Bavarian, who fought for American independence during the Revolution. The bill was amended in the Senate, then passed, specifying the following boundaries: Beginning at the corner between Smith and Cannon Counties on the Wilson County line near Alexandria and running thence south twenty-three degrees east with the old line between Wilson and Smith Counties eight miles to a point on said line; thence south forty-eight degrees, east eleven and three-quarter miles to the Warren County line at John Martin's; thence north eighty-three degrees, east seven miles to a point twelve miles north from McMinnville; thence south eighty degrees, four and three-quarter miles to Caney Fork River at the mouth of Barren Creek; thence down said river with its meanders to an oak on the road from Sparta to Dibrell's Ferry, four miles from said ferry; thence north thirty-seven and a half degrees, east nine and three-quarter miles to a point on the stage road from Sparta to Carthage; thence north two miles to a corner between White and Jackson Counties on Cane Creek; thence south seventy-five degrees, west sixteen and a half miles so as to strike the northwest corner of Cannon County, on the Caney Fork River; and thence with the line run by Thomas Durham between Smith and Cannon Counties to the beginning.

From time to time the line has been changed, slightly, however, in most instances. On January 2, 1844, for instance, the Alfred Hancock property was taken from DeKalb and added to Cannon County. The Hancocks came from Virginia about the time the Overalls, Turneys, and others arrived, and have been among the foremost citizens of their section for more than a hundred years.* On February 1, 1850, the legislature so altered the line between Smith and DeKalb as to include the residences and farms of Nicholas Smith, Andrew Vantrease, John Robinson, and others in the latter county, as well as the farm and residence of John F. Goodner, near Alexandria.

On Monday, March 5, 1838, the following citizens, holding certificates as magistrates of the county, met at Bernard Richardson's, on Fall Creek, and organized the county court by electing Lemuel Moore chairman: Lemuel Moore, James Goodner, Jonathan C. Doss, Reuben Evans, Joseph Turney, Watson Cantrell, Thomas Simpson, John Martin, Watson Cantrell, David Fisher, William Scott, Samuel Strong, Henry Burton, Martin Phillips, John Frazier, Joel Cheatham, Jonathan Fuston, Peter Reynolds, and James Beaty.

The various county officers elect exhibited their cer-

---

*It is told of Alfred Hancock's kindness to the poor that in times of drought he refused to sell his corn to those who could pay cash, but sold it on time to the needy at much less than he could get from the well-to-do.

tificates of election, qualified, entered upon the discharge of their duties, and the county was organized.

The county court continued to meet at the home of Richardson until a log courthouse could be completed. The circuit court was also organized at Richardson's, the first term beginning on the second Monday in August, 1838, Judge A. J. Marchbanks presiding. The chancery court was organized in 1844 by Chancellor B. L. Ridley. (See the chapter headed "The County Seat.")

The county is bounded north by Smith and Putnam Counties, east by Putnam and White, south by Warren and Cannon, and west by Cannon and Wilson. Its population in 1840 was 5,868, ten years later it was 8,016, and by the commencement of the War between the States it was 10,573.

About two-thirds of the county lies on the Highland Rim. The Highlands occupy the eastern and northern parts. The western part lies in the Central Basin and embraces several valleys of considerable size and great agricultural value, separated from each other by irregular ranges of hills, while there are some peaks and ridges which mount up to a level with the Highlands. The valley of Caney Fork is long, winding, and irregular. It begins below the falls between Warren and White Counties near the southeast corner of DeKalb; runs toward the northwest, then westerly, till it opens out in the Basin in the northwestern part of DeKalb. It is narrow at the upper end; below Sligo Ferry it has an average width of half a mile. Its greatest width is about a mile; its length, following the general direction, about thirty miles. The valley of Smith Fork extends from south to north through the western part of the county. Its length is about fifteen miles and its breadth variable, spreading out in some places for a space of two or three miles, while in others it is cut in two by projecting spurs on each side. Each of Smith Fork's tributaries has a valley of its own, and these small valleys contain many valuable tracts of level land.

The best lands in the Highlands are found on the hillsides and along streams. In these situations there are numerous excellent farms. The timber of the barrens includes a number of valuable varieties, such as black oak, chestnut, hickory, post oak, and white oak. There were once some pine groves at the head of Pine Creek and between Smithville and Sligo. In the Central Basin the timber was once dense and heavy, owing to the disintegrated limestone—beech, sugar maple, walnut, oak, poplar, and other varieties.

Orchards are not so numerous in the valleys as they were a half century ago, but are numerous and profitable in the Highlands. Fires ("log heaps") in the orchards for protecting fruit against late spring frosts were used by some of the pioneers.

The leading crops are corn, wheat, rye, and oats, though the first settlers grew flax, cotton, and tobacco. Some of the finest mules driven South before and after the War between the States were raised on DeKalb County farms. In 1840 Tennessee was the greatest hog and corn State in the Union, and this county produced its share. Small fortunes have been made in hog-trading. Early traders were Francis Turner, William B. Stokes, Matthew Sellars, Edward Robinson, Robin Forrester, William G. Stokes, and others. The last named, a son of Thomas Stokes, of Temperance Hall, disappeared before the war on a trip South and was never heard of again. Buyers after the war were C. W. L. Hale, W. G. Evans, Gips West, Fox Frazier, and others. Hogs handled by the earlier dealers were from two to three years old when fattened. They were driven across country south, mainly to Georgia. Ten drivers could manage one thousand hogs, and one route was through Liberty, up Clear Fork, by McMinnville, over Walden's Ridge, across the Tennessee River, and on to Marietta, Milledgeville, Macon, and various Southern towns. Thirty-five days were allowed to go from Liberty to Georgia. The animals traveled from two and a half to ten miles a day. Dr. Foster imparts the interesting fact that in the "flatwoods" years ago there were many wild or feral hogs, belonging to no one but claimed by many. Descended from domesticated stock, "they developed immense tusks and long, heavy coats of hair."

In the Basin, where there were once large maple groves, maple sirup and sugar became a considerable industry in ante-bellum times, and these articles could be purchased for some years after the war. To hear the old slaves tell of the sugar camps, it would appear that the industry was pleasurable as well as a source of income.

The county is well watered, the principal streams, besides Caney Fork, being Smith Fork, Clear Fork,

History of DeKalb County

Sink Creek, Pine Creek, Fall Creek, Eagle Creek, Hurricane Creek, Hannah's Branch, Holm's Creek, Indian Creek, Mine Lick, Hickman Creek, Walker's Creek, Helton, Dismal, Falling Water, the Canal, Adamson's Branch, and Dry Creek. Dry Creek sinks some distance east of Dowelltown, then emerges at the Big Spring in that hamlet and flows into Smith Fork.

The malignant "milk sickness" breaks out occasionally, mainly on the headwaters of Holm's Creek and probably on Hurricane, though it is unknown after reaching the top of the Highlands. Cattle and a few people have been victims of the poison.

The southeastern part of the county is a great poultry section. There are also numerous nurseries, the income from which amounts to many thousands of dollars yearly. On the east side of Caney Fork, near the White County line, there are beds of iron ore extending several miles. This ore also exists on the west side of the river and was once worked at a bloomery on Pine Creek by the pioneer Jesse Allen. State Commissioner Killebrew wrote in 1874 that "the county is very rich in iron."

The first things considered by the early settlers were good springs, dwellings, and mills. The earliest mill in the county was no doubt Adam Dale's, at Liberty, erected about 1800 and patronized by the Dale and other settlements. Jesse Allen settled on Eagle Creek in 1801 and soon built a small mill, in connection with which were a cotton gin and distillery. Other mills soon followed—Fite's, on Smith Fork, just west of

Dowelltown, a part of its dam being visible still; Fite's (later Crips's), on Dry Creek, the water furnishing its power coming from a large cave; Durham and Farrington's, on Pine Creek; Abraham Overall's, on Clear Fork; Hoover's, on Hickman Creek; Bate's, on Helton; and that which became known as Nicholas Smith's, on lower Smith Fork. In later years, in addition to those mentioned in the sketches of various towns, the following citizens have erected mills in different parts of the county: T. H. W. Richardson, Washington Reynolds, James Oakley, W. G. Crowley, John Bone, and James Kelton.

There are (1914) in DeKalb County 3,235 homes. Of this number, 2,407 are farm homes, 1,511 being owned by their occupants and free of mortgage incumbrance. The mortgaged farm homes number only seventy-seven, while renters occupy 815 farm homes. On the other hand, 828 homes are urban, the number of owners of town homes being 329. Eleven of these homes are mortgaged, and 300 are free of incumbrance. There are 472 rented urban homes.

With the county organized, many of its citizens displayed an anxiety to "save the country." Politics at length became strenuous and has remained so. Prior to the War between the States a majority of the people in the Basin—below Snow's Hill—were Whigs, Know-Nothings, and Opposition; after that event they were called Unionists, Radicals, or Republicans. Most of the voters of the sixth, seventh, and ninth districts —above Snow's Hill—with a sprinkling elsewhere, were Democrats before the war, Confederates during the struggle, and Democrats after hostilities ceased.

The two opposing parties down to 1861 were almost evenly divided; then came many unexpected changes. To give one illustration: Abe Lafever, of the Mine Lick section, had been a dyed-in-the-wool Democrat; after the war he was known throughout the county as a rabid Republican and a leader of that party locally. Again, certain Unionists, like Joseph Clarke, became strong Democratic partisans.

One of the old-timers says of the partisan zeal of the days of the Whig party: "It was not an uncommon thing to witness a Whig speaker, say for Representative, draw a coon's tail from his pocket and wave this emblem of Whiggery. When Clay and Polk were candidates for the presidency, Polk adherents would drive into Liberty with their oxen's horns ringed with poke juice, while their cart beds were striped with it. Directly another cart, driven by a Clay supporter, would enter the village having a mammoth clay ball in each corner of the cart bed and the horns of the steers smeared with clay. When Dr. J. A. Fuson was elected to the legislature in 1845, the Fuson supporters to a man wore red ribbon on their hats on which was printed *Fuson*." This illustrative anecdote also survives: Moses Spencer ("Blackhorse"), who was in the battle of New Orleans and a Whig in politics, was once solicited to vote the Democratic ticket, the solicitor kindly presenting him with a bag of cured hog jowls. Carrying to his home in Liberty this necessary ingredient of the famous dish of greens, Mose threw it down on the floor and observed to his wife: "Barbara, Colonel Tubb has asked me to vote for a Democrat the coming election. Barbara, now you hear this Blackhorse that fit an' bled under Andy Jackson: I'm a Whig an' have always been one, an' I would not vote for a Democrat for even a bag o' middlins."

The greatest orators of the State were developed in the days of the Whigs and Democrats. Some of the forensic giants had appointments in the county. Probably the most noted discussion of political issues took place in 1855 between Andrew Johnson, Democrat, and Meredith P. Gentry, Whig, with Know-Nothing leanings, for the governorship. It came off on the Fulton Academy grounds at Smithville, and the crowd was very large.

The Know-Nothing party was a secret organization and was aggressively opposed to the Catholic Church. There were both Whigs and Democrats in the new party, and it was thought that it would poll one hundred thousand votes in the State at the end of the 1855 campaign.

Johnson was not "flowery," but was a most effective speaker. Gentry, nominated by the remnant of Whigs and the Know-Nothings, was one of the best orators in Tennessee. In his excoriation of the Know-Nothings Johnson was extremely bitter, arraigning them for their signs, grips, and secret conclaves, and declaring that they were no better than John A. Murrel's clan of outlaws. "Show me a Know-Nothing," he stormed, "and I will show you a monster upon whose neck the foot of every honest man should tread!" Gentry was "hacked." In a lofty manner he defended the party which nominated him, but his party was not satisfied with his reply. Many Democrats forsook his cause, and Johnson was elected.

Neil S., Aaron V., and John C. Brown all spoke at various times in the county; also Isham G. Harris, William B. Campbell, D. W. C. Senter, William B. Stokes, James D. Porter, Horace Maynard, B. F. Cheatham, R. L. Taylor, A. A. Taylor, G. G. Dibrell, E. W. Carmack, John H. Savage, and even Squire Yardley, the Knoxville negro who canvassed the State for the governorship.

The citizens for many years were politically swayed by oratory, and those of DeKalb had an opportunity to hear other forensic giants besides the men named. A campaign almost as exciting as that in which Johnson destroyed Know-Nothingism came off when the question of secession was discussed pro and con by John Smith Brien, William B. Campbell, and others; also that after peace was made in which Stokes and Senter stumped the State. Of the last-named canvass, something will be said farther along.

A digression is made to present as full a list as can now be made of the county officers from the organization of the county to 1914:

County court clerks: P. M. Wade, William Lawrence, Wash Isbell, M. T. Martin, G. W. Eastham, P. G. Magness, E. J. Evans, Z. P. Lee, H. K. Allen, J. E. Conger, W. B. Foster, John E. Conger.

Circuit court clerks: David Fite, W. J. Givan, J. B. Gibbs, J. T. Hollis, W. T. Hoskins, T. M. Christian,

History of DeKalb County

T. W. Shields, James Fuson, Felix Hellum, J. M. Young, Jack S. Allen.

Clerks and masters: Thomas Whaley, Wash Isbell, J. T. Hallum, John P. Robertson, W. W. Wade, M. A. Crowley, J. B. Moore, Sam Foster.

Sheriffs: P. M. Thomason, James McGuire, E. W. Taylor, J. L. Dearman, J. Y. Stewart, John Hallum, W. L. Hathaway, Charles Hill, Henry Blackburn, M. F. Doss, C. S. Frazier, B. M. Merritt, H. S. Gill, S. P. Gill, W. H. C. Lassiter, Silas Anderson, Ben Merritt, Louis Merritt, John Odum, B. B. Taylor, Everett Love, George Puckett, A. Frazier.

Registers: Daniel Coggin, Wash Isbell, David Fite, J. Y. Haynes, John K. Bain, W. H. McNamer, Judson Dale, J. C. Kennedy, J. B. Atwell, John Harrison, B. M. Cantrell, E. W. Taylor, John G. Evans, Dabner Lockhart, Dave Worley, E. G. Pedigo, W. H. Hays.

County trustees: Rev. Joseph Banks, Aaron Botts, W. A. Nesmith (1861-62), Bluford Foster, Eli Vick, Brackett Estes, Sr., W. P. Smith, James Fite, James Fuson, H. C. Eastham, W. G. Evans, Pope Potter, Lee Overall, J. W. Reynolds, J. A. Newby, W. N. Adcock, William Taylor, J. A. Phillips, Thomas Crips, Matt Bratten.

The county had no Representatives until 1843, while a part of the time it was in a floterial district with the Representative from some other county. These DeKalb Countians have filled the office: Twenty-Fifth General Assembly, 1843, Daniel Coggin; Twenty-Sixth, 1845, John A. Fuson; Twenty-Seventh, 1847,

History of DeKalb County

John A. Fuson; Twenty-Eighth, 1849, W. B. Stokes; Twenty-Ninth, 1851, W. B. Stokes; Thirtieth, 1853 (first session held in the new State Capitol), Horace A. Overall; Thirty-First, 1855, M. M. Brien; Thirty-Second, 1857, A. M. Savage; Thirty-Third, first session 1859, second 1861, third April, 1861, J. J. Ford; Thirty-Fourth, first session 1861, second 1862, adjourned to Memphis, no Representative; Brownlow's Legislature of 1865-66, session held in April, 1865, John A. Fuson; Thirty-Fifth, 1867, W. S. Robertson; Thirty-Sixth, 1869, W. A. Dunlap; Thirty-Seventh, first session October, 1871, second March, 1872, James P. Doss; Thirty-Eighth, 1873, none; Thirty-Ninth, 1875, none; Fortieth, first session January 1, 1877, extra December, 1877, none; Forty-First, first session January, 1879, second December, 1879, none; Forty-Second, first session January, 1881, extra December, 1881, second extra 1882, none; Forty-Third, 1883, Horace A. Overall; Forty-Fourth, first session January, 1885, extra May, 1885, J. M. Allen; Forty-Fifth, 1887, J. M. Allen; Forty-Sixth, 1889, extra session 1890, M. L. Bonham; Forty-Seventh, 1891, J. H. S. Knowles; Forty-Eighth, 1893, Henry C. Givan; Forty-Ninth, 1895, Samuel Wauford; Fiftieth, 1897, A. T. Phillips; Fifty-First, 1899, W. T. Dozier; Fifty-Second, 1901, P. C. Crowley; Fifty-Third, 1903, L. Driver; Fifty-Fourth, 1905, L. Driver; Fifty-Fifth, 1907, J. H. S. Knowles; Fifty-Sixth, 1909, J. E. Conger; Fifty-Seventh, 1911, A. N. Cathcart; Fifty-

HISTORY OF DEKALB COUNTY

Eighth, 1913, extra session, Norman Robinson; Fifty-Ninth, 1915, Horace M. Evans.*

The following DeKalb Countians were members of the State Senate: Caleb B. Davis, 1851; W. B. Stokes, 1855; J. S. Goodner, 1857; Wingate T. Robinson, 1865; John A. Fuson, 1867; Joseph Clarke, 1872; M. D. Smallman, 1881; M. D. Smallman, 1883; B. G. Adcock, 1893; P. C. Crowley, 1903.

It is noted that Hon. Horace A. Overall represented the county when the General Assembly met first in the State Capitol, newly erected, October 3, 1853. The fact suggests that the first legislature of the State met in Knoxville, which was for a while the seat of government, in 1796. In 1807 the legislature met at Kingston, but in a few hours adjourned to Knoxville. Nashville was the place of meeting in 1812, 1813, and 1815, then Knoxville again in 1817. In 1819 it met at Murfreesboro and continued to meet there until 1825. The sext session (1826) was held in Nashville, as have been all succeeding sessions.

---

*Mr. James Dearman writes: "I understand that James McGuire represented the county sometime in the forties." The name is not found in the records, however.

CHAPTER III.

THE OLDEST VILLAGE.

ON his arrival at the site of Liberty from Maryland in 1797 Adam Dale, who came by way of East Tennessee and over Cumberland Mountains, Mr. Riley Dale says, must have been impressed with the country, for he sent back in some way a report to his friends which induced the coming of a colony consisting of William and John Dale, Thomas West, William and George Givan, Thomas Whaley, Josiah and T. W. Duncan, James and William Bratten, Henry Burton, the Fites, Truits, Bethels, and many others, some of whom were young married couples.

It is not certainly known that he had a companion during the something like three years before the arrival of the immigrants. If he was alone, life must have been lonely at times. The descendants of all the pioneers who have talked on the subject, repeating the stories handed down, join in saying there was no wagon road through from Nashville after the first few miles. One, perhaps W. G. Bratten, told the agent for Goodspeed's history of the State that the colony "came down the Ohio River, up the Cumberland to Nashville, and from that point made their way overland to the Dale settlement in wagons." Another, perhaps a descendant of Rev. John Fite, stated to Rev. J. H. Grime, author of "A History of Middle Tennessee Baptists": "When he [Fite] landed here in the very beginning of the nineteenth century, he found

History of DeKalb County

this country still a wilderness. . . . He helped to cut away the cane and underbrush to construct the first road to Liberty, the work consuming a period of nineteen days for a number of hands." We may assume that there were roads a short distance eastward from Nashville, but it may be taken as true that a part of the fifty-six miles to Liberty was almost primeval forest. Doubtless game and fish abounded, and these occupied Dale's mind by day; but the snarl of the bobcat or other noises of the night, together with the solemnity of the great woods, were necessarily spirit-depressing, even if he had no fears of Indians.

We are told that he passed his first months in a rude shack built on the bluff overlooking the creek on the north side of town, about where the Whaley lime kiln was for a number of years. After his friends came he erected a small dwelling on the west side of the turnpike beyond the bridge going north. This writer saw the building carried off by the flood near the beginning of the War between the States, at which time the small mill Dale erected, but at the time belonging to Daniel Smith or the Lambersons, was wrecked.

Mrs. Jean Robertson Anderson, wife of Gen. Kellar Anderson, of Memphis, is a great-granddaughter of Adam Dale. Her mother was Mrs. James (Anne Lewis Dale) Robertson, the third daughter of Edward W. Dale, who was the oldest son of Adam Dale and the only one to leave issue. From a letter of Mrs. Anderson dated November 4, 1914, these facts are gleaned: Adam Dale was born in Worcester

County, Md., July 14, 1768. He was a boy volunteer of the Revolution. In 1781 this company of boys from fourteen to sixteen years was raised in Snow Hill, Md., to oppose the progress of Cornwallis through Virginia. Receiving land grants with his father, Thomas Dale, for service, he settled in Liberty, Tenn., in 1797, after having married Mary Hall February 24, 1790. He raised, equipped, and commanded a company of volunteers from Smith (DeKalb) County and fought under Jackson at Horseshoe Bend and other battles of the War of 1812. Removing to Columbia, Tenn., in 1829, he died at Hazel Green, Ala., October 14, 1851, and was buried there. His wife died in 1859 in Columbia. To this couple were born ten children.

Mrs. Anderson says further:

When the surviving children of Adam Dale had his body removed from Alabama to Columbia after his wife's death, his body was found to be absolutely perfect—petrified. The picture is from an old daguerreotype made shortly before his death. I have several letters from him to his grandchildren. One minutely describes the battle of Horseshoe Bend. Another tells of his English ancestry and their coming to America. I also have the newspaper clipping of the eulogy on his career as soldier, patriot, citizen, and friend published at the time of his death. Among his descendants are Mrs. W. D. Bethell, Denver, Colo.; Mrs. John M. Gray, Nashville, Tenn.; Mrs. Thomas Day, Memphis, Tenn.; Mrs. E. M. Apperson, Memphis, Tenn.; Mrs. J. S. Van Slyke, Dallas, Tex.; Mrs. Joseph Houston, Denver, Colo.; and Mrs. W. R. Holliday, Memphis, Tenn.

Adam and William Dale were probably sons of Thomas Dale, who came to Liberty with the Marylanders. Josiah Duncan married a daughter of Thomas; while another, Sophia, was the wife of William Givan. There are many descendants of these Dales in Tennessee and other States. Among them is Mrs. H. P. Figuers, of Columbia, whose father, W. J. Dale, was born in Smith (DeKalb) County in 1811 and removed to Maury County in 1822. Another is Mrs. Bertha L. Chapman, of Alexandria. She has a Bible containing these entries:

Sophia E. Dale was married to William Givan June 26, 1802. They had children: Nancy, born January 11, 1804; George, born September 21, 1806; Elizabeth, born May 1, 1810; Sarah, born April 11, 1812; Thomas, born March 20, 1814; Mary Ann, born June 23, 1816; Robert Johnson, born August 9, 1818; and Martha Laws Dale, born November 5, 1820. Martha Laws Dale Givan was married to James D. Grandstaff September 19, 1839. Mrs. Grandstaff lived in widowhood from 1844 to 1893.

Riley Dale has in his possession a letter from his grandfather, Rev. William Dale, dated February 28, 1844, containing this genealogical note:

I was born on the Lord's day, the 4th of May, 1783. My place of nativity was Worcester County, Md. My father's name was Thomas Dale, of John Dale, of James Dale, both of Londonderry, Ireland. My mother's name was Elizabeth Evans, of John Evans, of William Evans, from Wales.

Thomas Dale, who was a Revolutionary soldier, enlisting in Gen. Charles Smallwood's command, soon became captain of a company of the Maryland line. He owned a great deal of land around Liberty, in which village he erected a house. This was on the lot on which Will A. Vick more recently built. His son-in-law, Josiah Duncan, was settled on the land last owned by the W. G. Bratten heirs. Erecting a house on the farm now owned by George Givan, a mile south of Liberty, he died before moving to it. His widow, with his son-in-law, William Givan, removed to the farm, and it is in the possession of the Givan family in 1914. In the family graveyard in the rear is a limestone slab with this legend: "In memory of Thomas Dale, born March 5, 1744; died January 6, 1812."

The colony set about preparing homes and the community soon took on a more encouraging aspect. The mill was erected on Smith Fork Creek north of Liberty, and the place became widely known as the Dale Mill Settlement. As the little cluster of houses grew larger, the name of Liberty was given it by its founder. It is possible that the mountain between Liberty and Smithville was named Snow's Hill by him in memory of the place where he enlisted for American independence. There is not a Dale in what was once called the Dale Mill Settlement. A grandson of Rev. William Dale, Riley, resides on his farm, several miles from Liberty, aged seventy-two.

There is a diversity of opinion as to who was the first merchant. Goodspeed says he was a Mr. Walk; James Givan thinks his name was Vaught. George Givan, on Clear Fork, it is interesting to state, now owns a well-preserved wash kettle purchased from the first merchant about a century ago.

The earliest dwellings were supposedly built by William Givan, Josey Evans, and Henry Burton, who came with the Maryland settlers. All three were carpenters. Other pioneer merchants were Fite & Duncan, Ben Blades, Joshua Bratten, and Moore & Price.

From Dr. Wright's daybook it is seen that the following firms were in existence as early as 1832-33: Fite, Whaley & Co., Ray & Reed, woodworkmen and smiths, Davis & Wood, Derickson & Braswell, saddlers, York & Bailey, and Whaley & Son.

Some years prior to the War between the States the following were in various businesses: Eli Vick, William Vick, Hale & Hays, merchants; W. G. Foster, Frank Foster, William Whaley, and William Ford. Among the merchants after the war were Eli Vick, William Whaley, C. W. L. Hale, William Vick, J. H. Overall, Overall & Hollandsworth, M. C. Vick, D. D. Overall, Elijah Bratten, Vick Bros., George Turney, James Pritchett, Isaac Whaley, H. L. Hale, Blue Givan, W. T. Hale, and others. The business directory for 1914 shows: Maud Spurlock, Robinson & McMillan, Whaley Bros., general merchants; Bright Bros., vehicles; W. L. Vick, harness; Will Fite, hardware; Turner & Son, groceries; Bratten Bros., grain; William Organ, Jr., tinner; Tom Lamberson, blacksmith; Hugh Gothard, liveryman; H. L. Hale and Joe Conley, produce; Grover Evans and J. C. Stark, insurance; L. Woodward, photographer; W. C. Smith, painter.

As early as 1832-33 the neighborhood around the village must have been thickly populated or many patrons of the stores came from the Smithville and Woodbury communities. Some of the names on Dr.

History of DeKalb County

Wright's daybook are: J. G. Roulstone, S. J. Garrison, David L. Ray, W. C. Garrison, Lemuel H. Bethel, David Fite, Reuben Evans, Eli A. Fisher, M. A. Fricks, German Gossett, Francis Turner, G. Shehane, Henry Fite, Charles Jenkins, James Stanford, George L. Givan, John Floyd, Zach Williamson, Brackett Estes, John L. Strong, Joel N. West, John Stark, Peter Hays, Joshua Bratten, B. F. Wood, T. W. Duncan, James Wilder, Moses Fite, Joseph Cameron, Louis Y. Davis, Thomas Allan, Lem D. Evans, Richard Arnold, Matthew Simpson, John Little, John Griffith, James Bayne, William Boyd, Joseph Fite, Alfred Wallace, Capt. William S. Boswell, David Thompson, Thomas Allan, David Fricks, Richard McGinnis, John Stark, John Hays, John E. Dale, W. T. Cochran, Wyatt Pistole, Shadrick Trammel, Moses Spencer, Thomas and Moses Pack, Shadrick Kelley, Tilman Bethel, Lewis Parker, Milka Strong, Rev. William Dale, James Pendleton, Capt. Joseph Evans, Aaron Davis, Moses Allen, Capt. James Spurlock, Alex Armstrong, David Dirting, John Owen, Nancy Kelly, Mrs. Mary Hart, Henry Hart, P. W. Brien, William A. Wisner, George Barnes, Joseph Snow, Henry Horn, Rev. James Evans, George Foster, Hugh Smith, Joseph Atnip, R. H. Parkison, John Martin, Nancy Givan, William Blair, Charles Hancock, Luke McDowell, Lewis Parker, John Hollandsworth, Jordan Sellars, James Baity, Benjamin Clark, Dempsy Taylor, Archibald McDougle, Benjamin Goodson, Lemuel Moore, Abner Evans, Leonard Fite, Richard Bennett, Isaac Pack, George A. Rich, Smith Brien, Peter Turney, Augustin Vick, Thomas Underwood, Nathan Wade, John Candler, James Carney, Wingate Truitt, Littleberry Vick, Leonard Lamberson, James Perryman, Lewis Ford, William Estes, Wiley Wilder, Crag Parsons, Leven Gray, William Brazwell, William Carroll, Alfred Wales, Thomas West, A. W. Ford, William Measles, Harriet C. Roulstone, John Conger, Joshua Ford, Wiley J. Melton, Samuel Hays, James Robinson, Mathias S. West, John Frazier, Alex Dillard, Friday Martin, Robert Wilson, Samuel Bryson, James Yeargin, D. H. Burton, Benjamin Avant, Edward Sullivant, James Pistole, Washington Gossett, William Gossett, S. C. Porterfield, Gideon B. York, Green Arnold, Tilman Foster, Mrs. Kesiah Alexander, Thomas Bratten, U. G. Gossett, Moses Mathews, Sophia Givan, David H. Burton, Ed Evans, Gilbert Williams, Samuel Williams, Silas Cooper, John R. Dougherty, Goulding Foster, J. M. Farrington, John Reed, Mikel V. Ethridge, Dr. Samuel Tittle, Moses Spencer, Emerson M. Hill, Edmund T. Goggin, Giles Driver, P. C. Watson, Bryant Spradley, Peter Reynolds, Josiah Spurlock, Jonathan Fuston, John Curtis, Nathan Evans, A. Overall, J. A. Wilson, Thomas Bratten, O. M. Garrison, Matthew Sellars, Joab Hale, John Burton, W. H. Burton, Thomas Taylor, Sally Evans, Welles Adamson, W. A. Nesmith, Acenith Fite, Washington Bayne, Lee Brazwell, Coleman Johnson, James Bayne, Thomas Close, W. B. Stokes, Jane Lawrence, Joseph Hendrickson, Lewis Stark, Phillips Cooper, Henry McMullin, Sally Woodside, Robin Forester, Cantrell Bethel, Jesse B.

Jones, Col. James Tubb, Jacob Page, Thomas Pack, John Dodd, William Botts, Thomas Whaley, Jacob Overall, John M. Leek, Adam Bratten, Abe Adams, Benjamin Pritchard, Isaac Bratten, Gilbert Williams, Nancy Burton, George Grizzle, Onessimus Evans, W. S. Scott, Joseph Evans, Solomon Davis, Edwin Shumway, John Merritt, Matthew McLane, Benjamin Blades, F. S. Anderson, and Randall Pafford.

There is a certain pathos connected with the changes that have come about in the personnel of the population during the past fourscore years. For instance, a leading family of Liberty in other days was that of Gossett; there is now not a person of the name in the village or in the county. The Dales, as shown, have also disappeared from the town.

Mrs. Rachel Payne wrote in 1914:

> I well remember the Liberty of sixty-two years ago, my father, Frederick Jones, having bought Duncan Tavern in 1843. In that year the first schoolhouse was built, not far from the Methodist church. Mr. Chambers was the first teacher in it. I was one of the later pupils. Most of the houses were of logs back then. I went to school in the log church that stood by the graveyard. The seats were split logs, with holes in them for the insertion of legs. The first person buried in Salem graveyard was Major Lamberson's girl, Martha. Nearly all the old-time people are gone to their reward. Aunt Polly Youngblood is the oldest resident. She was a Miss Avant, of Dismal Creek. I was only six months old when she became the wife of William Youngblood, and I was sixty-eight years old September 23, 1913. There were about thirty houses in Liberty when I was a child, and nearly all the public travel was by stagecoach.

HISTORY OF DEKALB COUNTY

In a gossipy letter Dr. Foster names some of the residents of about 1850: Mr. Dean (blacksmith), Dr. J. R. Dougherty, Joshua Bratten and his son James, Dr. J. H. Fuson, Dr. J. A. Baird, Aunt Sallie Bratten, Len Moore, Bill Thompson (blacksmith), Jim Crook (wagon maker), Leonard and Clint Lamberson, William Youngblood, Dr. G. C. Flowers, Isaac Whaley, Tom Price, Elijah Strong, J. P., Bob, Hilary, and other Dales, Frederick Jones (tailor), W. G. Foster, Arthur Worley, U. D. Gossett, Ben Blades, Eli Vick, Seth Whaley, James Hollandsworth, John Woodsides, William Gothard, Bill Avant (tanner), John Evans, John Reid, and John Perryman. Dr. Foster adds:

I can see other things as I look back to Liberty: Aunt Polly Blades's ginger cakes, set on a little shelf as a sign; Aunt Hettie Bratten selling good whisky for ten cents a quart; Dr. Flowers's John with his bowlegs; Jim Crook and his legs; Alex Bayne and his snow-white steers; and Sam Wooden as he hits and raises a knot on Bill Pack's head. I go around to Reuben Evans's farm and see his sons, Ed, Will, Ike, Mose, and Jim, and his daughters, Nancy, Matilda, and Martha, and his wife, Aunt Clara, as well as a dog named Danger, that bit Jim Youngblood on the hindmost part. Likewise I see old Dr. Tilman Bethel and his black horse and his sons, Chess, Greene, Blue, Fayette, and John; Louis Vick, Jim Bratten, and Clint Lamberson (the last three died when yet young men). Then I look on Polly Stanley, the best "fisherman" with a pole and line in the county and a good fiddler; Sam Barger, fat and squat, who wore his shoes when he rode to Liberty, but came barefooted when he walked. Coming on down several years, I was in the village the night Montillius Richardson died. That was after the battle of Fishing Creek, and I was on furlough. (I belonged to the Fifteenth Mississippi Confederate Regiment.) Sixty-five years ago, when I was a ten-year-old boy, changes were going on, of course. The physicians were George C. Flowers, E. Wright, John A. Baird, Horace Sneed, Samuel Little, J. A. Fuson, and J. R. Dougherty, with Tilman Bethel, a steam doctor, living a mile or two west. The magistrates for that district were Reuben Evans and Joe Clarke. The constables were William Blackburn and Josiah Youngblood. Church Anderson was one of the merchants. The blacksmiths were Bill Thompson and Greene Perryman, but preceding them were Goolsberry Blades and a man named Brooks. Later smiths were W. G. Evans and Bill Givan; miller, "Chunky" Joe Hays (who was not chunky), his wife being Aunt Sukey, mother of Mrs. William Blackburn; shoemaker, John Woodside; saddlers, W. G. Foster, U. D. Gossett, John A. Carroll, George Warren, G. F. Bowers, and others; saloon keeper, James G. Fuston; cabinet workmen, James Hollandsworth, Bob Burton, and Isaac Whaley; brickmason, Berry Driver; tailors, Joe Perryman and Len Moore. The Lamberson boys were also millers, running the old Dale water mill. Liberty had a horse saw mill and a rope factory—the latter about where the tanyard was afterwards. Wagon makers were Jim Crook and Perry Wells. Perry and Jim Wells put up a store on Dismal Creek after the Clay and Frelinghuysen canvass, and some one got off this doggerel:

> "Hurrah! hurrah! the country's risin';
> Perry and Jim are merchandisin'.
> One sells liquor, and t'other sells goods;
> And when they start home—get lost in the woods!"

Liberty was incorporated January 17, 1850. The boundaries were: Beginning at a sour oak near Leonard Lamberson's wellspring, thence south to Smith's Fork, thence down said creek with its meanders to the mouth of the branch west of the town spring, thence west to a chinquapin oak standing on the north side of the Liberty and Dismal Creek road, thence south to the beginning; provided that the west boundary shall not include any of the land owned by Leonard Lamberson.

Revived after the war, the corporation was abolished soon after the passage of the four-mile law of 1877. William Blackburn and Elijah Bratten were postbellum mayors.

The people of Liberty for some years had to go as far as Carthage to mail letters. This was changed when the stage began to run, maybe before. The earliest postmaster recalled by the old people was "Grandaddy" Dougherty, who carried the mail around in his hat, collecting the postage. Perhaps Dr. Wright preceded Dougherty, as in his daybook various persons were charged "cash for postage." Wright was a son-in-law of James Fuston, third host of Duncan Tavern. In 1844 Isaac Whaley succeeded Dougherty, holding the position until 1888, with the exception of a few months when, at the beginning of the war, Frank Foster was postmaster for the Confederacy and when, after the war, M. C. Vick held the office a short time. H. L. Hale succeeded Mr. Whaley in 1888. Mrs. Cannie Whaley was appointed some years later. C. L. Bright is the present postmaster.

It should be noted that there were no envelopes until a late day. The writer has before him now a letter addressed in 1827 to "Mr. M. S. West, Liberty, Smith Co., Ten." It is a sheet of paper folded and fastened with a small bit of sealing wax, the amount of postage, ten cents, being marked on the outside. It was mailed at Haysboro, Davidson County, Tenn., and shows that postal rates were high.

In an interview with Isaac Whaley several years ago the writer obtained these facts bearing on the old times: "The letter postage was once six cents from Liberty to Alexandria, seven miles; ten cents to Nashville, fifty-six miles; over four hundred miles the postage was twenty-five cents, double that if the letter consisted of two sheets. Like registered letters to-day, a record of every letter was made on a 'way bill,' each postmaster receipting for it to the postmaster back on the route."

The physicians of Liberty have been numerous. These are recalled: Early, J. R. Dougherty, J. A. Baird, E. Wright, George C. Flowers; Tilman Bethel and Dr. Little, herbists; Horace Sneed, George R. Givan, J. A. Fuson, Thomas Black, J. S. Harrison. Later, A. S. Redman, J. W. Campbell, T. J. Sneed, W. H. Robinson, W. A. Whaley, J. H. Johnson, J. G. Squires, W. A. Barger, Robert Estes, T. O. Bratten, J. R. Hudson. Present, T. J. Jackson, T. J. Bratten, Harrison Adamson.

Dr. Foster mentions the old miller, "Chunky" Joe Hays, whose service was after Adam Dale's time. The Lambersons and Daniel Smith owned the mill still later. W. C. Youngblood and Edward Robinson were owners of the steam mill when it was burned by the troops of Gen. John T. Wilder, Federal.

Allan Wright, of Maryland, came to Liberty in 1866 and built a mill on the site of the one which had been burned, the first to be erected in the county after peace came. For many years the patronage of this mill was very great. Among those who have been connected with it since the war were: E. W. Bass, Jep Williams, George Wood, L. N. Woodside, J. H. Overall, John L. Lamberson, and George Bradley.

A water mill was erected by Buck Waters about 1873 or 1874 a few yards below the site of the Dale mill, the dam which supplies the big turbine wheel being one hundred and twenty-five yards wide and twelve feet high. It was sold to Vannata & Hicks. Within the next few years it was owned by Vannata & Stark Bros., H. L. Hale & Stark Bros., and H. L. and Bruce L. Hale. About 1884 a stock company was formed and the roller process installed, the stockholders being R. L. Floyd, George Turney, R. B. West, Sams Sellars, T. G. Bratten, W. C. Youngblood, B. L. Hale, and C. W. L. Hale. The capital stock was $6,000. On the death of B. L. Hale, in 1898, R. B. Floyd and C. W. L. Hale bought all the shares. The property is now owned by Bradley Bros.

The earliest attempt at publishing in Liberty was made by H. L. and Will T. Hale. The paper was small, miserably printed, and called the *Imp*. Only one issue appeared (September 20, 1879); and had it been larger, its failure would have deserved what the father of the young men cheerfully called it, "a stupendous abortion."

The *Liberty Herald* was established April 1, 1886, by Will A. Vick. Mr. Vick spent considerable money on the plant, and the journal, existing several years, became very popular in DeKalb and surrounding counties.

The Bank of Liberty was established by A. E. Potter and J. J. Smith in 1898. The latter became President, H. L. Overall, Vice President, and A. E. Potter, Cashier. Directors: D. D. Overall, J. J. Smith, H. L. Overall, H. C. Givan, C. D. Williams, E. J. Robinson, Will A. Vick, L. D. Hamilton, A. E. Potter, W. R. Robinson, and J. W. Reynolds. Mr. Potter was Cashier until 1895, when D. D. Overall became President and W. H. Overall, Cashier. The officers in 1914 were: John W. Overall, President; Thomas M. Givan, Vice President, T. H. Chapman, Cashier; J. C. Stark, Assistant Cashier. Directors: T. M. Givan, W. H. Overall, T. J. Jackson, J. F. Turner, B. W. Robinson, T. H. Chapman, John W. Overall, and Tom W. Overall.

The American Savings Bank opened for business December 8, 1905. This bank, like the other, has been successfully conducted. The first officers were: T. G. Bratten, President; W. H. Bass, Vice President; J. M. Bradley, Cashier. Directors: G. B. Givan, D. B. Wilson, J. B. West, R. B. Vannata, S. J. Chapman, Mrs. M. J. Corley, J. R. Corley, W. L. Evans, W. F. Hooper, H. M. Evans, J. E. Williams, and J. L. Lamberson. These officers, or all that were living, held their positions until 1914. The President's health became such that on January 10, 1914, the following officers were elected: L. A. Bass, President; G. B. Givan, Vice President; J. M. Bradley, Cashier. Directors: L. A. Bass, G. B. Givan, H. M. Evans, R. B. Vannata, J. M. Bradley, H. A. Bratten, D. B. Wilson,

A. L. Reynolds, A. J. Williams, J. E. Hobson, J. L. Lamberson, W. L. Evans, and S. J. Chapman. H. M. Evans, T. M. Bright, and C. G. Givan, as finance committee, have served since the organization.

Among landmarks reminding this generation of a past era are Lamberson's wellspring and the town spring. The former was on the southwest, with a sweep and the "old oaken bucket." Here on baptizing days the crowds going to and from the place of baptism higher up Smith Fork Creek would stop to quench their thirst and to gossip. The town spring, on the north side, was of more romantic interest. The pioneers greatly appreciated a good spring. It for a while furnished drinking water for almost the entire village. It was walled up, while a long flight of stone steps led down to the entrance on the east side, where a bucketful of the sparkling fluid could be easily dipped up. For half a century it was a Sunday meeting place for the young folks. Seated in couples on the steps or under the big oak on the bluff, they engaged in light badinage or love-making. The spring is yet held in pleasant memory by many elderly people.

There is one other landmark demanding notice, the pioneer cemetery on the northwest edge of Liberty. It is referred to by H. L. Hale as the "old Methodist graveyard." It lies on a gentle slope facing the sunrise, and at one time it must have been a beautiful spot. Pathos now hovers over it. But few stones are standing, and these are the stone pens covered with broad slabs of carefully worked limestone. Not a flower can be seen in the most gorgeous summer save the wild rose. No one walks there to meditate over the departed. A century ago children's voices were heard, and relatives of the dead walked among the tombs to pay the tribute of a sigh. Now nobody cares. James H. Burton writes: "My grandfathers, Ebenezer Burton and John S. Woodside, my father and mother, W. H. and Nancy Burton, and Uncle John Woodside are buried there." H. L. Hale writes: "Few names on the two or three tombs are legible. On a little 'house of rock,' the last home evidently of a husband and wife, this only could be read: '—— Daugherty. Born 1770, died 1828.' Near by was this: 'Caroline Arnold. Died July 22, 1828.' On another tomb: 'D. E. S. Kenner. Died December 4, 1809; age seventy-seven years.' One other: 'Nancy Fite, born 1805; died July 22, 1828.' Judging from the grave of D. E. S. Kenner, the cemetery was used at least one hundred and five years ago, and the slumberer was born the same year Washington was, 1732."

Liberty, fifty-six miles east of Nashville, has suffered much from fires. It is in one of the finest agricultural sections of the State, with a population estimated at five hundred, and perhaps it is of more romantic interest than the other towns in the county.

CHAPTER IV.

Pastimes of the Foreparents.

We should not think of the past in terms of the present, but remember that social advantages of a century ago were far inferior to those of 1914. The society of the grandparents, then, as in all primitive communities, was somewhat rude. The crudeness varied, being less apparent in the villages than farther in the backwoods. While there was some degree of refinement among those who could buy books and visit the outside world occasionally, the majority were plain citizens. Amusements were few. There were parties, sometimes called frolics. Candy-pulling and frumenty boilings were often the outcome of a quilting, log-rolling, or corn-shucking. Such plays as "thimble," "snap," "slapout," and "Jake's a-grinning" would be engaged in. Others would be accompanied by songs on this order:

> The higher up the cherry tree,
>   The riper grows the cherry;
> The sooner you court a pretty girl,
>   The sooner you will marry.

The dances were usually rough in outlying communities. The more cultured, especially near the middle of the nineteenth century, enjoyed the Virginia reel and other less boisterous dances; their plays, too, were more refined.

With people of Anglo-Saxon stock the favorite musical instrument in the first stages of society is the violin. General Stokes and Hon. Horace Overall performed on this instrument. In the mercantile account book of Dr. Wright General Stokes, Richard Arnold, and Green B. Adams are charged with "piano songs" in the first third of the nineteenth century. Does this mean that there were pianos in the county as early as that? Possibly the music was bought to be sung without piano accompaniment. The fiddlers in the county from 1800 to 1875, including black and white, would have no doubt numbered several hundred, and some were so popular that they were in demand on all nearby social and public occasions where music was a feature.

The race course was encouraged and well patronized. There were quite a number of locally famous horses, and some had prestige beyond the borders of the State. Dr. Foster writes:

> The stallions Old Pete, George Boyd, and Steamboat were as well known in the western part of the county about 1845 or 1850 as the most prominent citizens. William Gothard, of Liberty, was a great lover of horses. Lemuel Moore, the tailor, once sold a small "scrub" for thirty-five dollars. The animal turned out to be a racer and soon afterwards sold for eighteen hundred dollars.

Tan Fitts, of near Temperance Hall, owned Dock Alvin, Elizabeth Johnson, and Tom Hal, noted racers.

The most noted animal in the county was Ariel, a quarter horse. The owner was William B. Stokes. It was told that he won so many stakes that few would bet against him, and through a prejudiced cabal he was ruled off the tracks. Whereupon his owner painted him a different color and won other races, but the paint eventually took off the hair. Of course this was apocryphal. Stokes's daughter, Mrs. Leath Calhoun, told the writer that Ariel's leg was broken and that her father gave him to his brother-in-law, Horace Overall, then a lad. Horace and the little slaves put some sort of juice or homemade liniment on the afflicted limb. As it did some good, boylike, they decided to anoint him all over, thinking a greater improvement would result. This denuded him of his once glossy coat. In a conversation with the writer in 1899 Mr. Leander Hayes said: "I recall having passed Colonel Overall's one day and saw the animal standing in the lot by the road. All the hair had slipped from him except that on his belly and the ends of his ears. He was a woeful sight."

What became of Ariel? The next heard of him is through Oliver Taylor's history of Sullivan County, East Tennessee. Taylor says in one place:

Sullivan County wheat took first prize over the world at the Vienna Exposition in 1872, and the bones of the swiftest horse of the racing days between 1845 and 1860 moldered on a field on the old Fain farm east of Blountville.

Farther along in his chapter devoted to politics are these notes:

When General Stokes and De Witt Senter were opposing each other for Governor [in 1869] they engaged in a discussion at Blountville. Stokes was the owner of Ariel, the famous race horse. He appealed to the horse-breeding and agricultural spirit of his countrymen. "The bones of Ariel," said he, "are moldering in Sullivan County soil." Replying to this, Senter said: "I grant you it is a great honor to have the resting place of the fastest horse of the times; but, gentlemen, the bones of an ancestor of mine, who fought in the battle of King's Mountain, are sleeping in Sullivan; and what are the bones of the fastest horse in the world compared with the sacred dust of a man who fought for your liberties?"

It is possible that Ariel, after recovering from the broken leg, was bought and carried to East Tennessee for breeding purposes. Dr. T. J. Jackson, of Liberty, says that he once read a description of Ariel in pamphlet form, and his natural color was described as "snow white."

There were company, regimental, and brigade musters in the first half of the nineteenth century. They became less frequent about 1855.

Solomon in his glory was not much more resplendent than the superior officers at these gatherings. Especially noticeable were their long black or red plumes. When the time came to muster, some one would take a position at some point on the street and cry out: "Oyez, Oyez! All who belong to Captain ———'s company form in a parade here." Another would call the same to a different company a hundred or two yards distant, and so on until all the militia was in action. After forming they, with drum and fife (field officers on prancing horses), would march to a commodious field and evolute and march to the admiration of the surging crowds. Dr. Foster writes:

> As the muster at Smithville was a bigger affair than that at Liberty, it must have been a brigade muster. Colonel Cotton, Major Atnip, and Captain Perkins took great interest in these affairs. The officers' hats, as I remember, were of the stovepipe pattern. Horses not used to the noise and

crowds reared and pranced, but Captain Perkins seemed to enjoy the prancing of his roan steed. In the language of old Tom Askew, all the officers "felt the weight of the argument."

Mr. H. L. Hale, who was almost six years of age when the war began, recalls a muster he witnessed at Liberty and writes:

I think Peter Adams was then colonel of a DeKalb regiment. I can see Colonel Peter sitting his gray charger in a deep Spanish saddle, with high boots and spurs and three-cornered or crescent-shaped hat and large feather or tassel. He was, I thought, the finest and greatest man I ever saw or could expect to see. Tall and straight, he had a military bearing as long as he lived; and, small as I was when I saw him on this occasion, I thought he took special pains to "daddle" that plume by some movement of the head.

He says further: "These companies always marched to the stirring music of fife and drum. There was a Liberty company called the Blues and another the Greens. Ike Lamberson and Jim Bethel, negroes, were noted fifers and drummers."*

---

*Among the State archives are many commissions of muster days. Thus, Thomas Patterson was made captain of the Forty-First Regiment September 18, 1812, George Turney lieutenant, and Josiah Spurlock ensign. Joseph Fite became a captain in the regiment January 28, 1813. Lemuel Moore was commissioned lieutenant of the same regiment June 14, 1813, and Moses Garrison September 14, 1814. In the last-named year Shadrack Moore was made a second major of the Sixteenth Regiment March 21, while Beverly Strange (or Strong) became captain April 13. James Malone figures as early as August 31, 1813, as lieutenant.

Shooting matches were greatly appreciated, and there were crack shots celebrated throughout the county, W. G. Evans and John McDowell among others.

The chase is appreciated in all new countries, and it was so in this county. Until long after the War between the States some farmers kept packs of fox hounds. It would be interesting to know their breed. But they were black and tan, with an occasional grayish or pied animal, lank, with long pendulous ears, calling to mind Shakespeare's description: "Ears that swept away the morning dew, . . . matched in mouth like bells." Farm neighbors would meet each other with their packs on some high point in the hills and spend the hours from dark to dawn's approach and listen and listen and listen. The charm born of night in the woods around the fire waiting for the hounds to open up! The music of the trailing pack wafted over hill and hollow! The man who takes part in all this once soon finds the lure irresistible, and the chase becomes a habit.

The writer has heard his mother describe the corn-shuckings and the shanty songs sung while the men were at work. A banquet would follow the husking of the big piles of maize about midnight. Though the corn-shucking meant work for the negroes, they enjoyed any occasion where they were free to indulge in antics and humor. Whisky and brandy were plentiful on these occasions. The report of a "husking bee" held in the northern corn belt some years ago showed that a champion shucked ten and a half bushels in an hour. Something like that was probably turned out at the corn-shuckings mentioned.

Superstition prevailed, and, indeed, it still prevails to some extent. The writer does not claim freedom from it and admits that he will not willingly pass under a ladder, pare his nails on Sunday, tell a dream on Friday morning before breakfast, nor step over another's feet! The inculcation of superstitious notions has been laid to the slaves; but our ancestors were as much to blame, if any blame can be said to attach, since the wisest minds now give credence to the occult.

The social visit, as it was of old, might well be classed with amusements. There was still a genuine hospitality existing, and for neighbors, though not related, to pay each other a visit Saturday afternoon and remain until Sunday afternoon was no uncommon thing. This was called "going abroad"; by the children, "goin' on a broad." Perhaps Saturday night was the most interesting part of the visit. Around the great wood fire in winter or upon the porch in summer the gossip of the neighborhood would be discussed, then would follow stories of adventure and the supernatural, relieved with humorous anecdotes. Greatly enjoyed, too, was the evening call, when neighbors would merely "drop in" and sit till bedtime.

Reverting to the society of the foreparents, it should be stated that looking on wine when it was red and corn whisky when it was white was almost universal. In 1840 there were 1,274 distilleries in the State. The best citizens made, sold, and drank intoxicants. There was scarcely a gathering where men did not drink—musters, races, elections, and weddings. The bibulous frequently disturbed camp meetings. Children were "treated" on Christmas morning. Of course there were temperance advocates. When Bird S. Rhea and H. A. Overall were candidates to represent the county in 1853, the former was defeated, it is thought, because of his temperance principles.

DeKalb County had its share of the 1,274 "stills." Perhaps the first was put up about 1801 by Jesse Allen on Eagle Creek. The writer's maternal grandfather, Abraham Overall, was a distiller, and from his old account book we get an idea of the cheapness of ardent spirits and realize how the best people kept a supply. Among his customers were Thomas Richardson, Moses Allen, Dr. Flowers, Dr. Jefferson Sneed, William Goggin, Josiah Fuson, Samson Braswell, John Allen, Josiah Hale, Matthew Sellars, Samuel Barger, William Pistole, Joseph Hays, James Stark, Hiram Morris, Joseph Turney, Daniel Ford, Francis Turner, Isaac Turney, Jacob Adams, Henry Powell, Goolsberry Blades, 'Bias Wilson, and Peter Clark. Polly Stanly and Polly Huchens purchased largely, perhaps to sell. The latter on July 17, 1841, was charged $3 for six gallons. Under the same date is this entry: "Three gallons whisky in evening of the election, $1.50." Here are the purchases of one farmer for about seven months of 1844. The buyer's name is withheld, although on the book: April 12, one gallon of brandy, .62½; April 17, one gallon of whisky (order), .37½; April 27, one gallon of whisky, .37½; May 1, one gallon of whisky, .37½; May 9, one gallon of whisky, .37½; May 23, one gallon of whisky, .37½; May 29, one gallon of whisky, .37½; June 18, one gallon of whisky, .37½; June 27, one gallon of whisky, .37½; July 12, one gallon of whisky, .37½; July 17, one gallon of whisky, .37½; August 24, one gallon of whisky, .37½; November 6, one gallon of brandy, .40.

CHAPTER V.

Farming and Merchandising.

THREE early land offices had been opened in Tennessee at different times. That for Middle Tennessee was opened in 1783. A military reservation was laid off to satisfy bounties promised the Revolutionary soldiers of North Carolina. Thousands of acres were taken up. As no method of selecting land was used (the holder of a warrant could explore and locate anywhere and in any shape), the best was taken up, and poor tracts were left in every section. The North Carolina demands for her old soldiers were allowed even after Tennessee became a State. Each private was given 640 acres; each noncommissioned officer, 1,000; each captain, 3,840; each colonel, 7,200; and so on. Gen. Nathaniel Green was granted 25,000 acres.

Many warrants were located on DeKalb County lands. Not all the soldiers or their heirs desired to locate here, though some came. So numerous claims were bought up by speculators, Linn Cocke being one of the best known.

Early crops were hemp, cotton, and tobacco in more than one portion of the county. Neither cotton nor hemp is now grown here. Wheat to-day is one of the main crops, but the pioneers grew so little of it that wheat bread was with a host only a Sunday morning luxury. Wheat had to be cut with hand sickles and threshed with a flail or tramped out by horses and oxen, and making it into flour was not easily done. The grain was ground between rough millstones and the product bolted by hand. Before the turnpike was built, corn, which has always been the American pioneer's stand-by, could not be carried to distant markets with profit, and this may be one reason why there were so many distilleries in the early years. Cotton and hemp were used largely in making clothing for the slaves, for there were many in the county. John K. Bain, whose father, Peter Bain, settled near the mouth of Sink Creek in 1812, says: "The productions of that section were corn, wheat, oats, and rye. Reaping was done with hand sickles. Plows used were bull tongues. Iron cost twenty-five cents a pound. The range was good. Hogs got fat on beech mast, dry cattle lived on the range all winter, and there was no thoroughbred stock." Dr. Foster writes: "Corn about 1845 sold for $1 a barrel, or ten cents the bushel if you went to the country after it. I remember when the best horses sold for $40; then the price went up some, and as fine a horse as I ever saw in the county was bought by John F. Moore at Liberty for $100. Hauling was done mostly with oxen, many men driving two yokes. As fine apples grew in the Basin as anywhere."

An account book of 1844, once belonging to Col. Abraham Overall, gives an insight to farm products and prices of that period; they were probably about the same throughout the county. Hemp retailed on the farm at about five cents the pound; tobacco, four cents; flour, $1.50 per one hundred pounds; apples and sweet potatoes, twenty-five cents the bushel.

Freight by wagon from Nashville to Liberty was sixty cents per one hundred pounds.

If the foreparents did not generally have pure-bred stock, they had good crosses, judging by the great herds of hogs driven south yearly. The Copperbottom horse was popular, as was the Morgan. Doubtless the Narragansett was known, since for years pacing was an appreciated gait. William B. Stokes, T. W. Fitts, and others made a specialty of fine horses in ante-bellum days. It might be interesting to dwell on such breeds of poultry as the old dominique and shanghai, once prized but now differentiated into brahmas and cochins. Likewise vegetables like peachblow and London lady potatoes and the small varieties of tomatoes or "love apples," as they were then called.

The grandparents lived well. Vegetables were carefully stored for winter use. Smokehouse and larder were full. Maple sirup and New Orleans molasses were used, as sorghum was not introduced into America until 1853. Loaf sugar was a delicacy, though there was a cheap quality of brown sugar.

The earliest merchants of the county doubtless carried small stocks. One reason was that merchandise was hauled long distances. Another was that every village had its hatter, tailor, shoemaker, and saddler. Handmade things were the rule. Much cloth was manufactured at home (housewives vying with each other in weaving) and made up at home or by the tailor. Isaac Whaley once gave this pointer to the writer: "Our people generally wore homespun clothes

—the women cotton dresses striped with indigo and turkey red, though some had silk. The men's clothing was usually made by tailors, our first tailor at Liberty being Bill Cochran; the second, Joe Perryman. The best of our early hatters was Mathias West, who made considerable money. Wool and fur hats were made. Mr. West could make as fine a 'stovepipe' as you will see. The price was $7 or $8, and when the fur was worn off the hat was brought back and made as good as new. The wealthiest people, like Francis Turner, Ned Robinson, and Abraham Overall, had fine broadcloth suits made by the tailors." The old people have always claimed that merchandise was frequently brought from New Orleans, necessitating high prices with the middlemen, for the trip by keel boat required five months. Even the Liberty merchants may have got some of their wares by water, for this item is found in Dr. Wright's daybook: "John Conger, credit for raising flatboat and keeping her till next boating season in Caney Fork, $20."

By 1830, however, stocks of goods were no doubt enlarged, and Alexandria may have made the innovation. Dr. Foster writes that "the people of that town were always more dressy than in other parts of the county"; while the writer remembers the remark frequently made by Squire Len F. Woodside just after the War between the States: "Yes, sir, the Petersons don't send to Paris, but to Alexandria, for the latest fashions with which to illustrate their magazine."

But Dr. Wright's daybook indicates that his stock was full enough for a village store. It also indicates that his patrons bought on time; moreover, there is not an item charged at five cents. Joshua Bratten is charged twenty-five cents for half a pound of powder; Col. Abe Overall, $2 for eight pounds of coffee and 12 cents a pound for sugar; Hariette C. Roulstone, 43 cents for two yards of "apron checks"; Thomas Cameron, 75 cents for three yards of domestic; David L. Ray, $1.50 for three yards of calico; Leonard Lamberson, 62½ cents for a fourth of a pound of tea; John R. Dougherty, 62½ cents for a pound of raisins; E. Wright, 12 cents for two dozen eggs; John M. Leake, $1 for a bandanna handkerchief; Irving Gray (hatter), $2.50 for six yards of calico; Jacob Overall, 12 cents for two gimlets; Littleberry Vick, $5.75 for twenty-three yards of homespun; Louis Y. Davis, 25 cents for two pounds of "homemade" (maple) sugar; Col. Abe Overall, $7.50 for a mill saw (probably the straight sort); Elizabeth Overall, $2.25 for a cotton umbrella, "to be paid for in brown jeans"; Liberty Lodge, No. 77, "to cash to pay postage, 6½ cents"; William Blair, two reap hooks, $1.50; Asia Cooper, one dozen button molds, 6½ cents, and one paper of tacks, 18½ cents; W. B. Stokes, four pounds of nails, 50 cents; W. G. Stokes, one drab hat, $8.50, one cravat stiffening, 12½ cents, and one vial oil of cinnamon, 25 cents; Bartimeus Pack, one hymn book, 75 cents; Richard Arnold, one fur hat, $6. Calico was worth 50 cents the yard; nutmegs, 6¼ cents each. A lady is charged 87½ cents for three and a half yards of domestic and 60 cents for a pair of cotton hose. T. W. Duncan buys a dozen gun flints for 6½ cents, and John Canler a paper of ink powder for 18¾ cents. James B. Pistole is charged $8 for "one Tom and Jerry hat"; William C. Garrison, $3 "for Webster's speeches"; William B. Stokes, 62½ cents for "one piano song"; L. H. Bethel, 37½ cents to pay postage; Thomas E. Bratten, 75 cents for a gallon of molasses. There is a charge of $1.20 for four pounds of loaf sugar. Loaf sugar was in conical packages and came ready wrapped in dark-blue paper. Somewhat pathetic is this charge of eighty-two years ago, "Two boys' balls, 6½ cents," for one cannot help wondering what came of the boy or boys. A farmer is credited $2 for twenty-four and a half pounds of butter and another $2.16½ for six and a half pounds of wool.

The leghorn hat was fashionable then and later. Was it also called a "poke" bonnet? A writer in the Liberty *Herald* in 1892 stated that the "leghorn bonnets were a foot and a half long, more or less, without any artificials, simply a plain ribbon drawn across the top and tied under the chin."

The Dunstable bonnet was much in vogue. One is charged in the following bill to Miss Elizabeth O. Hall: "One Dunstable bonnet and trimmings, $6; six yards blk. silk, $6; seven yards calico, $3.50; pair side combs, 12½ cents; one best fancy handkerchief, $2; twelve strands beads, 87½ cents; one black bobbinet veil, $2.50; one black bandanna handkerchief, $1; two and a half yards bobbinet lace, $1.56½."

Among the products of the farm in 1832-33 were cheese and flax seed. David Griffith's account was credited with 62½ cents for one and a quarter pounds flax seed; and at the time Jordan Sellars was charged $9 for "one fine fur hat," he was credited with 85 cents for eight and a half pounds of cheese.

Since Isaac Whaley's reference to the clothing worn by the foreparents has been introduced in this chapter, it will be only a second digression to quote the words of an old DeKalb Countian who wrote from Missouri to the Liberty *Herald* April 6, 1892, of before-the-war days:

> For Sunday many of the well-to-do men wore a blue or black broadcloth coat which cost from four to ten dollars a yard. They were usually cut with a frock or "claw-hammer" tail and rolling collar. The black and white satin vest, double-breasted, was worn by the fashionable. Pants were made very loose and had wide or narrow flaps before, invariably. A black silk cravat, doubled crosswise, was worn around a collar of uncertain dimensions. The dress described was worn by the fashionable, such as Eli Vick, Jasper Ruyle, Pete Adams, Len Walker, Joseph Clarke, Peter Clark, and others on Sunday. Later Dr. Horace Sneed, Dr. J. S. Harrison, the Hayes boys, the Turners, and the Turneys were the leaders in fashion. Many women sometimes wore silk dresses—not gaudy-colored, but plain black silk. A calico dress was seldom seen. Nearly all dresses were made with two widths of cloth and a gore on each side. Hoop skirts were as rare among women as drawers among men. All young women wore their dresses fastened behind. No such institution as a corset was thought of. The hair was usually parted in the middle, a strip bent around each ear, and wound up with a large horn comb at the back of the head.

The people did much trading by exchanging one commodity for another. The amount of money in circulation must have been negligible. For instance, this note was made by Colonel Overall, who was not poor, but owned perhaps twenty-five hundred acres of land, a score of slaves, a mill, cotton gin, and distillery: "The amount of money that I have spent since the 26th of August, 1844: September 10, $1; September 18, 50 cents; September 20, 50 cents; October 1, $1; October 20, $2; October 25, 45 cents; November 9, 50 cents; December 6, $5."

Life was "slow" compared with this age that goes the pace that kills, but it had its advantages. One worth $10,000 or $12,000 was in easy circumstances. With his slaves, abundant crops, and loaded tables, he made a social impression that is not now made with thrice that amount. He had time to read; he indulged in hospitality; and, free from business cares, behind his grave demeanor lurked a trace of humor tragically absent from the countenances of the nervous men of the present.

CHAPTER VI.

Relating to Education.

We owe a debt of gratitude to the old field tutors who for poor pay labored in the cause of mental and moral attainment when we had no adequate public school law. Of course there were many instances in the county where parents were able to send their children to schools where the advantages were greater. James Givan, speaking for the Clear Fork country, has said: "The settlers from Virginia—they were called the upper ten by their neighbors—in some instances sent their children back to the Old Dominion for schooling or to well-established boarding schools." But the old field teacher was the main reliance of the masses.

Dr. T. W. Wood, who was reared in Cannon County and who is past threescore and ten, says: "I have heard my father speak of having studied Dillworth's speller and Johnson's dictionary. I used Webster's speller (which has never been surpassed), Kirkham's grammar, McGuffey's reader, Smiley's arithmetic, Walker's dictionary, Davies's algebra, and Mitchell's geography and arithmetic." Dr. Wood adds: "It was nothing uncommon for free schools to last only six weeks or two months. Teachers were paid from $20 to $30 per month, frequently holding forth in log cabins with dirt floors and wooden benches without backs. The writing desk consisted of a broad plank attached to the wall. More attention was paid to penmanship, reading, spelling, and arithmetic than to-day. The true basis of education is more neglected now than then." John K. Bain wrote in his eighty-seventh year: "From 1836 to 1842, or later, there were no free schools in my section—all subscription. The teacher took his seat and made each scholar stand beside him to say his lesson. He kept a long switch, fully four feet, sticking up over the door. There were no classes. The books used were Webster's speller, Smiley's arithmetic, McGuffey's readers, and geography. One of my teachers was Glasgow Harper, who finally became a Methodist preacher and moved down near Liberty or on Smith's Fork." Dr. J. B. Foster gave this information in 1914: "The schoolbooks sixty and seventy years ago were Webster's speller (my copy, however, was yellow, not blue, and I recall having written on the inside 'bird foster'), McGuffey's readers, Smith's grammar at Liberty and Kirkham's at Smithville, Smiley's and Pike's arithmetics, and Olney's geography. There were others for advanced pupils. At all old field schools two pupils would choose spellers and have a 'spelling battle' on Friday afternoons. When a pupil wanted to 'go out' in some instances he (to keep tab) had to carry a crooked stick, and on his return he hung it back on a nail in the wall. The presence of the stick meant 'all are in; now you can go out.' It was a sort of passport. Blackboards were not then in use. Big and little were whipped when the teacher thought they needed chastisement. The pupil who reached the schoolhouse first 'said' his lesson first; 'recite' was not used. At the writing hour the girls practiced first and then the boys. Goose quill pens were common. Vials took the place of inkstands. In each was a piece of cotton, holding the absorbed ink in case the bottle was turned over, and when not in use the bottles were suspended on nails by strings. The larger pupils were allowed to sit outside and 'cipher,' study grammar, and the like. Boys and girls did not play together, and young teachers were partial to boys who had pretty sisters."

Corporal punishment was indeed in vogue. Often it was severe, even for some years after the close of the War between the States. Sometimes as effective a punishment as could be administered was to make a mischievous lad sit beside a girl. Thus exposed to gaze, he was the pink victim of snickering playmates. Doubtless that course would not embarrass young America to-day.

Geographies being scarce, once a day, usually late in the afternoon, the entire school stood against the walls and "sang geography," the teacher leading. Nations or States with the capitals and the names and height of mountains were the main things learned in this way. The chanting would run somewhat thus: "Ar-kan-sas, Ar-kan-sas—Little Rock, Little Rock;" or, "Copenhagen, Copenhagen—Denmark, Denmark."

School hours were from sunrise to sunset, with a "recess" in both forenoon and afternoon, and "playtime" took up an hour in the middle of the day. The lunch brought by children to be eaten during recess was called "recess," not "snack" or lunch. The games played were town ball, bull pen, Ant'ny-over, marbles, knucks, and fox chase. The favorite relaxation of the girls was jumping the rope. From time out of mind the shouting of "school butter" by a passer-by was resented by the pupils and maybe the teacher. Chief Justice John Marshall was now and then, he tells us, chased for uttering the challenge and could not explain why it caused resentment or how it originated. Recently through the Nashville *Banner* a Tennessee lady has said that "school butter" is a corruption of the taunt, "the school's better"—that is, the school's superior. If caught, the challenger was ducked in the nearest stream or mudhole and punished for his temerity.

The writer was a pupil of these first schools. Often, when among new friends in his experiences in the daily journalism of various cities, he has forgotten them and thought of his boyhood playmates. His affection for the latter was on one occasion expressed in the following lines, which, if not of historical interest, may yet appeal to survivors of the old times:

The time for cakes and ale is gone for us of grizzled hair—
But that can't make our hearts forget how old school days shone fair.
Outside the house—the waving woods where rose the brown bees' hum,
And the wild roses that appeared dead lovers' vows in bloom;
Within—the boys in homespun suits, the teacher's mighty frowns,
And girls, though plainly dressed, as plump as those in silken gowns.
And Zekle Moore and Abner Smith, Sue Brown and Mary Strong!
Your plain, old-fashioned names are fit to grace the sweetest song.

Where are you, tow-head boys who felt each day the birchen rod,
And knew how well to place the pin and aim the paper wad?
Where are the girls on whom back there we cast admiring eyes—
Whose smiles brought back to earth once more some hints of Paradise?
Old time has been as rough with them no doubt as with us blades,
And some are fat-and-forty dames and some perhaps old maids! . . .
But there was one of pleasant mien I think of oft and long
And wish she knew a thought of her throbs through this little song.

In all probability the earliest school in DeKalb County was taught at Liberty. Among the early teachers there were a Mr. Chambers and William Gay. Their names recur more persistently to the older people than others of the ante-bellum years. The latter married a daughter of the merchant, Seth Whaley, and is described by Dr. Foster as having "two or three fingers missing from one hand and parting his hair in the middle." Mr. and Mrs. Gay removed to Missouri. Mrs. Rachel Payne, as will be seen elsewhere, says that Mr. Chambers was the first to keep school in the first specially erected schoolhouse, the long one-story frame building which stood from about 1843 to some time during the war, when it was torn down by order of Col. William B. Stokes and the lumber used for making cabins for the officers of his regiment about the stockade, northwest of the Methodist church.

Richard Carroll, a lame pedagogue, came from Smith County with Frederick Jones, tailor and tavern keeper. John Collins, who also may have taught at Alexandria, was for a while in charge of a school at Liberty. Writes Dr. Foster: "Collins and C. G. O. Smith were teachers who occasionally imbibed—kept intoxicants hid out." Among other ante-bellum teachers were Professor Crane, who married Miss Amanda Seay and who, being Northern-born, returned to Indiana during the secession excitement, C. W. L. Hale, W. D. G. Carnes, and Roland Foster. This writer started out during Mr. Foster's time to lay the foundation of an education, being very small, tow-headed, and bare of feet. Reaching the door with his brother Horace that summer morning, he espied Billy Gothard sitting astride one stove and George Smith astride the other. They were being punished thus for some mischief. This startled him, and he shot under the house, where he remained long enough to devour his "recess," and then took to his heels in the direction of home.

Dr. Foster refers further to teachers at Liberty prior to 1851, naming Joseph Perryman, A. M. Jones, Robert Yeargin, and Mr. Woodward. The last named remained only a short while.

The writer recalls these later teachers: W. D. G. Carnes, John Truitt, Miss Cynthia Fuston, Miss Hattie Woodside, Mrs. Thomas Adamson (from Iowa), Rev. D. P. Searcy, John F. Roy, Horace M. Hale, Miss Callie Sneed, W. D. Gold, Miss Sallie Coward, W. A. Barger, John Bryan, Miss Amelia Bryan, Hood and Baker (from the North), Jones and Renick, Mr. Friece (from the North), Rev. James Turner, Thomas Turner, Professor Paschal, Miss Stevens, S. B. Sherrill, Alona Gossett, Robert Smithson, Professor Rose, Professor Crewes, E. W. Brown, J. H. Killman, and Matt Bratten. The teachers in 1914 were: Horace L. Smith, principal; Misses Gene Crowley and Bessie Saunders, assistants; and Miss Mildred Mathis, music teacher.

It is believed that the first building put to educational purposes was the old log church, Salem, then the new frame which took its place. After the war of 1861-65, the latter was again used; so was the Methodist church; and Miss Cynthia Fuston kept school awhile in a log cabin in the eastern part of the village. In 1869 the Masonic Academy was erected, the first teachers being H. M. Hale, principal, and Miss Callie Sneed, assistant. In the present decade the high school building was erected.

It should be stated that shortly after Masonic Academy was built differences arose between some of the patrons as to how the common school fund should be managed. As a result another house, William Blackburn leading, was put up near the pioneer graveyard north of the village. A few sessions were held in it, when it fell into disuse.

Old residents of Alexandria think that the first school kept there was by Wyley Reynolds in a log house about 1820. Persons who remember him say that he was above the average as an instructor. Later in a frame house John Collins taught the young idea how to shoot. A frame building was about 1840 especially erected for educational purposes. According to

Goodspeed's history, Masonic Academy followed in 1856, and in 1858 Lawrence College. The two latter, attractive and substantial structures, gave evidence of the people's love of learning, and in their time turned out many well-informed men and cultured women.

Prior to the great war subscription schools were also taught by Miss Bettie Minor, Miss Mary Mortimer, and Mrs. Susan Bryant.

Other teachers besides Reynolds and Collins have been: John Ogden, Thomas Bunday, William Rust, Frank Smith, Messrs. Pirkey, Joy, McKnight, and William Hi Smith, Mr. and Mrs. Sawyer, Mr. and Mrs. Blackington, Mr. and Mrs. Davis, Mr. and Mrs. Magoffin, James Turner, Thomas Eastes, H. L. W. Gross, Mrs. T. L. Gold, J. L. Boon, and others. Professor Boon was in charge in 1914, his assistants being Misses Odom, Lucas, and Coles.

Very little is known relative to early Smithville schools of the old field variety, but there were such. Dr. Foster recalls the following, who taught after 1851: William Eastham, Thomas Bunday, William Dawson, and Mr. Moore.

In 1838 Fulton Academy was chartered. This, a commodious brick building, became famous locally within a few years for its able instructors. The trustees of the institution were Thomas Durham, Moses Pedigo, Samuel Allen, Martin Phillips, and Bernard Richardson. The following taught in the academy: William Hi Smith, of Williamson County; H. G. Hampton, of Franklin County; Mr. Bentley, of Maury

County; John F. Moore, of Vermont; R. F. Sanders and J. J. and W. R. Smith. About 1880-81 Pure Fountain College was erected. It was three stories and cost about $12,000. It was burned, and a building of two stories took its place. One of the teachers at Pure Fountain College was Prof. T. B. Kelley, of Maury County. He took charge in 1883.

A noted ante-bellum school was Union Institute, a mile and a half out on the Sparta road. Mr. Ghormsley, who established it, was a minister of the Christian Church and a thorough instructor. He finally engaged in horse-trading, driving the animals south. Becoming bankrupt, he left the country.

Names of present tutors: J. S. Wood, A. Colvert, Miss Ocie Powers, Miss Janie Miller, and Mrs. Oma Foster, teacher of music.

In the sketches of Temperance Hall, Dowelltown, Laural Hill, and Forks-of-the-Pike will be found educational notes as to those sections. These names should be added to the list of men and women who have taught in the county at one time or another: W. G. Crowley, Mrs. Peter Adams, Miss Lizzie Simpson, Alex Robinson, his son William, Milton Ward, Robert C. Nesmith, Glasgow Harper, Terry Trapp, Mr. Whitlock (of Dismal Creek), Uncle Johnnie Sneed, James A. Nesmith, H. C. Givan, Dan Williams, and H. L. Overall.

The following have been Superintendents of Public Instruction: Terry Trapp, who served from the organization of the free school system until 1880, when he was succeeded by J. W. Overall; Alvin Avant,

1881; Dick Goodson, 1887; M. T. Martin, 1889; E. W. Brown, 1891; W. J. Gothard, 1895; J. E. Drake, 1899; R. H. Lankford, 1903; Martha Robinson, 1907; J. S. Woods, 1909; J. F. Caplinger, 1913.

The Board of Education for 1914 selected teachers for the schools of the county as follows:

Upper Helton, Richard McGinness; New Hope, Wiley Dinkins.

Green Hill, Otis Turney; Goggin School, Gertrude Wilson; Pea Ridge, C. H. Vickers and Harrison Ashford; Adamson's Branch, Tommy Cripps.

Possum Hollow, Robert Fuson; Church School, Miss Hattie Sanders; Cripps' School, V. R. Fuson and Miss Hildah Fuson; George School, Less Fuson; Crossroads, Floice Vickers and Virgil Gilreath, co-principals.

Helton, Howard Hobson, principal; Miss Corinne McNelly, assistant.

Pisgah, Mack Reynolds; Capling, Mrs. Carrie Jones; Bluff School, C. A. Malone.

Four Corners, Miss Willie Bell, principal; assistant to be supplied.

Temperance Hall, Leroy Smith (principal), Miss Stella Young (assistant); Cove Hollow, Claude Christian; Long Branch, L. L. Braswell; colored school, Lizzie Stokes.

Bethel House, Grady Kelley; Walker's Creek, Hugh Robinson.

Cooper's Chapel, M. C. Bratten (principal), Miss Mai Robinson (assistant); Dowelltown, Starnes and

Malone; June Bug, Robert White; colored school, Maggie Talley.

It was ordered that the pay of the teachers be the same as for 1913, which was for secondary schools, $45; primary, $40, excepting Bethel, Green Hill, Goggin, Mud College, Jones House, Rock Castle, and Dale Ridge, which were placed at $35. The salary of assistant teachers was $30 for teachers with experience and $25 per month for the new ones. Colored teachers receive $30 per month.

In 1823 the first public school law in the State was passed, providing for the application of public funds to establish "poor schools" or to pay the tuition of poor children in other schools. From this is dated the long-time prejudice against public schools, which were called "poor schools" down to recent times. The first efficient system became a law in 1867; while the present system, which has been added to and strengthened from time to time, was instituted in 1873.

CHAPTER VII.

Religious History.

THE first ministers to locate in Tennessee were: Samuel Doak, Presbyterian, who also established the earliest school; Tidence Lane, Baptist, who arrived almost as early as Doak, about 1780; and Jeremiah Lambert, Methodist, who came in 1783. Rev. Charles Cummings, Presbyterian, often visited the East Tennessee settlers before the coming of any of the aforementioned, but he resided at Abingdon, or Wolf Hills, Va. In 1810 the Cumberland Presbyterian Church was organized in Dickson County. The Lutherans formed an organization in 1825, the Christians in 1826, the Episcopalians in 1827, and the Catholics in 1830.

It is probable that the earliest church in DeKalb County was erected by the Baptists of Liberty. In Grime's history of Middle Tennessee Baptists it is said that Cantrell Bethel, born in Maryland December 17, 1779, and died near Liberty October 22, 1848, came with the colony that "marked the establishing of the first town in Tennessee between Nashville and the Cumberland Mountains" and settled half a mile west of Liberty. Not long afterwards he became converted; and as there were no Baptists in that section, he joined Union Church, in Warren County, Ky. On his return from Kentucky he began his ministry, gathered a band of his faith at the present Brush Creek, in Smith County, and constituted a Church there May 29, 1802; and then, securing an "arm" from

Brush Creek at Liberty, established Salem Church at the latter place in August, 1809, becoming the elder or pastor.

But an even earlier preacher who became prominent in the Baptist Church was Rev. John Fite. He also located west of Liberty. He was born in Maryland in 1758 or 1759 and was a Presbyterian minister when he came to this section. Becoming a Baptist preacher in 1812, he died near Liberty February 18, 1852. Elder Fite was the father of Moses and Henry Fite, also grandfather of James, Robert, and Thomas Fite, who are yet living in other States and maintaining the prestige of high citizenship established by their ancestors.

Salem Baptist Church, at Liberty, was constituted an independent body in August, 1809, with thirty-one members. The first building was of logs and was 25 by 30 feet. About 1849 a frame building took its place, and this in turn was replaced by the present frame structure, 40 by 70 feet, about 1880. The membership has been large in recent years, numbering three hundred and twenty-one in 1902. Pastors: Cantrell Bethel, 1809-37 (William Dale supplying a part of this period while Bethel was on a missionary tour); Joshua Lester, 1837-46; Henry Fite, 1846-47; Nathaniel Hays, 1847-68; L. H. Bethel, 1868-71; J. W. Hunt, 1871-72; J. R. Bowman, 1872-73; J. W. Hunt and J. R. Bowman, 1873-75; J. W. Hunt, 1875-76; T. J. Eastes, 1876-83; J. M. Stewart, 1883-86; William Simpson, 1886-87; T. J. Eastes, 1887-1902; William Wauford, 1902-13; R. L. Bell, 1913.

History of DeKalb County

It may be well to name some of the early clerks of this historic Church: Adam Dale (the first Liberty settler and miller), 1809-16; William Givan, 1816-20; Tilman Bethel, 1820-50; Seth Whaley, 1850-51; James Bratten, 1851-71; J. A. Fite, 1871-72; James Allan, 1872-78; I. N. Fite, 1878-79; L. J. Bratten, 1879 until his death, more than twenty years. Among the deacons were the following: John Horn, Nehemiah Garrison, William Dale, James Evans, E. Parsons, Joseph Hays, Moses Fite, 1822; Henry Fite, Sr., 1829; George Givan, 1845; Seth Whaley, 1845; Thomas Givan and James Hollandsworth, 1851; James Stark and Thomas Fite, 1871; I. N. Fite and William Robinson, 1878; T. M. Givan and J. A. Bass, 1886; Henry Fite, Jr., 1886; F. M. Turner and J. C. Bass, 1889; H. M. Fite and J. D. Smith, 1891; T. G. Bratten, 1891; Horace Evans and James Stark, Jr., 1897.

Salem has sent out this list of ministers: John Fite; Nathaniel Hays ("Uncle Natty"); William Dale, 1815; John Horn, 1819; James Evans, 1825; R. Wilson, 1819; Henry Fite, 1837; Lafayette Perryman, 1872; J. H. Vickers, 1881; R. E. Smith, 1886. The following were licensed as exhorters in the old days when this custom was in vogue: Jonathan Hendrixon, John Haas, Lemuel G. Griffons, William Gossett, Moses Fite, and others. Among former elders or pastors, these sleep in Salem Cemetery: Cantrell Bethel, James Evans (who died early from the kick of a mule, and was said to have been the first adult buried there), William Dale, Archamac Bass, Nathaniel Hays, Henry Fite, John Fite, and J. W. Hunt.

History of DeKalb County

The writer recalls a number of ministers of the county who were living during the war and shortly afterwards and pauses to pay them his tribute. One was Rev. Nathaniel Hays, born about 1807, ordained to preach in 1846, preached his first and last sermon at New Hope, and died October 28, 1868. Such was his life that he was not molested by either side during the war, though the antagonisms of that struggle brought something like chaos to the country. One can hardly estimate the good he accomplished after the war. A big man physically, he was strong-souled also, and people had faith in him. Hundreds of ex-soldiers listened to him, forgot heart bitternesses, and took the straight and narrow way. When the writer dreams of real heroes as they appeared to his boyhood eyes, he thinks of Natty Hays, Hall Bethel, Moses Fite, and two or three consecrated Methodists who for more than a generation stood unfalteringly for the cause of God.

New Hope is situated south of Alexandria. Rev. William Dale, who bought the farm known in later years as the Eli Rowland place, began preaching at Thomas Finley's home, but in 1818 established the Church with eighteen members. A building was erected, and the earlier pastors were: William Dale, W. P. Hughes, Archamac Bass, Henry Fite, Nathaniel Hays, T. J. Eastes, J. C. Brien, J. R. Hearn, J. M. Stewart, William Simpson, A. C. Webb, J. F. McNabb, and Stephen Robinson.

The Smithville Church was constituted August 25, 1844, with fourteen members, in the Methodist church.

A house of worship was erected about 1858. The pastors have been: Jesse Allen, 1847-60; Hall Bethel, 1860-70; J. C. Brien, 1870-73; J. R. Bowman, 1873-75; A. J. McNabb, 1875-76; T. J. Eastes, 1876-78; J. J. Martin, 1878—; J. J. Porter, about 1880; J. C. Brien, about 1881-85; J. T. Oakley, about 1885-88; N. R. Sanborn, 1889-90; William Simpson, 1890-91; W. H. Smith, 1891-92; J. H. Grime, 1893-95; J. T. Oakley, 1896—; and A. P. Moore. Clerks to 1902: J. L. Bond, Abner Witt, P. P. Johnson, J. A. Wilson, and L. W. Beckwith.

Indian Creek Church, eight miles north of Smithville, dates back to 1844. First named Caney Fork Church, it was changed to Indian Creek in 1848. Among its pastors were Henry Fite, J. C. Brien, William Simpson, J. M. Stewart, D. C. Taylor, D. W. Taylor, A. J. Waller, and W. E. Wauford.

A noted old log church, known to the present generation only as a Methodist church, was Goshen, on Dismal Creek, north of Liberty. It was constituted a Baptist Church in July, 1821, by Cantrell Bethel and John Fite. Fite was the only pastor it ever had, as not much interest was aroused, and the Church was dissolved in 1837. From then on for years the Methodists controlled the religious sentiment of the community. About 1879 Rev. J. C. Brien began preaching in the neighborhood. As a result Cooper's Chapel was constituted in 1880 with nine members. J. C. Brien was the first pastor. Others have been: J. R. Hearn, J. H. Vickers, William Simpson, W. E. Raikes, A. C. Webb, J. F. McNabb, J. A. McClusky, and

Stephen Robinson. The Church was named for Isaac Cooper, a Mexican War and Confederate veteran. Though a Methodist (but afterwards uniting with the Baptist congregation), the erection of Cooper's Chapel was due mainly to his efforts.

Mount Zion is situated near Temperance Hall. With fourteen members the Church was instituted June 30, 1851, in an old schoolhouse. Soon after its constitution Nicholas Smith was received by letter. He went to work arousing interest in the need of a church. It was erected and the first services held in it June, 1858. Pastors to 1902: Henry Fite, Nathaniel Hays, J. C. Brien, T. J. Eastes, S. S. Hale, William Simpson, J. M. Steward, A. C. Webb, J. F. McNabb, and W. E. Wauford. Clerks: T. P. Jones, W. M. Crowder, Z. P. Lee, R. W. Mason, A. P. Smith, W. A. Washer, H. A. Hill, S. M. Williams, E. L. Lawrence, T. D. Oakley, and L. C. Martin.

Until recent years the only Churches in Alexandria were the Methodist, Christian, and Cumberland Presbyterian, the first two having been established prior to the War between the States. As the result of a doctrinal debate in the town in January, 1887, between Elder Moody, Baptist, and Dr. T. W. Brents, Christian, the Baptist citizens resolved to organize. This was done during the month of the debate, and in time a neat and commodious church was erected. This was destroyed by lightning some years later, but in 1914 a new and handsome structure was built on the ruins. Some of the pastors have been: J. B. Moody, at one time editor of the *Baptist Reflector,* N. R. Sanborn,

W. H. Smith, J. B. Fletcher, Rutherford Brett, T. J. Eastes, and R. L. Bell. Early clerks: J. A. Walker, J. M. Walker, C. E. Bailiff, and C. B. Bailiff. Deacons in the first years: L. E. Jones, Isaac Cooper, Levi Foutch, J. H. Snoddy, H. H. Jones, A. P. Smith, G. A. Measle, Samuel McMillan, J. A. Walker, J. S. Rowland, and James Stark. Livingston Tubb is the present clerk.

Dry Creek Church was organized through the instrumentality of J. M. Stewart and J. H. Vickers "near a straw stack in Dr. J. A. Fuson's lot," says Grime. A neat building was erected, the early pastors having been J. M. Stewart, William Simpson, J. H. Davis, J. H. Grime, and Stephen Robinson.

Wharton Springs Baptist Church was constituted three miles south of Smithville in 1889 in the dwelling of E. B. Allen. Among its pastors were William Simpson, J. A. McClusky, J. H. Davis, J. M. Stewart, and J. T. Oakley.

The Snow's Hill Church was instituted in 1897, the following having been early pastors: A. J. Waller and Stephen Robinson.

Pastors of the Dowelltown Church, which was organized in 1894, were: J. W. Stewart, J. H. Grime, J. F. McNabb, W. J. Watson, J. H. Whitlock, and W. E. Wauford.

Sycamore Fork Church, having in 1902 the largest membership of any in Salem Association, is on the line between DeKalb and Cannon Counties, and was instituted through the efforts of Rev. Henry Bass in 1871. A house of worship was built in 1895. Of the pastors, these are recalled: Henry Bass, Hall Bethel, J. R. Hearn, William Simpson, J. H. Grime, G. A. Ogle, Stephen Robinson, and W. J. Watson. Of pathetic interest is the fact that one of the young ministers trained in this Church, J. T. Hancock, was called to its care, but died before his first appointment.

Other Churches are Beech Grove, at the mouth of Holm's Creek, established in 1858; Wolf Creek, near Laurel Hill, 1846; and New Union, near Frank's Ferry, southeast of Smithville, 1870.*

The Primitive, or "Hardshell," Baptists have a small membership in the county. Of the two noted Churches, Bildad and New Bildad, both south of Smithville, the latter is the most noted. Among the well-known Primitive Baptist ministers, these are recalled: Revs. Isaac Denton, Terry Trapp, James Snow, L. Pope Potter, and Mr. Byers.

In reply to a letter of inquiry, Rev. G. L. Beale, Secretary of the Tennessee Conference, M. E. Church, South, writes:

The records of the Tennessee Conference are very incomplete. The minutes were not printed prior to 1879, except at rare intervals. The written journals were destroyed by fire in the Publishing House in 1871. In the fall of 1812 the first Conference appears. That same year Stones River Circuit first appears in the minutes. Smith's Fork Circuit first appears in 1823, with William Algood and John Rains as pas-

---

*At the meeting of the Central Association of the Missionary Baptist Church at Trezevant, Tenn., in September, 1914, reports showed that the membership in the State (white) was, in round numbers, one hundred and ninety-two thousand.

tors—no boundaries given. In 1838 the name of Short Mountain Circuit is given, with J. A. Walkup as pastor (no boundaries). I have no data by which I could tell you when the societies at Liberty, Alexandria, or Smithville were started. Neither Alexandria nor Smithville became a circuit until after the War between the States.

In examining such records as remain, the following preachers, among others, are named as having been pastors at various times from 1830 to the war:

Smith Fork Circuit: L. Lowery, Jacob Ellinger, John Kelley, Elisha Carr, W. Ledbetter, Miles S. Johnston, John Page, S. Carlisle, Abe Overall, N. L. Norvell, J. T. Sherrell, E. J. Allen, John Bransford, F. D. Wrother, J. J. Foster, Fountain E. Pitts (P. E.), John H. Mann, William Jarred, C. Evans, Asbury D. Overall, John Hill, Joseph Willis, Russell Eskew, S. H. Reams, John Sherrell (P. E.), J. C. Putnam, G. L. Staley, F. S. Petway (P. E.), J. J. Comer, J. W. Prichard, J. G. Ray, J. R. Harris. During the war (there were no Conference sessions in 1863-64): J. A. Orman, J. J. Pitts, Fletcher Tarrant.

Short Mountain Circuit: J. A. Walkup, John H. Mann, J. B. Hollis, Abe Overall, A. Bowen, Isaac Woodward, J. W. Cullom, Joseph Banks, Daniel P. Searcy (in 1855-56, afterwards with the "Northern wing"), J. A. Reams, Carna Freeman, F. S. Petway (P. E.), T. S. Brown, W. D. Ensey, R. A. Reagan. During 1861 and 1863: R. A. Reagan, William Burr (P. E.), A. C. Matthews.

Caney Fork Circuit: W. Deskin, Uriah Williams, Peter Borum, J. D. Winn, Jere Williams, John Kelley,

S. Pressley, P. P. Hubbard, Jacob Custer, J. H. Mann, J. Lewis, J. A. Jones, Isaac Woodward, B. F. Ferrell, Jehu Sherrill.*

In 1865 Rev. U. S. Bates was appointed to the Smith Fork Circuit, the first circuit rider at Liberty after the war. George L. Staley was presiding elder. In the same year John H. Nichols and A. H. Reams were appointed to the Short Mountain Circuit.

No doubt many of the before-the-war ministers were in their time well known personally to the Methodists throughout the county as well as over their particular circuits.

The Tennessee Conference of the M. E. Church, South, in October, 1914, made the following appointments in the county, with H. B. Blue, P. E.: Alexandria, J. D. Robins; Keltonsburg Mission, J. R. Crawford, supply; Liberty Circuit, J. B. Estes; Smithville Mission, J. W. Estes.

It appears certain that a Methodist society was organized at Liberty long prior to the building of the church, which was about 1825, for the itinerants often preached in the people's homes. The substantial church erected so early supports this view. It was built by the pioneer carpenters, William Givan, Josey Evans, and Robert Burton, Maryland people, and was about 30 by 40 feet, two stories, with a good bell and belfry. The second floor had a large opening over

---

*The writer may be pardoned for his personal interest in the ministers of 1859. It was in June of that year that, at Liberty, his father, C. W. L. Hale, and Rev. W. J. Hale were converted.

the pulpit and altar on the first floor, that the slave members, who occupied that floor, might see and hear the minister. The framework of the building was so stanchly mortised and dovetailed and pegged that citizens said it would not have come apart had it been blown from its foundation and rolled out of the village. This church was occupied by negro soldiers in the war of 1861-65, and when they left the hogs and town cows appropriated it. Soon after peace the Methodists put it in as good condition as possible, and it was used for Church and school purposes until about 1874, when the present building was erected. The writer recalls the church's appearance well. The doors faced east and west, and on the eastern end of the roof comb was the belfry, a favorite place for bats and owls. The membership seems never to have been very large; but, considering the intolerance which used to prevail, it was "game." Some of the pulpit orators of ante-bellum days were heard in this old building, among them Fountain E. Pitts, J. J. Comer, and Ferdinand S. Petway. Dr. Foster wrote in 1914: "Sixty or sixty-five years ago one of the grandest characters I ever knew lived in Liberty—Stephen Moore, a Methodist preacher. He was goodness personified, and his wife was a worthy companion." In the same year Mrs. Polly Youngblood, the oldest inhabitant of Liberty and the widow of William Youngblood, said: "Yes, I ought to remember Brother Moore, as he officiated at my wedding." Joseph Banks and Isaac Woodward (the latter from Warren County) often preached at Liberty.

Among the Southern Methodist circuit riders since the war who served at this place and other Churches in the county, the following are recalled by H. L. Hale: U. S. Bates, J. A. Orman, John H. Nichols, W. B. Lowry, John Allison, W. J. ("Dod") Hale, John G. Molloy, J. J. Pitts, Joseph Webster, Wade Jarred, N. A. Anthony, J. T. Blackwood, G. B. McPeak, I. N. Napier, Mr. Gilbert, J. L. Kellum, Mr. Baird, T. A. Carden, J. B. McNeill, R. N. Chenault, W. M. Cook (the pastor in 1914). The presiding elders: J. M. Allison, J. J. Comer, J. W. Cullom, Berry Stephens, R. P. Ransom, J. T. Curry, George Anderson, T. G. Hinson, W. B. Lowry, W. V. Jarratt, John Ransom, T. L. Moody, and J. T. Blackwood.

Among the old papers of Jasper Ruyle was found this list of the members of the Church just preceding the War between the States: M. S. West, Lemuel Moore, Katherine Moore, Elizabeth Garrison, Littleberry Vick, Rhoda Vick, Sarah Vick, Jacob E. Moore, Mary Lamberson, Christina Smith, Jane Vick, Isaac Whaley, Lucinda Evans, Martha Martin, Matilda Bratten, Rebecca Yeargin, Susan Vantrease, Jasper Ruyle, Rebecca Ruyle, Mary E. Gossett, E. Jane Vick, Edward Gothard, Josiah Youngblood, J. C. Youngblood, Mary Jane Kersey, Matilda Neal, Malinda Moore, Eliza J. Moore, T. H. W. Richardson, Elizabeth Richardson, Matilda Richardson, L. F. Moore, Amanda Bratten, Cynthia D. Sneed, Martha J. Moore, A. Tennie Evans, Sarah Hall, Montilius Richardson, C. W. L. Hale, W. J. Hale, J. F. Youngblood, T. R. Foster, J. H. Burton, E. W. Whaley, W. C. Vick, T.

B. Adamson, E. Jane Whaley, A. T. Vick, M. C. Seay, Matilda Burton, B. W. Seay, Mary F. Seay, Ellen Seay, Lydia A. Barkley, James Foster, John W. Lamberson, and Len F. Woodside.

Goodspeed's history, published in 1888, says the Methodists of Alexandria first had a log church, but a frame church was built in 1835. In 1885 they put up the present handsome building.

Since the war of 1861-65 these, among other ministers, have occupied the Methodist pulpit at Alexandria: B. G. Ferrell (1866), John G. Ray (P. E.), John C. Putnam, J. B. Allison (P. E.), W. J. Hale, J. J. Comer (P. E.), W. H. Bellamy, W. H. Johnson, B. M. Stephens, William Doss, G. L. Staley, Z. W. Moores, H. S. Lee, T. H. Hinson, B. G. Ferrell, W. W. Graves, T. L. Moody, R. P. Ransom, J. T. Blackwood, G. B. McPeak, George L. Beale, B. H. Johnson, G. W. Nackles, B. F. McNeill, B. H. Jarvis, W. E. Doss.

Relying further on Goodspeed, the first Methodist church at Smithville was built in 1848 and was a brick structure. (There was a Methodist house of worship of some kind in 1844.) It was followed in 1856 by a frame building. Among the post-bellum pastors have been the following: A. H. Reams, W. B. Lowry, John Jordan, W. H. Riggon, J. H. Nichols, J. J. Comer (P. E.), S. H. Andrews, R. T. McBride, J. F. Corbin, G. B. McPeak, David G. Ray, E. K. Denton, C. S. Hensley, E. L. Jones, G. W. Anderson (P. E.), J. T. Blackwood, Z. W. Moores, L. C. Young, N. A. Anthony, W. H. Lovell, G. L. Hensley, J. A. Chenault,

J. G. Molloy, H. W. Carter, D. M. Barr, J. W. Pearson, J. W. Estes (Smithville and Keltonsburg Circuit).

Goshen, on Dismal Creek, was well known for its Methodist gatherings before and after the war. This can be said also for Bright Hill, near Smithville, Asbury, near Liberty, and the camp ground at Smithville. Some of the old-time ministers became popular because of their eccentricities as well as piety, among them: Mr. Wainwright, "Uncle" Jakey Hearn, "Uncle" Ike Woodward, "Uncle" Joe Banks, Elisha Carr, James Stanford, Ben Turner, and Caleb Davis.

Rev. Jerry W. Cullom, aged eighty-six years and the oldest member of the Tennessee Conference, writes June 12, 1914: "In 1854 I was the young pastor of Asbury Church. It was there that I had the greatest meeting I ever had or saw. All Liberty must have been there. Uncle Joe Banks, one of my local preachers, assisted me. It was there that we struck water. The year 1854 was the dryest I ever knew. The question with everybody was, 'How shall we get water for the meeting?' Some one discovered a moist place in the sand under the bluff back of the church, and a few strokes of a hoe unearthed a fine spring."

It should be explained here that it has been told for the truth that the preacher prayed for water, and the spring was sent in answer. Mr. Cullom states the facts, as he found the spring. This stream, we are told, is yet flowing.

"Rev. Joe Myers," proceeds Mr. Cullom, "declared in his sermon one night at Asbury that he saw a great ball of fire enter the door and roll over the congregation; so the dear old Baptists said the Methodists had brought water from the earth and fire down from heaven. There were over two hundred conversions on the circuit that year, among whom I may mention Judge Robert Cantrell and wife, both of whom I baptized by immersion at Smithville. And I mention Colonel Stokes and Dr. Foster. Stokes was lying stretched full length on the floor when he was powerfully converted. I saw him in Alexandria after the war, when Stokes's Cavalry had become history, and we gladly greeted each other. Years afterwards I was sent up there as a presiding elder for four years—1871-75. Holding a quarterly meeting at Asbury, I found Uncle Joe Banks present, and we had a great service. Though he was now in the Northern branch of the Church, we met in the altar at the close of the sermon and fell into each other's arms, and the thing was 'catching' all over the house.

"Abe Overall and Uncle Jakey Hearn often preached for me in 1853-54. Uncle Abe was present at Round Top when I performed my first immersion, and of course I made a botch of it, as I was a new hand. He got a good deal of fun out of my awkwardness. Some one, speaking of Uncle Jakey Hearn's home conveniences, said he could lie down at night and by pulling a string lock every door on his farm.

"John Savage and I were great friends. He owned a hotel at Smithville when I was pastor and gave me a room, board, and stall for my horse free."

In a second letter Mr. Cullom says: "The preachers for Smith Fork Circuit in 1854 were Revs. Joe G.

Myers and Russell Eskew. They were rather unique. Myers assisted me in the Asbury meeting. Arch Bain was a young preacher famous for leading the songs at camp meetings. Ferdinand S. Petway was the finest singer I ever heard. After the great meeting at Asbury, let me add, it fell to my lot to immerse more than a score of converts in Smith Fork. Six young ladies decided to kneel in the water and have it poured on them—'went down into the water' and were baptized by water or with water. Judge Robert Cantrell and wife professed at Bright Hill, three miles from Smithville, and joined our Church at Smithville after immersion. In 1873 or 1874 I stood on the scaffold and preached John Presswood's funeral before the swing-off by request of the sheriff. Some eight thousand people were present. At Smithville lived Wash Isbell, a hopeless cripple, but for many years he was county court clerk. William Magness, a brother of Judge Cantrell's wife, was a prominent merchant. So was Bob West. The hotel belonged to John Savage and was conducted by Mr. Stewart, whose wife was a sister of M. M. Brien."

In 1845 the Methodist Church divided into the Southern and Northern "wings." The latter was not represented in DeKalb County or the South until after the war of 1861-65.

When the Federal army gained possession of East Tennessee many of the Methodists in that section desired the services of the M. E. Church—that is, the Northern wing. In 1864 its first Conference was organized. Soon the ministers of that wing were preaching in DeKalb. As a lad the writer remembers when they appeared at Liberty, one of the ministers preaching being a Mr. Stephens, who had located at McMinnville. Then there was Rev. D. P. Searcy, who had been a Southern Methodist prior to the war. Rev. Joe Banks, of the county, also joined the Northern wing. It seemed that it made more advancement around Liberty than elsewhere. There was considerable hard feeling for a time between the two wings. Mr. Searcy located at Liberty, and shortly he and his interesting family became much beloved by all the neighbors. He was a son-in-law of Alex Robinson, of the county.

A few churches were established. That at Dowelltown was erected first in 1880 and has been wrecked twice by storms. The second wind, in 1913, entirely demolished it. The following have served as pastors there: D. P. Searcy, J. N. Turrentine, J. F. Turner, O. O. Knight, W. B. Rippetoe, A. Barnes, J. L. Chandler, S. L. Clark, W. C. Carter, D. L. McCalebs, W. P. Banks, T. J. Stricklin, S. H. Creasy, J. R. Conner, G. W. Nunally, H. P. Keatherly, D. P. Hart, E. C. Sanders, and C. W. Clayton.

The Dowelltown Circuit has five churches—Asbury, Snow's Hill, Indian Creek, Fuller Chapel, and Dowelltown—with more than five hundred members. Rev. W. P. Banks, who died in July, 1914, wrote early in the year as to Asbury:

It is the oldest church in this vicinity. The early settlers built for themselves a small, incommodious house for Church and school purposes, and at an early date a Methodist Church was organized here. Who the preachers were, I do not know. This house was finally burned to the ground by an incendiary, and a commodious house for that time was erected in its place. This house also was used for Church and school purposes. About twenty years ago the members of the M. E. Church bought the property, tore down the old house, and erected an up-to-date building, perhaps the best country church in the county, with a thriving membership of one hundred and a Sunday school that has run more than fifteen years consecutively. The organization was effected by Rev. D. P. Searcy. Thomas Chapman was the first to join and was followed by Joe Banks, Jep Williams and wife, and about fifteen others. Judge W. T. Robinson and wife also joined soon afterwards.

Mr. Banks wrote of others, but was so modest about his own work that this writer feels it a duty to add: He was fifty-seven years of age in 1914 and was a retired minister on account of broken health. His grandfather, Rev. Joseph Banks, was not only a moving spirit in the organizations of DeKalb County, but a great revivalist in his day; while his father, Enoch Banks, was a local deacon and did some pastoral work on circuits as a supply. At the age of twenty-two, after spending four years in Tullahoma College, W. P. Banks entered the Central Tennessee Conference of the M. E. Church and became an itinerant preacher. He served as pastor of circuits sixteen years and as presiding elder of the Nashville District six years. While presiding elder the finances of his district increased one hundred per cent, an increase equal to that of any twelve years before or after his term of service for the same territory. For eight years he was secretary of the Annual Conference and twelve years the editor and publisher of the Conference minutes.

Rev. Enoch H. Banks, mentioned, for many years kept up monthly appointments and revivals in the fall at some of the schoolhouses adjacent to Dowelltown.

There are a small number of Cumberland Presbyterian congregations scattered throughout the county. For some years the only church on Dry Creek south and east of Dowelltown was a small building located at the head of that stream and called Cave Spring Church. It had a scattered membership. Its pastor for some forty years was the eccentric but really intellectual I. L. Thompson. He was also pastor of Banks Church, on Short Mountain, as well as a little society at Possum Hollow Schoolhouse, on Dry Creek, midway between Cave Spring and Dowelltown. Of the three, only Banks Church was remaining in 1814.

In 1881 the Cumberland Presbyterians erected a Church at Alexandria. Prior to the War between the States preaching was had in the Turner M. Lawrence College. The following, with their families, were early members: James Doss, John Bone, W. R. Lewis, Al Edwards, Monroe Doss, J. D. Baird, W. W. Patterson, J. A. Davidson, V. H. Williams, J. B. Stevens, C. D. Baird, T. Macon, also Mrs. Mary E. Ford, the Kings, Simpsons, Fousts, and many others, all among the most influential citizens.

Names of pastors, including the present one, Rev. Joseph Barbee: Mr. Dillard, Reece Patterson (before the war), Dr. Burney, J. F. Patton, J. H. Kittrell,

Baxter Barbee, H. Lamon, J. R. Goodpasture, Ira W. King, and Mr. Sanburn. A number of theological students from Cumberland University have from time to time held services in the church.

The Church of Christ, or Christian Church, has been very strong in the county for many years. In Alexandria the members erected a church as early as 1835. It was succeeded by a new frame in 1851, or near that time. About 1873 a church was built at Smithville, and at Liberty another prior to 1890, dedicated by Mr. Woolen. In all there are nine churches in the county, others besides those named being at Temperance Hall, Keltonsburg, Belk, Young's Bend, Falling Water, and Cherry Hill. The total membership is between six hundred and eight hundred. The oldest church is that at Falling Water, it is believed.

One of the most active ministers of this denomination for the past twenty years is Rev. H. J. Boles. His son, Rev. H. Leo Boles, who is now President of the Nashville Bible School, labored with him for some years in strengthening the congregations.

Among the pioneer preachers of the county were the following, in addition to H. J. Boles: Tolbert Fanning, Caleb and Jesse Sewell, Sandy Jones, J. M., C. C., and W. T. Tidwell. Later: J. M. Tidwell, Wiley B. Carnes, Mr. Sutton, Luke Melton, Mr. Gilbert, Mr. Woolen, and others. The resident ministers of the county in 1914 were Rev. H. J. Boles and Rev. O. P. Barry.

Among the prominent citizens who have been identified with the congregations may be mentioned Dr. Drake, Dr. T. J. Potter, Judge J. E. Drake, Prof. H. L. W. Gross, Brackett Estes, Samson McClelland, Hon. J. M. Allen, Judge W. G. Crowley, Judge M. D. Smallman, editor and educator W. D. G. Carnes, William Floyd, Dr. T. P. Davis, the Lincolns, Wades, Magnesses, Cantrells, Griffiths, Webbs, Martins, Hayses, Tyrees, Potters, Pritchetts, and Smiths.

After the War between the States a religious awakening became apparent throughout the county. The writer, then a lad, saw some of the manifestations of fervor at Liberty, and especially at the Baptist church. The war had somewhat demoralized the people, and during revivals at the church named well-patronized ginger cake and melon vendors held forth on the bluff less than one hundred yards from the church. At night mischievous persons would cut harness and saddles. There were many indictments, moreover, for disturbing public worship.

CHAPTER VIII.

ANNALS OF ALEXANDRIA.

THIS town is on the Lebanon and Sparta Turnpike, forty-nine miles east of Nashville. The nearest railway points are Watertown, six miles west, and Brush Creek, two and one-half miles north. The tradition is that it was named for one of its pioneers, James Alexander, who came from Virginia. Showing that it was a village of Cannon County in 1837, in which year DeKalb County was established and the Lebanon and Sparta Turnpike chartered, the following Alexandrians appointed commissioners of the road are named as citizens of Cannon: Jacob Fite and James Goodner.

The act incorporating the village was signed January 31, 1848, the boundaries being as follows: "Beginning at the southwest corner of Leander Scott's lot and running north to Hickman Creek; thence east with the meanders of said creek to the northwest corner of Thomas Allison's lot; thence south to the west end of Gin Alley; thence east with said alley to the northeast corner of lot No. 13; thence east to the east corner of McDonald's lot, including Elijah Dobb's lot; thence west to Jacob Fite's line; thence north with the said line to the beginning, including the Methodist church and schoolhouse." During the War between the States the corporation fell into "innocuous desuetude." After hostilities ceased it was rehabilitated. One of the ante-bellum mayors recalled was the late John Batts, while one of the most vigorous mayors just after the war was Robert Yeargin. As with other Tennessee towns of small population, the charter was surrendered shortly after the passage of the four-mile law to get the benefit of that statute. In 1913 the town was again incorporated, with Rev. O. P. Barry as the first mayor and J. W. Parker city attorney.

The first settlers of the community, it is believed, arrived about 1795. The following list includes as many of the early business men as it is possible to give at this late date: James Alexander, Joshua M. Coffee & Son, Jacob Fite (father of Judge John Fite), James Goodner, Samuel Young, Church Anderson, William Floyd, J. D. Wheeler, Bone & Bro., Thomas Compton, Reece & Ford, Turner Bros., Wheeler & Jones, John F. Moore, S. W. Pierce, Lawrence & Roy, William Geltford, L. D. Fite, James Baird, Jack Baird, and Dexter Buck. The last named was the only merchant doing business during the latter part of the war. Since the war the following are recalled: James and Jack Baird, Turner Bros., Stokes & Wood, Dinges & Lincoln, Hurd & Co., M. F. Doss, Bridges & Smith, George Evans, Rutland & Goodner, S. W. McClelland, Dinges & Co., Roy & Yeargin, J. W. King, John Jost, Tubb & Schurer, Edwards & Rutland, Gold & Newman, Jones Bros., John Garrison, and Batts & Garrison. Business directory for 1914: Livingston Tubb, Goodner & Son, Roy & Jones, Roy & Seale, Lester's Department Store, Adamson Grocery Co., D. A. Stark, Dinges Hardware Co., Rutland Bros., Sampson Grocery Co., O. P. Barry Produce Co., Style Millinery Co. (Miss Daisye Vantrease), Donnel & Patton, Griffith Livery Co., H. H. Jones, J. W. Measle, and Shelby Malone, insurance.

The pioneer bank of the town and county is the Alexandria Bank. This bank was the first established between Lebanon on the west and Rockwood on the east. The original capital was $10,000, it being a private concern owned by J. F. Roy and Ed Reece. About 1891 it was chartered as a State bank and the stock increased to $20,000. Mr. Roy was the first Cashier and then President. C. W. L. Hale, of Liberty, was once Vice President, and William Vick, of the same place, was a stockholder and an officer. J. F. Roy is now President, and Frank Roy, Cashier. This bank, which was established in 1888, has been successful from the start.

The second bank in point of time is known as the D. W. Dinges Banking Company. It has also wonderfully prospered. It opened for business January 24, 1900, with the following officers: D. W. Dinges, President; J. A. Walker, Dib Dinges, Brien Tubb, and W. H. Lincoln. On January 7, 1904, the capital was increased. Large dividends have been declared each year. The capital at present is $150,000, with a surplus of $14,000. Present directors: D. W. Dinges, J. A. Walker, O. P. Barry, Livingston Tubb, J. W. Measle, G. R. Lester, Dib Dinges, W. T. Jones, Paul Tubb, D. C. Dinges, and E. T. Dinges.

The earliest paper published in the county was the Alexandria *Independent*. It was established a year or two prior to the war of 1861-65, but suspended when the great struggle commenced. While its publisher and editor, W. H. Mott, was said to have been from the North (marrying a Southern girl, Miss Vantrease), he joined Col. R. D. Allison's company of Confederates. With the Twenty-Fourth Regiment in the battle of Murfreesboro, he was severely wounded, and soon after having been brought home he died. All efforts to secure a copy of the *Independent* have failed, though its jottings would be both interesting and illuminative of the times.

In 1882 J. W. Newman began publishing the *Enterprise,* continuing it about two years.

The Alexandria *Review* was published about 1892 by E. C. King. In that year it was sold to James Tubb, according to a communication to the Liberty *Herald* of April 6, 1892.

The initial number of the *Times* appeared April 4, 1894. A stock company was publisher, and Robert F. Jones editor. Rob Roy and R. W. Patterson purchased the plant two years later, but the latter soon retired. Since the change Mr. Roy has been publisher and editor. In the eighteen years of the *Times's* publication no less than twenty-nine newspapers in DeKalb, Smith, and Wilson Counties have started and suspended.

The War between the States is recalled in connection with two of the early enterprises of Alexandria, the flour mill and the fair. It is tradition that the name of the first miller was a Mr. Hoover, whose little plant on Hickman Creek was equipped for grinding corn and sawing, the saw being of the horizontal, or sash, variety. The splendid flour mill built about 1852, which Gen. John T. Wilder, Federal commander, put out of business by twisting and bending the machinery, was under the management of Yan and Lon Wood. After the war—about 1887—a stock comany, composed of Ed Reece, J. F. Roy, B. F. Bell, John Rutland, L. E. Simpson, D. W. Dinges, and others, was organized, and a fine roller mill was erected. Brown Bros. once operated this plant in the eighties. Barry & Smith operated it in the nineties. This finally burned, and Lon Compton operates a plant erected somewhat recently.

A county fair association was formed prior to 1858, and in that year the first fair was held. The war then interfered, and Federal soldiers, principally Stokes's men, camped on the site and practically destroyed the property. The site was on the William Floyd farm, on Hickman Creek. In 1871 the DeKalb County A. and M. Association was formed, and the present-day fair resulted. The first directory was composed of J. P. Doss, J. D. Wheeler, J. F. Roy, J. H. Kitchen, J. A. Jones, John Bone, J. J. Ford, John Rollins, M. A. Wood, H. B. Smith, W. H. Lincoln, Jacob Measle, and Gen. William B. Stokes. Of these directors, only one, J. F. Roy, is living. This is believed to be the oldest fair in Tennessee. The State is said to be a stockholder. From 1871 to the present the fair has been held every year except 1881, when the severe drouth prevailed. On the morning of June 27, 1914, all the buildings were burned, entailing a loss of $8,000 or $10,000, Rob Roy being the largest loser. Undaunted, tents and circus seats were procured, and the fair of 1914 was made a success.

A fact worthy of note, reflecting credit on the negro population of the county, is that for several years the colored people have held a fair at Alexandria, the managers in 1914 being Henry Belcher, R. E. Preston, and Dib Burks.

Among the early citizens of this community, in addition to many already mentioned, there are recalled: Bartel Carter, King Herod, James Malone, Robert Dowell, Rizer Duncan, Louis McGann, William Kiser, Phil Palmer, Benjamin Garrison, John Vantrease, Jonathan and Steward Doss, Thomas Simpson, William Wright, Aaron Botts, Louis Y. Davis, Edward Turner, James Goodner, William Grandstaff, Paschal Brien, Henry Rutland, Tom Minor, Beverley Seay, Samuel Pierce, Stephen Pledger, Bartley James, Thornton Christy, Richard Rison, Turner Lawrence, T. Allison, James Link, Oliver Williams, Sr., James Jones, John Pierce, Spencer Bomar, J. Yeargin, J. F. Goodner, Jack Baird, William Johnston, Peter Davis, Tom Price, Caleb Davis, Hez Bowers, John Bowers, Al Bone, William Bone, Peter Turner, James Turner, Yan and Lon Wood, Jefferson Sneed, and William Floyd. The last-named brought to the county the first thresher and piano.

William Floyd was also a before-the-war postmaster; so was Joshua M. Coffee; so was Samuel W. Pierce. Other postmasters have been Stephen Pledger, James Turner, Al Edwards, R. M. Bone, S. B. Franks, J. W. Parker, and J. Moores Pendleton.

As to professional men, the lawyers who have lived at Alexandria were Col. John Fite (born there), Manson M. Brien, John Botts, William B. Stokes, Dan Williams, and J. W. Parker.

Dentists: Drs. H. I. Benedict and L. D. Cotton.

Early physicians: Drs. John W. Overall (about 1830, and born in the Shenandoah Valley, Va., before his parents removed to the neighborhood of Liberty, Tenn.), Jefferson Sneed, James Dougherty, William Sales, Cornelius Sales, George Gray, William Blythe, Richard Blythe, T. F. Everett, Nicholas Mercer, E. Tubb, Horace Sneed, Isaac J. Miers (or Mize), Mayberry, Bobo, McConnell, and Flippin. Later: T. J. Sneed, Jr., C. L. Barton, Dr. Fletcher, O. D. Williams, T. A. Gold, Thomas Davis, Sam McMillan, and J. R. Hudson.

This tradition is told by the older people of Alexandria: Dr. Miers (or Mize) was of French extraction, locating in Alexandria long before the War between the States (about 1848 or 1849), and wooed and won a Miss Paty. He was impatient to build up a practice, and it was charged that, going to Woodbury one day and procuring smallpox virus, or "scabs," he returned to his home with a sinister scheme. Inviting a young Mr. Turner to go hunting with him with flintlocks, he managed to inject his companion with the virus. Soon there was an epidemic of smallpox.

During the illness of Turner, who resided near the present Brush Creek, Miers visited him, saying his condition was serious, but did not hint that the malady was probably smallpox. As a consequence of the visits of friends and relatives the disease soon spread. The doctor was suspected and forced to leave the neighborhood. It is said he went to Virginia, then removed to Illinois, and in the latter State engaged in a similar scheme to boost business, when he was indicted and punished.

There are two well-kept cemeteries at Alexandria— South View, the pioneer graveyard, and East View, much larger. In the latter many soldiers of the Civil War, as well as a few veterans of earlier contests, are sleeping. Among the Confederates: Col. John F. Goodner, J. P. Doss, J. A. Donnell, Joshua M. Floyd, G. M. Bowers, Wiley Jones, Nelson D. Eason, Dr. C. L. Barton, R. A. Lawrence, J. W. Batts, Capt. J. D. Wheeler, L. H. Fite, Billy Foust, J. D. Martin, Monroe Doss, O. B. Wright, W. H. Lincoln, R. B. Floyd, J. B. Palmer, John Bomar, William Talley, Thomas Dunn, William Mooneyham, W. E. Foust. Among the Federals: J. H. Kitching, Monroe ("Pud") Bradley, W. F. Batts, J. E. ("Rome") Goodner, J. B. Yeargin, Dr. O. D. Williams, John Garrison, Sr., John C. Garrison, W. A. Palmer, Monroe Hall, Len Robinson, James Pass, J. M. Walker, P. L. Wood, Robert Alvis, T. W. Eason, John Lawrence, and Gen. W. B. Stokes.

The writer has had access to an old ledger which belonged to Dr. John W. Overall, who resided in Alexandria. It covers a period from 1830 to October, 1834, and no doubt the names listed therein include a number of the pioneers of Alexandria as well as a number in other counties but in the town's "sphere of influence." The names follow:

Caleb Davis, Nehemiah Dowell, Sterling Davis, Daniel Coggin, James P. Dale, Elisha Dowell, Smithson C. Doss, Stewart Doss, Prestley Dowell, Levi A. Durham, Col. E. Durham, John Dyournet, Joshua M. Coffee, Beverley Callicoat, Thomas Crutchfield, Lineas Cock, David Crowder, Samuel Casey, Robert Caskey, Winslow Carter, John S. Brien, Thomas Beckwith, Peter Barton, Roland Burks, Manson M. Brien, Aaron Botts, David Blue, Thomas Bomar, James Brien, Thomas Bradford, William Bennett, Willis Dowell, William Edwards, Cornelius Ellison, Jacob Fite, Amos Foutch, Floyd Davis, William Floyd, Joseph Fite, Shadrack Figgin, John Floyd, G. W. Grayson, J. M. Goodner, Benjamin Garrison, Stephen Griffin, Valentine Gates, William Grandstaff, Henry Helmantaller, Philip Hass, Henry Haley, Benjamin D. Hynds, Henton A. Hill, Joab Haflin, Josiah Hicks, Sterling Hale, John Hathaway, Hawkins Heflin, Grogan Harper, Levi Herod, Pendleton Hobson, Washington Hicks, Hardin Hardcastle, Benjamin Jones, Josiah Inge, Wyatt Jenkins, Nelson Kyle, James Kitching, Spencer Kelley, Edward Lawrence, W. F. Luck, James Lancaster, John Lucky, William Linn, Gregory Moore, William Marler, John Moore (hatter), David Malone, Joseph McCrabb, Maj. William Moore, James Askew, Don Allison, Robert Nixon, Levi Purnell, Overstreet Pritchard, Caleb Preston, Philip Palmer, Brittain Reynolds, Rison Roland, Augustin Robinson, North Reynolds, Henry Rollings, Daniel Ratlidge,

Peyton Randolph, George Reasonover, William Wright, Thomas Simpson, Randolph Sanlin, Fuller Sanlin, William Stokes, Jordan Stokes, George Simpson, Anderson Tibbs, T. J. Tyree, Edward Turner, Littleberry Turner, Wilson Tubb, Benjamin Tubb, Tolliver Turner, John Vantrease, Joshua Vick, Samuel Vanatta, William Vantrease, Jeremiah Whitlock, Anthony Ward, John Warford, Benton Wood, Abel Wood, James Winfrey, William Wellaby, Tucker Woodson, Jesse Wood, Pleasant Watson, David Warford, Duke C. Wright, and Dobson Yeargin.

CHAPTER IX.

Concerning Slaves and Free Negroes.

There was only one attempt of the slaves to start an insurrection in this State, as far as the writer can learn; that was in Stewart County. In 1854 and 1855 it became evident that the negroes meditated mischief, as they were known to be holding secret meetings on nights and Sundays. They were instigated by white preachers, it is thought, from the North. In December, 1856, a vigilance committee was organized, slaves from all parts of Stewart County were examined, and the suspicion of a plot was seen to be well founded. The slaves were on a specified day to overpower their masters and, after arming themselves, cross the country to Hopkinsville, Ky., then enter Ohio, where they hoped to be free. Six of the leaders were hanged at Dover before Christmas and a large number whipped. To make the punishment more impressive a citizen of Dover cut off the heads of the six blacks executed and had them paraded through the streets, Goodspeed tells us.

The negroes were considered by the forefathers the most docile of all races of savages. Whether this was correct or not, those of DeKalb County were not hard to control. Now and then one heard of "runaway" slaves, but they had no desire, it appears, to injure their masters.

The old type of darky has almost become extinct. It seems but justice to refer at some length to a number who became well known locally from one cause or

History of DeKalb County

another. There were a few who had the instincts of a gentleman, some whose individuality made them favorites with the whites, and many with striking traits that created more or less notice. Not only did the negroes prove the most amiable of savage races, but the writer dares say that he recalls no instances among the whites of anything finer than the humble dignity of Wolsey Givan, the gentle urbanity of Wells Allen, the Chesterfieldian politeness of Dave Sellars, the serene patience of Mary Fuston, or the tireless devotion of Violet Overall to the little babe left to her care by the death of Mrs. Horace L. Hale.

Slaves were numerous in the county. Scores of citizens owned from two to a dozen, while a few held a much larger number. The original stock in most instances was brought from the older States by the pioneers. There was not very much trafficking in this species of property in DeKalb County. Of the slave owners adjacent to Liberty, these are recalled with little effort: James Allen, John Stark, W. G. Bratten, Reuben Evans, Francis Turner, Isaac Turney, Abraham Overall, Ezekiel Bass, Edward Robinson, Henry Frazier, Dr. G. C. Flowers, Daniel Smith, Nicholas Smith, Horace Overall, W. B. Stokes, James Tubb, Isaac Turney, Thomas Stokes, John Bethel, Eli Vick, James Fuston, Joseph Clarke, William Vick, William Sellars, Jasper Ruyle, William Avant, Sampson Williams, Thomas Givan, Peter and Jacob Adams, Leonard Lamberson, the Brazwells, Hayses, Groomses, Roys, and Bates.

The Foutches, Sneeds, Wrights, Lawrences, Goodners, Rutlands, Grandstaffs, Turners, Floyds, Prestons, Davises, and others possessed "human chattels" at Alexandria; while well-known slaveholders around Smithville were W. H. Magness, Giles Driver, Nicholas Chambers, Thomas Bradford, and Bernard Richardson.

Free negroes were few in number. Lige Whitely, of Smithville, was one of a family of free men of color. He was a vendor of ginger cakes, holding forth at the courthouse well on days of occasion. From the letter of a correspondent out of the State this is quoted:

Often, thinking of Liberty, I see everything as plainly as sixty-five years ago—even Nat and Banks Evans, 'Lizabeth Flowers, Jim Bethel, Luke Turney, Wells Allen, Gib Clarke, Nye Givans, Wolsey Givan, Cato Bate, Strawd Overall, Jeff Overall (the old colonel's fiddler), Albert Smith (who assumed the name of Porter), Allen Fuston, Virg and Rans Robinson, Sut Bass, Pomp and Tom Ruyle, Burrell Stokes, Caleb Tubb, and Ike Lamberson. By the way, Ike passed as an infidel, the only one I ever saw among the colored folks. Any negro there who could claim descent from Wolsey Givan considered it a great honor. Strawd and Jeff Overall were noted characters.

Is the negro's religion mere emotion, signifying nothing? The writer testifies to a permanent change in the conduct of "Aunt" Violet, who was cook in his father's home for twenty-five years. Though she and her mistress grew up together, for a few years Aunt Vil would have "tantrums" two or three times a week, swearing like the army in Flanders and otherwise working off her temper. One day news came that her son Bill had been stabbed to death by Doc Allen, another negro. She made no hysterical outcry, but fell writhing on the floor in mental torture. Some months later she was converted, and from the day of her conversion to her death she was never guilty of profanity nor of giving way unrestrainedly to her temper. And when her mistress was dying she came shuffling from the kitchen, and the two, who had known each other for fifty-nine years, embraced.

There were three or four outlying negroes prior to the war. The most noted were "Arrington," "Jim," and "Old Yaller." According to the scant information obtainable, it appears that sometime in the first half of the nineteenth century Henry Hart, who owned large tracts of land on Dry Creek, decided to sell his realty holdings and move from the country. Several thousand acres were purchased by Henry Frazier, then a young man, who, after the War between the States, was slain on Snow's Hill by Capt. W. L. Hathaway. Hart disposed of his negroes in the South, including Tom, who was sold to a planter named Arrington.

Tom ran away from his new master, returning to DeKalb County, and hid in caves and cane thickets for quite a while. He was fed by such negroes as Ike Lamberson, Jeff Overall, the Allen slaves, and others. While not appearing vicious, he became a terror to the women and children, because, like the wild things, he prowled at night. It is possible that he did not hesitate to appropriate a lamb, fowl, or hog, or to raid a kitchen when moved by hunger. There were many large caves in the country and immense canebrakes, and it was not difficult to avoid detection by day. Arrington evaded capture four or five years, then disappeared. He may have sought new fields or died unattended in one of the caves that exist only in limestone sections.

The case of Jim is of interest from the fact that his trial for murder is given in the reports of the Supreme Court of Tennessee (4th and 5th Humphreys) and is the precedent for conviction in a capital offense on circumstantial evidence. Belonging to a farmer named Williams, he was tried for murder in 1843, was convicted, and appealed. The case was remanded and resulted in a second verdict of guilty in 1844. Appealing to the Supreme Court again, the case was affirmed. His lawyers were Sam Turney, Brien, and Haynes. Jim was hanged at Smithville, making a sensational statement on the gallows.

Isaac, the property of William Avant, was murdered in the kitchen of William Williams on Dry Creek on Saturday night, January 11, 1843. Proof showed that a slave named George (against whose owner executions were in the hands of an officer) and Jim (against whose owner an attachment had issued) were both in the neighborhood, concealing themselves in the woods, and were harbored by persons living near the place where Isaac was murdered. Isaac had been hired to catch George. The latter and Jim, both well armed, heard of Isaac's purpose and made frequent threats against his life. One night while Isaac was sleeping on the floor with his head to the fire he was shot twice by some one outside and died in about an hour. Dr. Fuson examined the body, and William Avant found tracks fifteen or twenty steps from the kitchen, where Isaac was killed. The night had been cold. The tracks were visible only at a mudhole near the kitchen and at the spring branch. They seemed to have been made recently by some one running, and showed a deficiency in one of the soles. When Jim was caught in a cave by Francis L. Boyd, it was found that a piece was wanting in the sole of the right shoe. The measure of the track with Jim's shoes corresponded with the width, but was about half an inch shorter than the shoes. David Coger, a witness in the case, testified from tests that tracks made while one was running would be half an inch to an inch and a half shorter than the shoe that made it, and the tracks would be shortest in soft ground. One of the negro women swore that Jim had admitted the deed, while others gave damaging testimony.

Some young physicians secured Jim's body and, to avoid detection, conveyed it from hiding place to hiding place, finally cutting it up, tradition says, and throwing the pieces and bones in Smith Fork Creek just below the Gin Bluff cave. The violation of graves was made a felony by the act of 1831, which explains the doctors' fears.

"Old Yaller" was Jim Stokes, a slave owned by General Stokes. From some cause he was always absconding, hiding in the neighboring hills. One morning he discovered from his hiding place that Col. James Tubb's residence was on fire and succeeded in putting out the flames before much damage was done. In gratitude Colonel Tubb purchased him from Stokes, a delight to "Yaller Jim," since his wife was one of Colonel Tubb's slaves. Jim was the father of ten or twelve children by this woman.

This is of pathetic interest: Caleb was Colonel Tubb's body servant—a very large black man possessed of much humor, who had a deep affection for every member of his master's family. He had superintended the digging of graves for all the burials that had taken place, and the Colonel had enjoined upon the survivors of the family the duty of burying Caleb next to himself at the head of the family section.

After the war freed him, and after Colonel Tubb's death, Caleb remained faithful, caring for Miss Addie Tubb, the youngest girl, and Mrs. Caroline Fite, a widow. When they died he went to Dowelltown, but suddenly left there and went to parts unknown. Years passed, when one day an old colored man asked the stage driver from McMinnville to Smithville for a ride. He was wanting to get back home to die and be buried beside his master and "the chilluns," as he pathetically explained. Though he was black and his language broken, in his old heart was a yearning as loyal as that expressed by Jacob: "Bury me not, I pray thee, in Egypt: but I will lie with my fathers, and thou shalt carry me out of Egypt, and bury me in their burying place." Before the stage reached Smithville the negro's life had gone out. James Tubb, Jr., was notified, and he carried out the promise exacted by his father as to the burial of old black Caleb.

According to the report of the Adjutant General of Tennessee in 1866, Col. J. P. Brownlow, the enlistment of negro troops in the Union army from this State numbered 17,770. A number may have been from DeKalb County, though the writer has heard of but one, Banks, belonging to Reuben Evans.

Some of the early laws relative to negroes were these: They were not permitted to practice medicine. When found off their master's premises without a pass, they were arrested by patrols. Before 1831, for certain offenses slaves (also free negroes) could be nailed to the pillory by the ears and have their ears cut off. By the act of 1831 free negroes were not allowed to remove to this from any other State and remain more than twenty days; while by that of 1833 no stage driver or boat captain was allowed to carry free negroes from one place to another without a certificate from the county court clerk; but if the black were a slave, verbal or written authority from the owner was sufficient. Free negroes were allowed to vote until 1834, when they were disfranchised by the new State constitution. A bill was introduced in the legislature of Tennessee in 1859-60 providing that all free negroes except certain minors should be sold into slavery if they remained in the State after May 1, 1861. It failed to become a law.

CHAPTER X.

STAGECOACH AND TAVERN DAYS.

QUITE a bulky debt was saddled on the State when the mania for internal improvements in Tennessee was on. But it brought us good roads, and no State can properly develop without these. It also brought an era of romance which made the people in isolated places better and happier and mentally broader.

It was a great event, as great as the construction of a railroad to-day, when the turnpike was extended from Lebanon in the direction of Sparta. On December 2, 1837, a company was incorporated with the following commissioners: John Hearn, John Muirhead, W. L. Martin, Joseph Johnson, O. G. Finley, J. P. Wharton, Solomon Caplinger, Wilson T. Waters, James Young, George Smith, J. M. Armstrong, Jonathan Bailey, and William Lawrence, of Wilson County; Abraham Caruthers, John Gordon, Francis Gordon, William McCain, and Nathaniel Ward, of Smith County; T. W. Duncan, Leonard Lamberson, E. Wright, Jacob Fite, James Goodner, James Tubb, and Joseph Clarke, of Cannon County (afterwards De-Kalb); William Glenn, William Simpson, Jesse Lincoln, and S. V. Carrick, of White County.

The commissioners were to open books for receiving subscriptions to the amount of $120,000, to be used in building the pike, "commencing at Lebanon," the charter not specifying at what point it should terminate. The $120,000 was to be divided into shares of

$50 each. The chief surveyor of the State marked the route, and that part going over Snow's Hill, a mountain in DeKalb County, the gorges and peaks of which suggest Alpine scenery, is said to be an extraordinarily fine example of surveying, with the exception of a few hundred feet. This variance was due, explains Mr. John L. Lamberson, grandson of one of the commissioners, to the fact that it was left to an assistant, the chief surveyor, becoming ill, having been carried to Lamberson's, where he died. For some reason, probably because of a lack of funds, the road for some years was completed only to the top of Snow's Hill; but the grading was completed to Smithville after the War between the States.

As soon as possible after securing the charter and making the survey work was begun. The route must have presented a bustling appearance, with the camps and the great ox teams (shod with triangular pieces of iron on each toe, we are told) drawing stone, sand, and gravel, and the toiling slaves and their overseers. The work was given out to various contractors—Nicholas Smith, James White, Daniel Ford, Leonard Lamberson, James Tubb, Abraham Overall, and others. It is said that the part running under the Allen bluff and beside the creek west of Liberty was constructed by Colonel Overall.

But one tragedy resulted during the building of this highway, so far as the writer can learn, though in some instances those upon whose premises the survey was made became very indignant. One farmer in the Alexandria neighborhood went gunning; but as the route was changed for the better in his neighborhood, no blood was shed. The tragedy was the drowning of a youth named Blades. "There under the roots of that big tree," said the widow White to the writer one day when he was visiting the old Gray cemetery in Dowelltown, "is buried Charlie, the only son of Benjamin Blades. He fell through the Liberty bridge before it was finished and was drowned. Near by is the grave of James White, who contracted to build a portion of the turnpike."

That women had an eye to business even so early as 1837 is indicated by the fact that Mrs. Sinia Foster superintended the building of the road some way up Snow's Hill. With her sons and employees, she bossing the job, a section of road was built that was probably unexcelled.

Mr. Caplinger, possibly one of the commissioners, constructed the old bridge north of Liberty, a covered wooden structure with two driveways; probably also that over Dry Creek, as both were alike.

The stagecoach was a familiar sight prior to the building of the turnpike; while the pike did not always follow the first highway. To illustrate, the old road passed along the western and northern brow of the Daniel Smith hill a quarter of a mile north of Liberty, and after a large half circle eastward came out near Dowelltown. The trace is clearly visible today. With the coming of the big, red, rocking coach there had to be stage stands and wayside inns providing "entertainment for man and beast." As far back as the oldest inhabitants can remember, Col. M. A.

Price was the mail contracter, an old one-eyed gentleman, who smacked his lips enjoyably over a glass of gin and was strictly business. Horace McGuire, an early stager, says the mail was carried from Nashville to Knoxville. Isaiah White, son of one of the road builders and now a citizen of Nashville, avers that the Colonel had mail contracts covering twelve thousand miles, and this particular route extended from Nashville via Knoxville to Richmond, Va. The coach was drawn by four horses a large part of the time, says James Dearman, another stager, and horses were changed every fourteen miles. "Colonel Price grew wealthy," says Mr. White. "My father had the contract to make the road from the foot of Snow's Hill to the top, taking the contract off the hands of Mr. Duncan and Dr. Wright; but they became bankrupt, and he received very little compensation. It was finished to the top of the hill, I think, about 1845."

After Price's time the route was gradually shortened, finally becoming insignificant. Sam Black followed Price. Other contractors have been: Jesse Walling, Colvert & Lewis, Hale & Lewis, Overall Bros., and Taylor & Robinson. From Watertown to Smithville a number of automobiles now run.

There were taverns at Liberty nearly a century ago —the Duncan at the north end of the village, and one somewhat south of the first-named, probably erected by a Mr. Fite. The latter was at various times occupied as a residence by W. G. Foster, John F. Moore (a Vermont immigrant), Frank Foster, and William Blackburn, father of Col. Joe Blackburn. It was at last torn down to give place for Will A. Vick's residence.

The pioneer, Josiah Duncan, had the Duncan Tavern built, and it was conducted by his son, T. W. Duncan. Some of the Duncans removed to Nashville. It is believed that the Duncan Hotel, in the capital, was named for one of these Duncans. They came originally from Maryland. Isaac Whaley, postmaster at Liberty for about forty-four years, once stated to the writer that within his memory Gen. Andrew Jackson was a guest at the Duncan. He added: "The General used to pass here in his carriage on the way to Washington and other points. One time he purchased some negroes and was bringing them to Tennessee. While here a young slave died. It was between 1834 and 1839. I made the negro's coffin. Of the Duncans who left Liberty, I believe the one to become best known was Cicero."

T. M. Givan, a relative of the Duncan family, has heard his father tell of a large delegation going as far as Snow's Hill to welcome Old Hickory on one occasion. Some genius had improvised a sort of cannon, and when it was "touched off" it escaped from its fastenings, disappeared somewhere down one of the gorges near the road, "and has never been seen since." On Jackson's arrival the county broke all records by the size of its crowd. Jackson was social and pleased his hearers by expressing admiration for the great hills and predicting a wonderful future for that section.

Mrs. Rachel Payne, daughter of Frederick Jones,

who bought the Duncan Tavern too late to entertain the hero of New Orleans, says she heard Mrs. Duncan tell how she once prepared a great feast for Jackson, but he would partake of nothing but milk and mush. Mrs. Payne states further: "When I was a child fifteen young men and the same number of girls passed through the village from Alexandria to Smithville to attend a ball. Coming back to the village with the purpose of having a dance at the Overall home, they found the creek past fording and stayed overnight with us, and that dance was the first I had ever seen. I recall two of the young ladies, Colonel Stokes's daughters, Miss Melissa (afterwards Mrs. Haskins) and Miss Leath (called 'Bug,' who became Mrs. James R. Calhoun). The fifteen couples were horseback, which would be a wonderful sight now."

Latter-day hotels at Liberty were conducted by Joshua Hollandsworth and Mrs. Cannie Whaley.

About the middle of the nineteenth century there was an excellent and popular tavern at Alexandria kept by Capt. J. S. Reece. "I remember a few balls at the tavern," writes Mrs. S. W. McClelland, formerly of Alexandria, "and among other attendants were Misses Ellen Johnston, Tump Sneed, Mary, Fannie, and Lorena Davis, Matt and Harriet Batts, and Messrs. Pope Rutland, John Sneed, William Bone, Joshua Floyd, and Capt. John F. Goodner, the gayest of the gay and a soldier of two wars. Next day we stood on tiptoe listening to a recital of the joyous events. When the circus came the old tavern was quickened into new life, and nothing was more delightful to us children than to get a peep in on the show folks, especially the show girls, this being accomplished through the friendship of Mary Reece, the innkeeper's amiable daughter."

Ed Reece, of Nashville, who was brought up in the Reece House, but who is now a prosperous Nashville man, says the building stood where Lester's department store now stands, on the south side of the principal street. "I think," he continues, "it was formerly conducted by Jack Baird, Sr., father of James and the late Jack Baird. My father exchanged property with James Baird for it and had it put in fine repair, opening it to the public in 1851 or 1852. My father was a Whig, and the Whigs all stopped with him. Among the guests of more than local repute I mention Jordan Stokes, Sidney S. Stanton, Gen. Bill Cullom, and Bird S. Rhea. There were balls there a plenty prior to the big war, and young people from Carthage, Lebanon, Gordonsville, and Nashville attended. An event I distinctly remember was the marriage of Horatio Betty—probably the grandfather of Willie Betty Newman, the distinguished Nashville artist—and Miss Mary Lawrence, daughter of William Lawrence, who lived in Wilson County, west of town. Betty lived at Gordonsville. The young married folks and their friends, about thirty couples in all, were horseback, and stopped for dinner on the way to Gordonsville for the 'infair.' As there was then no very great opposition to intoxicants, some of the gentlemen merrymakers imbibed freely. Two guests at the tavern when we had balls were the Misses Roulstone, relatives of the publisher of the first Tennessee newspaper, the Knoxville *Gazette*. One of them on one occasion highly incensed a guest by refusing to dance with him because he did not wear pumps."

The old people name John Vantrease as Alexandria's earliest innkeeper. Mrs. Sallie Browning kept a tavern prior to the days of the Reece House. The Reece House was in later years conducted by T. Williams and then by Joseph Lawrence. The present well-patronized hotel is owned by Byron Bell.

In 1846, or thereabout, a stock company built a large tavern at Smithville, the first host being Dr. G. W. Eastham, possibly. On January 2, 1852, it was incorporated. The incorporators were: Ransom Youngblood, John B. Tubb, Alex Goodwin, T. B. Fite, R. C. Sanders, Charles Schurer, Samuel Turner, Elect Tubb, James Tubb, William Floyd, Elias Barbee, W. H. Magness, W. B. Lawrence, W. W. Wade, William A. Duncan, and M. M. Brien. Was it leased at this time by Col. John H. Savage? The oldest member of the Tennessee Conference, Rev. J. W. Cullom, says Savage was in control of it in 1854. The builder of the tavern was said to have been David Morrison, the architect of the State prison. It changed proprietors frequently. It was once purchased by David James, who sold it to Matt Lee, then by B. M. Webb, and is now owned by B. M. Cantrell.

Beckwith Place, just east of Snow's Hill, became very popular in ante-bellum days, and is one of the best-known landmarks of DeKalb County. Mrs. Beckwith was a Miss Roulstone, of the Knoxville family just mentioned. Beckwith was in its prime when Bon Air Springs, on the mountain, was in its heyday. Travelers to and from that resort liked to spend a while at Beckwith Place. Many very notable guests have been sheltered there.

On Snow's Hill, four miles west of Smithville, Thomas Bradford kept a famous inn at the sign of the Two Cranes. A distinction claimed for the proprietor is that he had the earliest orchard in that section, not excepting that of Giles Driver, the pioneer, who lived to the age of one hundred and four. Luke McDowell's tavern was not far from Beckwith Place, a mile westward. After the War between the States, John L. Boyd occupied the McDowell Inn.

No doubt there was a tavern at Sligo Ferry, on the eastern side of Caney Fork River and on the stage road. It was a very important point at one time. Bird S. Rhea and A. L. Davis, who owned a large store and warehouse, operated the ferry and that end of the stage road. Sligo was the head of navigation, and the firm was able to do a very heavy business by loading boats at Nashville and transporting merchandise and other freight to Sligo. Price's stagecoaches traveled that way. The travel by stage, carriages, and freight wagons was tremendous. But when the Nashville and Chattanooga Railroad was constructed to McMinnville Mr. Rhea saw that it would injure White and DeKalb Counties and left the place for Nashville, where he became a factor in business circles, as is his son now, Isaac T. Rhea, President of the St. Louis and Tennessee River Packet Company.

History of DeKalb County

In this East Middle Tennessee section there is much picturesque scenery. Off the turnpike some miles are the Caney Fork "Narrows," where the river makes a nine-mile bend, but comes so close together at one point that one can stand on the ridge between and toss a stone into the current on either side. The views at Fall Creek and Culcarmac Falls, also in the boundaries of DeKalb County, are magnificent and inspiring. From the top of Snow's Hill (the turnpike passes over the summit, a distance of two miles) the sight may traverse long distances, especially south and west, taking in a bewitching panorama in winter or summer. On each side are deep valleys, gloomy and forested, and miles to the south the long, hazy crest of Short Mountain, suggesting the back of leviathan afloat upon the ocean surface. Traveling westward, there was once the well-kept Trough Spring. The water, gushing out of the hill, was brought down to the pike in wooden "spouts" to a very capacious trough. Here the stage horses were checked to allay their thirst, and it is doubtful if any passenger could pass without desiring to quaff. If in the night, the trickle and murmur awoke his thirst; if in the daytime, the sparkling streamlets dashing over mossy stones had the same effect.

Between Dowelltown and Liberty one of the noisiest streams, reminding you of Browning's "How the Water Comes Down at Lodore," issues from the Gin Bluff cave and finds silence in the Crowder Hole of Smith Fork. It used to run a cotton gin long ago. On Dry Creek the stream cast out of a cave has for three-quarters of a century furnished the power to run Crips's Mill.

Then you arrive at Liberty, resting like a sleeping hound at the feet of a dozen lofty hills—the Barger and Evans hills to the east, the Gin Bluff and Dismal hills to the north, to the west the Bethel and Lamberson hills, and to the south the Bratten, Givan, and Clarke hills—cultivated to the tops and hazy in summer, in winter drowsing to the winds' singing, "The heavens declare the glory of God, and the firmament showeth his handiwork." And in their embrace this: Smith Fork Creek forming a silver horseshoe, great bottom fields, the pioneer graveyard on a rise covered with pennyroyal and gashed with gullies, the battle ground where General Winchester fought the Cherokees, the more modern cemetery with three thousand sleeping inhabitants, and a village so queerly arranged that the son of a pioneer once described it as being three miles long and thirty feet wide.

Still going westward, the road crawls by the beetling Allen Bluff, then through other picturesque hills until Alexandria is passed and the Wilson County line reached, where the low grounds set in.

As a general thing, the stage drivers were "characters." Didn't they have a right to feel their importance and to exercise their prerogative of letting a boy swing onto the boot or driving him away with a great swipe backward with the whiplash? Uncle Sam depended upon them to be on schedule time with his mail; the traveling public was also beholden to them; and, sitting behind four horses, manipulating the lines cleverly if not pompously as the milestones were left behind, they certainly had some part in the nation's affairs. The names of a few have been preserved, and for the sake of the old-timers who knew some of them in the flesh and of the one-time boys whose cherished ambition was to be a stage driver and at night toot the bugle as the announcement of his approach to the post office they shall be recorded here: Ben Blades, Yance Lamb (a dandy), Tom Hearn, Josiah Youngblood, Mr. Angell, Mr. Kelley, Mr. Bridges, Mr. Sadler, Bob Witt, Abe Witt, Mr. Potts, "Scotch John," Horace McQuire, Jim Little, Mose and Charles Vannata, James Dearman, J. H. Meacham, Tom, Jim, and William Dearman, Isaac Borum (who drove about twenty years), William Lewis, Sr., William Lewis, Jr., and William Robinson (who drove about fifteen years).

So, while the first note of the bugle on the famous old stage road was a reveille, the last sound, lingering mournfully among the hills, meant taps forever, the old order giving way to the new.

The mail is now delivered to the four principal towns twice a day and once on Sunday. The postal system must have been very unsatisfactory to the people a century and less ago. It is said that the residents of Liberty for a long while had to go to Carthage, which was laid off in 1804, and other points to mail letters. As late as 1797 the mail to Knoxville, then the State capital, arrived only twice a month. It must have been several years later that there was a mail route to Liberty. In 1789, about eight years before the first settler came to Liberty, there were only seventy-five post offices in the United States. Postage was so high and ready money so scarce, as stated elsewhere, that letters often remained in the post office for weeks because the person addressed could not pay the postage. In the daybook of E. Wright, a Liberty merchant, his customers are frequently charged postage. It may be he was an early postmaster. Thus under date of June 23, 1832, is this memorandum, "Liberty Lodge No. 77, Dr., to postage paid on letter from G. States Secty., 66 cents," and this under date of August 20: "Lemuel H. Bethel, Dr., to cash to pay postage, 18¼ cents." The adhesive postage stamp was not used in America until 1847. The method was to fold a letter, fasten it with sealing wax (no envelope), and mail it, the receiver to pay the postage. The rates of postage from 1789 to 1816 were: For any distance under forty miles, 8 cents; under ninety, 10 cents; under one hundred and fifty, 12½ cents. From 1816 to 1837 they were: For distances under thirty miles, 6¼ cents; under eighty, 10 cents; over four hundred, 25 cents; and these rates were quadrupled upon letters which weighed an ounce.

CHAPTER XI.

THE COUNTY SEAT.

THE country adjacent to Smithville was settled by a most worthy class of people, second to none in any part of the county. Old names that come to mind are: Giles Driver, Jesse Allen, Martin Phillips, Tobe Martin, Britton Johnson, Allan Johnson, James Lockhart, John Wooldridge, J. C. Kennedy, P. G. Magness, Zach Lafever, D. League, Henry Cameron, Bernard Richardson, Samuel Chandler, Elijah Chambers, Edward Hooper, William Adcock, Luke McDowell, John Maynard, the Whaleys, Wades, Beckwiths, Atwells, Bradfords, Smiths, Gilberts, Dunlaps, Colverts, Potters, Cantrells, Pedigoes, Isbells, Bonds, Bozarths, Rheas, Davises, Dearmans, Wests, Fosters, Tyrees, Grays, Magnesses, Judkinses, Titsworths, Dentons, and others.

When the county was organized at Bernard Richardson's in March, 1838, a committee, composed of Joseph Clarke, Thomas Allen, Joseph Banks, Watson Cantrell, and Thomas Durham, was appointed to select a site for the seat of justice and erect a courthouse and jail. James Dearman, one of the middle-aged men of Smithville, thinks the center of the county was found to be a mile north of the present Smithville; but as Bernard Richardson had donated fifty acres of land for the town, it was located thereon. But Rev. W. P. Banks, grandson of one of the commissioners, writes under date of April 27, 1914: "My grandfather was the first trustee of the county and one of the men who located the county seat. It was first selected two miles south of the present town on the McMinnville road; but when on digging a well (the mound of dirt is there now plainly visible) the commissioners failed to get water they accepted the proposition of Mr. Richardson, provided they should find water for the public well. Grandfather was a leading spirit in all this."

The first name selected in the original bill for the seat of justice was Macon, but by amendment it was changed to Smithville in honor of Samuel G. Smith, one of the Secretaries of State, who died in 1835. He held this office from 1832 to his death.

The first courthouse was soon erected. Prior to 1844 it was replaced by a two-story brick building, costing about $6,000, while the log jail was replaced by a brick structure, costing something like $2,500. Subsequent to 1890 the present courthouse was erected.

It may not be out of place to chronicle the fact here that on August 28, 1890, when new county buildings were seen to be needed, an election was held to change the county seat. A site was offered by C. W. L. Hale on his farm, about halfway between Dowelltown and Liberty. Much excitement prevailed, the election resulting in a majority for no removal.

The following lawyers have been residents of the county at various times. If all are not included, it is not an intentional omission, but an oversight: M. M. Brien, J. J. Ford, A. M. Savage, J. H. Savage, W. W. Wade, Sr., W. W. Wade, Jr., John B. Robinson, Ralph Robinson, Solon Robinson, Joseph Clarke, J.

W. Clarke, Robert Cantrell, William B. Stokes, James A. Nesmith, Robert C. Nesmith, T. M. Wade, B. M. Webb, Boone Trapp, R. M. Magness, W. G. Crowley, M. A. Crowley, B. M. Cantrell, J. W. Overall, Alfred Smith, B. G. Adcock, P. T. Shore, Alvin Avent, Will T. Hale, Dan O. Williams, J. W. Botts, John Gothard, H. A. Bratten, W. D. G. Carnes, R. B. Anderson, I. C. Stone, M. D. Smallman, S. H. Collins, Richard Saunders, J. J. Foster, B. T. R. Foster, J. B. Foster, W. B. Staley, T. J. Bradford, Pallas Smith, White Turney, W. B. Corley, M. M. Brien, Jr., J. M. Allen, Albert McClellan, R. W. Turner, Joseph H. Blackburn, Caleb Davis, J. W. Parker, Eli Evans, D. M. Robinson, L. N. Savage, Thomas Fisher, Jr., J. A. Drake, J. E. Drake, P. C. Crowley, William O'Conner, J. B. Crowley, R. L. Cantrell, Brown Davis, and Dixie W. Floyd.

The following were practicing in the county in 1814: T. W. Wade, Alvin Avant, J. E. Drake, R. L. Turner, P. C. Crowley, E. G. Lawson, D. M. Robinson, J. B. Robinson, J. A. Gothard, Dixie W. Floyd, Brown Davis, Smithville; W. B. Corley, Dowelltown; James W. Parker, Alexandria; and H. A. Bratten, Liberty.

These have occupied the bench while residents of the county or after having removed therefrom: M. M. Brien, Robert Cantrell, M. D. Smallman, W. G. Crowley, W. W. Wade, Jr., Thomas Fisher, and John Fite.

The act to incorporate Smithville was passed December 4, 1843. The boundaries were as follows: "Beginning at the dwelling house of E. M. North, including the sawmill; thence to the southwest corner of the plan of the town; thence east with the line of the said town plan to the northwest corner of the lot of land which M. M. Brien purchased from John C. Cannady; thence with the lines of the same so as to include it in the town plan; thence a direct line to the stage road so as to include the dwelling house of P. M. Wade; thence north to Fall Creek; thence up the said creek to the chalybeate spring; thence a direct line, including the dwelling house of W. W. Wade, to the northeast corner of the original town plan; thence to the beginning." As in other towns of the county, the corporation was abolished soon after the four-mile law was enacted to secure the statute's educational benefits.

Among the first merchants were Willis W. Wade, P. M. Wade, and Samuel Chandler. Then came W. P. Harvey, P. G. Magness, J. M. Allen, W. H. Magness, J. L. Dearman, George Beckwith, J. Y. Stewart, S. B. Whaley, and Elijah Whaley. Still later the following were business men: R. B. West, Isaiah White, G. R. Smith & Son, Black & Bond, Smith Bros., T. B. Potter, S. D. Blankenship, J. L. Colvert, Hooper & Bro., D. S. Harrison, F. Z. Webb, A. L. Foster, and E. J. Evans. Business is carried on to-day by the following individuals and firms: W. H. H. Bond, general merchant and undertaker, in business 40 years; F. Z. Webb, druggist, 34; H. E. Mason, druggist, 10; Conger Bros., gentlemen's furnishing goods, 11; H. E. Staley & Son, dry goods and shoes, 25; J. C. Foster & Bro., grocery and hardware, 15; Mrs. W. R. Smith, millinery and dress goods, 20; S. C. Tyree, dry goods and notions, 15; W. H. Smith & Co., hardware, 10; J. C. Bond & Bro., groceries; Fred Robinson, groceries; Potter, Love & Hays, ladies' dress goods and millinery; W. L. Taylor & Co., general store and freight transferers; J. E. Foster, groceries; G. S. Davis, groceries; H. Calhoun, groceries; Burton & Jennings, groceries; James Burch, general store; Young & Conger, groceries and produce; Cash Hardware Company, W. F. Hooper manager; James Dearman, hotel and livery stable; A. H. Lane, livery stable; Mrs. E. M. Bailiff, hotel; Mrs. T. W. Wade, hotel; E. J. Evans & Son, spokes, also millers; Sam McGuire, barber; Mart Talley (colored), barber; Lafayette Pack, C. Shaw, C. H. Vickers, and George Summers, blacksmiths; Lee Magness and Thomas Beckwith, photographers.

Among the early physicians were: G. W. Eastham, Charles Schurer, J. C. Buckley, E. Tubb, J. C. Cox, P. C. Shields, J. S. Harrison, J. J. and Isaac Gowan, Dr. Evans, Dr. Barnes, and Ben Cantrell, herbist. Later: J. Z. Webb, J. S. Fletcher, T. W. Eaton, A. Avant, M. L. Wilson, and James Womack. Present: W. W. Parker, W. R. Parker, M. L. Wilson, L. D. Allen, C. A. Loring, and T. J. Potter.

Dentists, J. T. Bell and E. H. Conger.

The Smithville brass band of twenty-one pieces, J. K. Shields leader, has a well-merited reputation throughout DeKalb and surrounding counties.

A number of tanyards have been sunk in that section from an early day. Among the first were Tom Roe's, on Snow's Hill, and Henry Gray's, in town. J. L. Colvert, W. H. Magness, and D. T. Harrison were formerly in this business. D. T. and J. B. Harrison established a tobacco factory in 1879, and for years did a good business, as did the Mack Shores factory.

The town has been noted for its excellent schools, though no record was kept of the old field variety. Fulton Academy drew attention to the county seat a score of years before the War between the States. It was incorporated January 17, 1838, with these as trustees: Thomas Durham, Moses Pedigo, Samuel Allen, Martin Philips, and Bernard Richardson. For further references to this subject see the chapter on educational matters.

List of Smithville postmasters as far back as can be ascertained: J. Y. Stewart, George Beckwith, "Big Jim" Williams, George Bing, Felix Patterson, Robert Black, Ralph Robinson, J. S. Dunlap, S. P. W. Maxwell, E. K. Atwell, Dick Goodson, J. H. Christian, and (present) C. W. Moore.

Like Alexandria and Liberty, Smithville has two banks—the Farmers and Traders' (J. B. Moore, Cashier) and the People's. The latter was organized in 1903 with a capital of $15,000, with R. B. West, President, and J. E. Drake, Cashier. Its resources in 1914 were about $75,000. Present officers: W. H. Davis, President; F. M. Love, Cashier; W. L. Davis, Assistant Cashier.

Mention of the most noted Smithville taverns is given in the chapter on "Stagecoach and Tavern Days." It is thought that the earliest tavern keeper was Dr. G. W. Eastham. Then there were Bernard Richardson and James Erwin. Dave James was tavern keeper from 1850 to 1860, and Mack Shores in 1861-62. Tyree's Hotel has long been a favorite hostelry, as have the Dearman House and Bailiff House. A correspondent writes that many years ago there was a village adjacent to Smithville, a suburb, "just down the hill, across the creek and in the direction of Sparta," called Chalk Hill, and that Jack Frazier kept a tavern there. Six miles from Smithville is a popular summer resort called Seven Springs, J. T. Odum, proprietor.

Pearl-hunting in Caney Fork has been carried on for some years, pearls bringing from $500 to $1,800 having been found. John Windham, of Smithville, was one of the most successful dealers. S. L. Fitts, of Temperance Hall, is also a successful dealer.

There are no stories to tell of the old-time modes of punishment of criminals. Before Smithville was thought of, whipping, branding, pillorying, and cutting off the ears of criminals were abolished—in 1829 as to whites and in 1831 as to negroes.

Relative to the early transportation of freight, Mr. Dearman writes: "The produce from Sligo Ferry, on the Caney Fork River, was carried to Nashville in flatboats, and merchandise which the people needed was brought back on these boats. The boats were pushed up the Cumberland and Caney Fork, and it often required a week or two to reach Sligo. J. L. Dearman, who served as sheriff of the county three terms and twenty years as a magistrate, Levi Bozarth, William Bozarth, David James, Nat Parker, Dave Koger, the Phillipses, and the Dildines are some of the men who made runs down the river and back. While the work was hard, the men were hardy and won their way."

Through the kindness of Mr. Tal Allen, now an honored citizen of Nashville, this list of papers that have been published in the town since the war is furnished: The *Highland Sun,* A. Max Ford; the *Journal,* A. C. Carnes; the *Index,* W. D. Carnes; the *Watchman and Critic,* Dozier and Kelly; and the *Review,* Frank Wallace, later Eugene Hendon.

W. D. G. and W. B. Carnes were at one time connected with the *Index,* and M. L. Fletcher was once a Smithville publisher.

The following necrological note by a correspondent shows the sad changes that have taken place in the population in the last generation: "The following early citizens of Smithville are dead: W. G. Crowley, Chancellor for many years; Bernard Richardson, who donated the site of Smithville to the county; Jack Kennedy, Mexican War veteran and register for thirty years; J. T. Hollis, who served as County and Circuit Court Clerk and Clerk and Master; Mr. Dillard, druggist; Joe Stewart, sheriff and old-time slave trader; J. L. Dearman, sheriff, magistrate, and merchant; 'Sporting Ike' Hays; G. R. Smith, merchant and magistrate for twenty years; T. B. Potter, Confederate soldier, merchant, and banker; W. C. Potter, merchant and banker; Dave James, tavern keeper; Mack Shores, tavern keeper; O. B. Staley, merchant; J. B. Atwell, register for ten years; J. M. Allen, magistrate for thirty years and twice representative; J. L. Colvert, merchant; S. D. Blankenship, merchant; T. N. Christian, Circuit Court Clerk for sixteen years; T. W. Shields, Circuit Court Clerk for twelve years; Rev. J. M. Kidwell; Z. P. Lee, County Court Clerk for eight years."

But time, tide, and progress await no man. Smithville is to-day a pretty and thriving town of about one thousand inhabitants. "The turnpike from the town to Snow's Hill," writes a correspondent, "resembles an urban avenue—new houses all along where thirty years ago none were to be seen. From Smithville to Sparta you are never out of sight of new residences and barns. People from the Caney Fork River and hill country have been buying the land and moving to it. Even a dweller of the western section—the Basin—admits this fact: 'I am not sure but the flatwoods show more thrift to-day than any other part of the county.' Smithville has a flour mill, a spoke and handle factory, two banks, a paper, churches, and several general stores. The buildings are all comparatively new, only three or four of those built forty years ago standing; while every road leading out from one to eight miles is macadamized. Perhaps much of its prosperity is due to the enterprise of the farmers who have recently bought the lands surrounding and the awakened energy of the descendants of the pioneers."

Smithville is a charming and prosperous inland town and growing. Its distance from Nashville is sixty-seven miles.

CHAPTER XII.

HISTORICAL JETSAM.

IN a history of Kentucky by Prof. N. S. Shaler, who for more than a quarter of a century filled the chair of Agassiz at Harvard University, it is shown that by actual measurement the Tennessee and Kentucky soldiers in the War between the States were the largest in the army and in the world.

DeKalb County has been noted for its large and strong men. Commercial travelers and others have remarked upon the fact. It is safe to say that no county of the same population can show a larger number.

"Big" Bill Evans, once county trustee, weighed in his prime about two hundred and seventy-five pounds. Mrs. Matilda Huggins, his sister, weighed probably more. William B. Preston was about the size of Evans, and his mother weighed about three hundred pounds. Fox Frazier (hog trader), his brother Henry, John Parker (of Dismal Creek), Col. James Tubb, James Fuston (tavern keeper), Presley Adamson, Henry L. Turner, Francis Turner, James Stark, Landon Richardson, Bill Garrison, Aaron Frazier, Sr., William Estes, Moses and John Spencer, Jim Willis Thomas Roe, George and Thomas E. Bratten, Bart Pack, George Givan, Sr., William G. Bratten, Jack Tubb, Rev. Natty Hayes, Gips West—such men, weighing from two hundred and twenty-five pounds up, could be named in scores.

There were other men noted more for their strength

than for their size, though all were probably above the average in weight. Ben Cantrell, of the Smithville neighborhood, once lifted with apparent ease twelve hundred pounds of brass while in Nashville. Ben Denny was another noted strong man of Smithville. A pioneer shoemaker of Liberty, John Woodside, placed his shoulders under an average-sized horse and lifted him clear of the ground. John Spencer, also of Liberty, carried a bag containing five bushels of wheat (300 pounds) five miles to mill. There were three or four of these Spencers, all large and powerful. It is possible, even probable, that they were related to John Sharpe Spencer, the giant who lived in Sumner County in a hollow tree before James Robertson made his settlement at Nashville. A number of the pioneers went farther into the wilderness as the Cumberland country was settled.

As to men of great height, Dr. J. G. Squires was probably the tallest. He stood six feet seven and a half inches in his stockings, but would not weigh more than one hundred and forty pounds. "Curl" Jennings, who resided for some years at Dowelltown, was not less than six feet six inches and weighed close to three hundred pounds. A Mr. Brashear, over the average in size, had an attack of typhoid while boarding with Jennings. Each had a pair of trousers made from the same bolt. When recovering, Brashear decided to sit up a few moments. As it happened, Jennings's trousers were hanging on a near-by chair. Believing them his, he slipped them on. When he saw how they hung in great folds and bags on him, he fell back weakly on the bed, exclaiming: "Great heavens! If I've fallen off so much, there's no use trying to go about!" John Gann, of Liberty, was about as tall as Jennings and rather thin. One day in front of a saloon John Vandigriff, short and stocky, sidled up to him and said: "Mr. Gann, please hand me down one o' them buzzards flyin' over." Milton Ward, a well-known old field teacher, was about six feet six inches tall and required a special bedstead made for his use. Jim Willis, fist fighter, of Smithville, was six feet four inches tall, weighing about two hundred and twenty-five pounds. He was somewhat stooped, his arms were extremely long, while his eyes were deep-blue and deep-set. While he did not appear to delight in bloodshed, it is believed that he had a natural inclination to fight. During the war he lived in Missouri and belonged to Quantrell's guerrillas. One who knew him says that his scalp was as rough as a turtle's back, due to scars made by rocks, knife thrusts, and club blows. Landon Richardson, of Liberty, weighing two hundred and twenty-five pounds, was usually deputized in ante-bellum times to arrest dangerous characters who came to the village. He was not a "bully," but powerful and fearless. It is tradition that on one occasion he put to flight seven "bad men" from Helton Creek who had attacked him. Firearms were not used in brawls then.

The two men who had the distinction of being the smallest in the county were Frank Foster, of Liberty, and Thornton Christy, of Alexandria.

Mention has been made in the sketch of Temperance Hall of the disappearance of William G. Stokes. Other mysteries have puzzled the people and tried the souls of the parents of the missing men. Dr. Foster, who was given the story by an aged relative, says that Frank Givan, son of the second Circuit Court Clerk, started horseback to visit relatives in Maryland early in the nineteenth century. He was never heard from again, and he nor his horse could be traced out of the Liberty community. Was he murdered for his money? Did he sink in quicksand, then supposed to exist in the county? The wildest rumors were afloat. Years afterwards a skeleton was found in a hollow tree on Dry Creek, and some thought this the solution of the problem. Isaac Evans, son of Reuben Evans, went with W. B. Preston and others to California during the excitement over the finding of gold. He was heard from once, his letter stating that he had joined William Walker's filibusters. No other tidings have ever reached his friends or relatives, though sixty-five years have gone by.

Clay lamps, burning grease, were used in kitchens some years after the war. Candles, often made of tallow, were used by the grandfathers for illumination. As there were no matches in general use until about 1830, we know that the tinder box, flint, and steel were kept for starting fires by the early DeKalb Countians.

Dr. G. C. Flowers, an ante-bellum resident of Liberty, was regarded as the most extensively read man in the county in his day, as far as general literature is concerned. Dr. John S. Fletcher, who died in Smithville in 1877 (graduated from three universities, among them the University of Pennsylvania) and was surgeon in Gen. John C. Brown's brigade at the close of the war of 1861-65, had a distinction in after years similar to that of Dr. Flowers.

The county has produced some men of more than local reputation, but the writer recalls but one instance in which the people contributed of their means to erect a memorial to any DeKalb Countian. It is worth thinking about. The one thus honored was neither jurist, minister, statesman, editor, captain of industry, author, scholar, nor military chieftain. He was a very plain, unassuming man, who out of sympathy for the bereaved and their dead made it convenient to help dig the graves of his neighbors for nearly or quite threescore years. The marble shaft over W. H. (Hamp) Woodside's grave at Liberty is proof that a noble heart is still regarded as more than mere worldly success.

Mention might be made of many DeKalb Countians with rare or bizarre qualities, such as the one who could never be made to answer yes or no directly and another who spoke as if always quoting, as, "I'm not feeling well to-day, as the old saying is"; but to give the story complete much more space would be required than can be offered in this history.

Hundreds of names of citizens once familiar in the county are recorded in these pages, it will be noticed. Of their owners little more can be said now than that their graves are green. It is pathetic. But, to paraphrase Burns,

> Should auld cognomens be forgot,
> And *never* brought to min'?

A striking thing about the names is the absence of foreign ones. The foreparents were of Anglo-Saxon stock. Some names were queer: Esau Pack, Giles Driver, Sim Hathaway, Bob Prydy, Pack Florida, Enoch George, Gil Etheridge, Cantrell Bethel, Cicero Duncan, Caleb Davis, Seaborn Harts, Brown Harriman, Crofford Rankhorn, John Shehane, Daniel Ratlige, Poindexter Joins, Nehemiah Garrison, Congelius Burrip, Jonas Nokes, Iradel March, Conrad Lamberson, James R. Gapway, Brice Parsley, Zene Crips, John Canler, Seth Whaley, Archamac Bass, Crag Parsons, Acenith Fite, Brackett Estes, Thomas Durham, Edwin Shumway, Randall Pafford, King Herod, William Mooneyham, Cain Adams, Lito Hullett, June Driver, Leven Gray, Friday Martin, Samuel Casey, Tucker Woodson, Festus Moses (the great walnut buyer), Goodman Mallon, Telford Steele, Park Amonett, Vincent Manor, Bart Nonnelly, Emory Cubbins, Mikel Etheridge, Irwin Page, Fuller Sanlin, and North Reynolds. Others were musically alliterative: Edmondson Elkins, Nelson New, Mat Martin, Lee Lafever, Leonard Lamberson, Benjamin Blades, Sylvanus Stokes, Kern Clark, Rich Richardson, Elam Edge, Pleasant Pistole, Dempsey Driver, Fox Frazier,

Hardin Hardcastle, Henry Helmantaller, Hawkins Heflin, Rison Roland, Tolliver Turner, William Wellaby, Wylie Wilder, George Givan, Moses Mathews, Henry Horn, Alex Armstrong, Henry Hart, German Gossett, Philip Palmer, Henry Hass, Martin Murphy, Ben Brownin, Thomas Terry, James Jones, Thomas Tyree, Willis Wade, William Wright, Archibald Allen, Elial Elston, William Wilson, Shines Scribner, Abe Adams, Frank Foster, Hiram Hildreth, Travers Tarpley, David Dirting, Mickeral Manning, Morris Marcum, Hart Hinesly, Ephraim Evans, Arch Allen, and Samson Sellars.

As observed elsewhere, the names of a number of families figure no longer in the county's activities. Some of the settlers died; others moved to different sections. Now and then one hears of a few of their descendants: John C. Floyd, of Arkansas, and Frederic Barry, of Mississippi, who became members of Congress from their adopted States; M. M. Brien and Robert Cantrell, noted lawyers and jurists; Bird S. Rhea, Ed Reece, R. B. Wright, Cicero Duncan, Church Anderson, James Yeargin, and Len F. Davis, all prominent in the business world, Mr. Davis in 1914 having the distinction of being the senior of Nashville's wholesale merchants in point of service.

There were (and are still) in the county many racy local characters of a type one rarely ever meets in large towns, where personalities lose their distinctness of outline like coins which pass innumerable times across shop counters. Such were Jonas Nokes, Ross

Keith, "Sporting Ike" Hays, and others. Some were natural wits and humorists, whose drolleries have been kept alive by the joke-loving DeKalb Countians. The writer thinks none excelled four or five Liberty wits— Hamp Woodside, Blue Givan, Pole Woodside, Jr., Thomas Vick, James Burton, and M. C. Vick. Dr. Foster avers that Thomas Askew was the wittiest man he ever knew. Such little sallies as these, handed down from father to son, approach the character of folk tales:

Shed Lawson, who resided in Alexandria many years ago, was noted for his cheerful disposition, despite the fact that his treasury of worldly goods was small, and for his ready wit on any occasion requiring quick repartee. When the circus comes to town, the parade is sure to gather the crowd. One day Shed and his little son, who always accompanied him like his shadow, were following the clown. The latter, on his pony and diked out in conventional cap and bells, was shouting his badinage to the sight-seers. Seeing Shed, he said: "Here, mister, I want to hire that boy." Sensing a chance maybe to get his admission fee easily, the Alexandrian asked what he wanted the lad to do. "I want him to blow my nose," the clown said. "O, well, now," retorted Shed loudly and without hesitation, "ef you will jest wait a little while, jedgin' from appearances, the flies will blow it fer you."

Speaking of noses, Littleberry Vick, of Liberty, as well as the Duke of Wellington, possessed a prominent nose. One day he and William Burton were arguing over some political issue. Directly Mr. Vick, somewhat irritated, said: "Billy Burton, you never could see an inch beyond your nose." "And, Berry Vick," replied Mr. Burton, "if you could see an inch beyond *your* nose, you could see into another county."

Matthew Sellars, a pioneer of Dry Creek and a first-class citizen, had no blasphemy in his heart when, after a storm one night, he went out and looked on the wreck the wind had made of the timber and young corn in the new ground. Returning to the house, he said to his wife in a low tone: "Charlotte, don't whisper it above your breath; but, taking the Almighty up one side and down the other, it seems he does about as much harm as good."

There is no spot of earth where the people apply the title of uncle and aunt more industriously than in the DeKalb County Basin. When it is applied to a neighbor, it is an indication that he is getting old. It also signifies reverence. Some wag thereaway once observed: "There are four periods in the life of a man. As a child he is Bobby, as a young man he is Bob, in his prime he is Uncle Bob, and after threescore and ten he is Old Uncle Bobby." Some there were who objected to having the title of age thus thrust upon them, and one was William Vick, the Liberty merchant. One day he was sitting in front of his store. Dempsy Driver rode by and, bowing, said: "Good morning, Uncle Bill." Turning to a companion, Vick said dryly and somewhat resentfully: "Another nephew."

Thomas Askew was a soldier in the Mexican War.

Becoming ill, he died, to all appearances; doctors and nurses pronounced him dead. His coffin was brought in and placed near the cot where he was "laid" out. He revived when left alone for a few minutes and saw the coffin. Having been a DeKalb official, he reached for a pencil and wrote on top of the casket: "No property found. T. B. Askew, constable."

Reuben Evans, farmer, magistrate, and rock mason, was sincere and matter-of-fact. He was also cautious, extremely so, and one cannot imagine him guilty of exaggeration in praise or blame. While he was doing some stonework for C. W. L. Hale, the latter's child said something the father regarded as bright and cute. "Now, Uncle Reuben," said he, "wasn't that just too much?" "Really," Mr. Evans replied deliberately and carefully, "I can't say it was *too much*, but it *was* a good deal."

Dr. J. W. Campbell had a farm in a very deep hollow a mile west of Liberty. One afternoon his tenant hauled about two hundred and fifty pounds of hay to the village. As he passed Blue Givan's store some one remarked that it was a very small load for two horses to haul all the way to town. "But you must recollect that when you come out of a *jug* you have to come out with a small load," said Givan.

Jacob Adcock, south of Smithville and formerly a representative from Cannon County, bought a broken-down stallion for $15, fed him on roasting ears, groomed him all times of day, and kicked and punched him to make him gay. Then he got out on the fence to watch for a victim. Rev. William Dawson, riding by on a fine black mare, was bantered for a trade. "The horse is a top-notcher," said Adcock, "but too young and spry for an old man like me." As they approached the stable the horse saw his master, then, walling his eyes and snorting, tried to climb out of the stall. His coat glistened, so that he looked as well as he acted. The trade was made, the parson giving the black mare, a watch, and a note for $50 for the stallion. At the Short Mountain camp meeting some weeks later, after the stallion had retrograded to the $15 class again, Adcock professed religion. As he was going home Dawson overtook him, said he was glad God had pardoned his sins, then suggested that he ought to return some of the money he swindled out of Dawson through the horse trade. "I don't see it that way, Brother Dawson," replied Adcock. "When the Lord pardoned my sins he included the horse swap."

CHAPTER XIII.

SMALLER VILLAGES OF THE COUNTY.

Hon. J. M. Allen once averred that his father, Jesse Allen, a Virginian, entered the land on Smith Fork Creek from John Corley's farm to Lancaster, one mile on each side of the creek, but sold his rights for $400, after which he entered a tract in another part of the county that became DeKalb. Lower Smith Fork Valley is one of the most fertile sections in Middle Tennessee, and the wonder is that the pioneers could see no farther ahead.

Dr. R. M. Mason says Samuel Caplinger, a large landholder, built the mill and house which were later owned by Nicholas Smith and which formed the nucleus of Temperance Hall. The late A. P. Smith, son of Nicholas, has stated that the village received its name from the fact that the Sons of Temperance used to hold their meetings on the second floor of his father's residence. It was named then, after 1848, for the elder Smith in that year removed from Wilson County to Temperance Hall, the site being in Smith County. By act of February 1, 1850, the line was changed so as to include in DeKalb County the farms and homes of Smith, Andrew Vantrease, John Robinson, and others. By the same act John F. Goodner's farm, near Alexandria, was taken into DeKalb, as has been seen.

The men who located at and around Temperance Hall in the first years of the nineteenth century were, many of them, of unusual force of character and a number in affluent circumstances: Samuel Caplinger, Alex Robinson, Stephen Robinson, Nicholas Smith, Daniel Ford, John Mason, John Corley, James Simpson, Matthew Simpson, John Lamberson, George Kelley, Jack Reynolds, Peter Reynolds, the Drivers, Bates, Lawrences, Lancasters, Oakleys, Hayeses, Tubbs, Stephens, Kelleys, Fishers, Stokeses, and others.

Owing to the distinction to which two members of the Stokes family reached in the State (William B. and Jordan), it is pertinent to record that their father, Sylvanus, had started from North Carolina to locate on his land, near the present Temperance Hall, when his team ran away, and he was killed. Mrs. Stokes, with her three children, Thomas, William B., and Jordan, and a Mr. Kelly, continued the journey, reaching this country in 1818. Some years later the widow married Mr. Kelly and settled near or in Temperance Hall. To them were born Harry and Rufus Kelly and two daughters, one becoming Mrs. Mike Lancaster and the other Mrs. Thomas Lancaster. Thomas Stokes became a farmer. Of him a reliable citizen, a former neighbor, writes: "He was at one time the richest man in DeKalb County, having at the close of the war of 1861-65 about fifty negroes and large land interests. He was a fire-eating secessionist, as was his brother William at the beginning of the war, though the latter became a Federal. Everything Thomas had that was loose at both ends was taken from him by Federal soldiers. For intelligence and fine mother wit he was the superior of either Colonel Bill or Jordan, but his fault was a fondness for alcoholic drink. He gave way to this habit after the war and died poor and almost an imbecile. A son of Thomas was William G. I can just remember him. A year or more prior to the war he started south with a drove of hogs and was never heard of more. Sylvanus, another son, the youngest, fought through the war for the Confederacy and died a few years ago. He was one man in the county who, in a threatened difficulty, made Capt. W. L. Hathaway 'take water.'"

Early merchants of Temperance Hall were John Mason, Dr. Arch Robinson, and Mr. Rodgers. The two first were in business about 1851-52; the last-named, who was there about 1855 to 1860, was Northern-born and returned to that section. Present business men: L. Driver (who also twice represented the county in the legislature), Williams & Terry, J. H. Close & Son, Turner & McBride, J. R. Kelley, and L. B. Midgett. The flour mill is operated by the Temperance Hall Milling Company.

Dr. Arch Robinson, father of the late Dr. W. H. Robinson, of Liberty, was one of the early physicians. Following his death, his brother, Dr. William B. Robinson, located in the village. After the war Dr. Thomas Gold entered that field. Other physicians have been Drs. R. M. Mason, G. W. Martin, and S. C. Robinson. Dr. Samuel Walker was for some years practicing in that region.

One of the earlier teachers was Mrs. Stephens. Others were Mr. Bush, Mr. Hatcher, A. L. Reynolds, A. L. Malone, E. W. Brown, J. W. Thomison (now a lawyer of Nashville), Joseph Ford, Dr. Thomas Ford, and Frank Foster. The present teachers are Leroy Smith and Miss Stella Young. Miss Lizzie Simpson taught in the vicinity some years following the war.

The Southern Methodists have a good church in the hamlet. A Baptist church and Pisgah, the latter belonging to the Northern wing of the Methodists, are located a short distance out. The Disciples also have a congregation at this place.

Dowelltown, on the Lebanon and Sparta Turnpike and two miles north of Liberty, is on land settled some years after 1800. Thomas Dale, of Maryland, seems to have bought up some of the claims of Revolutionary soldiers of North Carolina. At any rate, he held warrants for much of the land around the village.

Levi Gray became possessed of a tract on the south side of the creek, living in the house east of the covered bridge, which was later occupied by Frank Dowell. It belonged to the Grays for years, and their family graveyard was across the turnpike west of the residence. The estate was inherited by Isaac Gray, who married a Miss Dowell. He died and left two children, Harriet and Melvina.

Frank Dowell married the widow Gray, his cousin, and lived on the farm until the close of the War between the States, when he removed to Arkansas. At one time he represented his county in the Arkansas Legislature. Dowelltown was named for him.

Frank Dowell sold the Dowelltown property to Rev. John Hunt, a Baptist minister from East Tennessee. Hunt exchanged it for land belonging to Sanford

Mann, who came from the North after the war and was the first ferrotype artist of Liberty after peace. Mann sold to Thomas Chapman. The present owner is John Robinson, a son of the pioneer, Edward Robinson.

The country adjacent to Dowelltown was settled by as high-class men as any mentioned in other sections of the county. Among them were Robin Forrester, William and Samson Williams, Matthew Sellars, Benjamin Avant, David Fite, Alex Robinson, George Barnes, Edward Robinson, the Yeargins, the Harts, the Fraziers, the Bankses, the Snows, the Turners, and others.

The first storehouse was erected about 1869 where the Barger Hollow Lane intersects with the Lebanon and Sparta Turnpike, and probably the first merchant was James Ashworth. In the same building the following successively had stocks of merchandise: James Fuson, William Wall, Bratten & Turney, Riley Taylor, Barney Taylor & Co., Thomas Curtis, Less Fuson, and John F. Turner. Other early merchants were Charles Pullen, Thomas Bright, Pat Geraty, and Robert F. Jones.

There are now six stores in the village, the present merchants being John F. Turner, N. R. Robinson, W. T. Robinson, A. R. Meares & Son, G. S. and W. T. Blackburn, and Less Bass.

In 1866 Col. J. H. Blackburn began the erection of a flour mill, which was finished in 1872 by Lieut. Wingate T. Robinson. The Big Spring northwest of town furnishes the power.

History of DeKalb County

In 1866 Allan Wright (born in Baltimore County, Md., in 1831) came to DeKalb County and erected the first flour mill in Liberty after the War between the States on the site of that burned by Gen. John T. Wilder during the war. In 1868 he erected and has since controlled the Dowelltown Woolen Factory.

As to physicians of the town, Dr. C. C. Robinson was the first to locate, remaining in the village until his death. Previous to this time Dr. John A. Fuson, of Dry Creek, did the practice. Dr. W. F. Fuson came next, then Dr. S. C. Robinson, a son of C. C. and now of Temperance Hall. Dr. C. B. White resides there at present. Dr. Howard Curtis, son of Rev. Mack Curtis, was graduated at Chattanooga University, but located at Allgood and is a leading physician of Putnam County. Dr. W. T. Robinson, a son of B. W. Robinson, was graduated at Vanderbilt and is meeting with success at Shelbyville.

The local dentist is Dr. J. T. Duggan. Dr. Hoyt Robinson, son of B. W. Robinson and graduated in dentistry at Vanderbilt University, located in Union City.

W. B. Corley and Hon. N. R. Robinson are resident attorneys.

Edward Gothard was probably the earliest blacksmith, then came Gothard & Self, then Self & Grandstaff. Isaac Burkett had a shop just north.

One of the early teachers of the neighborhood was Alex Robinson, a capable man. Other teachers: R. B. Harris, J. B. Green, T. A. Kilman, R. A. Underwood, Mr. Sykes, Mr. Myatt, O. B. Close, Rev. W. P. Banks,

N. R. Robinson, J. F. Caplinger, O. B. Starnes, and M. Malone.

The postmasters have been William Wall, Robert Yeargin, Alf Standford, R. F. Jones, M. A. Stark, Lucian Avant, B. W. Robinson, N. R. Robinson, and Fannie M. Robinson.

In 1885 an elegant school building was erected and for some years was properly appreciated. As in most villages, the public's appreciation of educational advantages is spasmodic, and in saying that there have been good schools here, followed by intervals of languor, we but repeat the history of most communities. Old Asbury Church was frequently used for schools before it was burned. Preceding it was a smaller structure erected by the pioneers for religious and educational purposes.

The village is surrounded by a fine agricultural region, and its population is prosperous and law-abiding. A considerable number of Federal pensioners live there and adjacent (though they are rapidly passing away), and their pensions have greatly added to the volume of business.

The Big Spring northwest is a notable feature of the community and was such before the village came into existence. It is deep, cold, and about forty feet in diameter. Formerly it was a great fishing place—for "gigging" by torchlight, angling, and lassoing with copper wire.

Near the Dry Creek bridge were the muster grounds, which in ante-bellum times provided a great gathering place. Near by was Gum Springs in a cavelike depression at the edge of the turnpike. "The water," Mrs. Pet White explained once to the writer, "was almost as cold as ice, dropping from the overhead rocks and falling into the tub made from the cut of a hollow tree. The young women and young men of the neighborhood congregated here on muster days and Sunday afternoons, so that you would be led to believe it some famous summer resort."

In the center of Dowelltown and on Mrs. White's land is the old Gray cemetery, a popular burying place a half century ago. Several members of the Gray pioneers sleep there, among the rest, Isaac C. Gray, born in 1807, died 1850; Leven Gray, born in 1812; C. E. Gray, died in 1852, in the sixty-fifth year of his age. Others interred there are: Rev. James Stanford, Matthew Williams, William Craven (Union soldier), James White, Isaiah White (born in 1806), and Charlie Blades. Time and the weather will crumble or hide these simple memorials before many years, then the humble sleepers will be as entirely forgotten as if they had never lived.

> For them no more the blazing hearth shall burn,
>   Or busy housewife ply her evening care;
> No children rush to lisp their sire's return,
>   Or climb his knees the envied kiss to share.

Laurel Hill, a pleasant village in the northern part of the county, was for a long while better known as Smutville, owing to the irreverence of the wag who does not let home pride interfere with his attempts at wit. The country adjacent is hilly but fertile and needs only good roads to make it an ideal section.

The citizens are mainly of North Carolina and Virginia ancestry—industrious, lovers of music and the chase, and of strong religious and political convictions.

Among the early settlers were: Coleman Helm, Riley League, P. W. Presley, James Isbell, William Garner, Isaac Burton, Riley Coggin, Jeremiah Hale, Willis Coggin, Peter Exum, Elisha Conger, Hezekiah Love, Andrew Carr (living in 1914 at the age of ninety-four), John Clemens, Mat Lee, David Lee, T. J. Lee, Ephraim Foster, Nelson New, J. H. Kerr, Jesse Haggard (yet living, aged eighty-four), Jesse Hale, Claiborne Vaughan, S. H. Smith, John McGuffey, Joseph Mitchell, Robert Maxwell, John Merritt, and the Johnsons. These were of the pioneer type of Americans—sturdy, conscientious, and level-headed. In politics they were, both Democrats and Whigs, of strong convictions. A majority of the old-timers were anti-slavery in sentiment. The village furnished several men to the Federal and Confederate armies, the larger number siding with the North. In 1914 only two veterans of the great war were surviving—J. S. Maxwell, Union veteran, and W. A. Moss, Confederate. During the war there was no local engagement between the belligerents, though not infrequently detachments and even regiments of troops passed through the community. It may be added that there was naturally considerable bitterness among neighbors of opposing political views, though this is now a thing of the past.

The Laurel Hill people are either Baptists or Methodists in religious faith, and both sects have comfortable churches. In 1876 and 1880 the old log structures were displaced by modern frame buildings creditable to any rural locality. Among the early ministers were Thomas Dodson, Alex Byers, David Lee, M. P. Gentry, D. P. Searcy, and Milton Pressley. Later ministers have been: J. M. Carter, Francis Deal, J. M. McNeil, J. B. Hitchens, Van N. Smith, and J. H. Keathly. Near Laurel Hill is Wolf Creek Baptist Church.

Among the old field teachers of the neighborhood were William Whitefield, S. H. Smith, Walker Brown, William Garner, William Isbell, and Jesse McDowell. These men were of rugged individualities. We are told that in the old days here the pupils sat in the schoolroom with hats on, studied aloud, and sang geography. They were followed by Napoleon Smith, J. E. Conger, Van N. Smith, and Misses Sallie and Emma McDonald. There are two schoolhouses on Wolf Creek and one north at the river, and school is still kept at these places.

The physicians have been: William Farmer, Gideon Smith, W. E. Sypert, W. E. Sypert, Jr., J. C. Fisher, and T. J. Smith.

Early business men: J. H. Kerr, Nelson New, S. H. Smith, and Joseph Mitchell. Later: T. J. Fisher, J. T. Exum, Smith Bros., D. G. Eaton, Bose Tyree, and J. E. Conger. Present: Noah Duke, Z. O. Medley, Allie Pressley, and Henry Sadler. Millers: K. D. Exum, Pinkney Coggin, J. S. Maxwell, and L. S. Exum. Blacksmiths: Coleman Helm, W. G. Stephens, John Alcorn, Pleas Randolph, and John New.

About 1906 the post office was abolished and rural route service established. Former postmasters were: J. H. Kerr, S. H. Smith, W. E. Bartlett, Van N. Smith, T. J. Fisher, and Henry Sadler.

In every community there has been some citizen whose bizarre qualities have attracted to himself unusual and pleasing attention above his local contemporaries. That of Laurel Hill is no exception to the rule. To illustrate, "Uncle Pink" Coggin, miller, will long be recalled with pleasure and amusement, and many anecdotes are told at his expense. Had Rev. Milton Pressley, another old-timer, been properly educated, it is probable that he would have been a leading minister of his day. "Chill penury" often indeed represses a noble rage. To this inland preacher one who knew him pays this tribute: "He could not read, but knew the Bible almost by heart. He also knew a few of the early day hymns. I have heard preachers of every type, but no scholar or theologian have I heard who had the power Uncle Milt wielded over an audience. He once preached before Methodist bishops and startled his cultivated audience with his untutored power. Sacred be his dust!"

There are a number of burgs throughout the county which sprang up after post offices were secured, but the rural route service has left them without official names. Perhaps the largest was Forks-of-the-Pike. The adjacent territory is very fertile, and the farmers are progressive. Among the older farmers were James Roy, John, Moses, and Henry Fite, Thomas West,

Eli Vick, Thomas Fite, Thomas and John Groom, and the Truits and Hayses. They were succeeded by Samson Sellars, Mrs. Ford, Grant Roy, F. H. Hayes, Tom Ford, John Bell Hays, William Hays, Robert Vannata, Sam Vannata, Henry Givan, P. T. Bragg, W. D. Evans, Sam Flippin, Jake Young, Joseph Clarke, and others. William Fite erected a storehouse just after the war, merchandising for several years. He was succeeded by Jacob Young, and Young by P. T. Bragg in 1880. The last merchant and postmaster was R. B. Vannata. Postmasters have been: P. T. Bragg, James J. Evans, and R. B. Vannata.

Four Corners, the village schoolhouse, has had many competent tutors, among them the following: Rev. and Mrs. P. A. Pearson, John W. Overall, Mr. Pendleton, the Preston brothers, Mr. Hood, E. W. Brown, Mr. Jones, Robert Hayes, Mr. Whitlock, Wheeler & Holmes, Matt Bratten, Lee West, Mr. Ford, Thomas Bryant, Prudie Sellars, Miss Mullins, Willie Bell, and Maggie Robinson. The Misses Bell were teachers in 1914.

Keltonsburg, a few miles from Smithville, was named for James Kelton, who built the mill there. This mill, it may be stated here, was transferred to Paris & Boles in later years, who sold it to Mr. Thompson. It is at present possessed by Mr. Mullikins. The village has two stores and a blacksmith shop, and the Methodists and Disciples have congregations there. The first store was under the control of B. M. Magness for many years. Keltonsburg is surrounded by a worthy class of citizens.

CHAPTER XIV.

IN THE EARLY WARS.

THE county was not in existence as such until about ten years prior to the war with Mexico, but many of those who made up its settlers had seen service in the Revolution and in the War of 1812. A large section, including Alexandria and Liberty, was in Smith County until 1835, when they were taken into the new county of Cannon. In 1837 the two first-named towns were included in the new county of DeKalb. Some years later the Temperance Hall section and John F. Goodner's land, near Alexandria, were taken from Smith and added to it.

The pioneer cemeteries and family graveyards—the latter are found on nearly all the large farms—have been long neglected. Such graves as had markers have in many cases crumbled or had the inscriptions effaced by the elements. No doubt a number of the followers of General Washington sleep in graves that were never marked. But from the wreckage of time the following names of Revolutionary veterans have been preserved: Adam Dale, builder of the earliest mill in the county (about 1800), but buried in Maury County; Thomas Dale, who owned several 640-acre tracts around Liberty (he having purchased the claims of old soldiers), buried south of that village, on the Thomas Givan farm; Philip Palmer, buried near Alexandria; John Fisher, buried in the eastern portion of the county. Also the names of the following who were living and drawing pensions in 1840: Rev. John Fite, aged eighty-one, residing then with his son, Henry; Leonard Fite, aged eighty-one (father of the late Thomas D. Fite and grandfather of Len F. Davis, of Nashville); Col. James Saunders, aged seventy-one, living with Joseph Saunders; Elijah Duncan, aged ninety; Joseph Rankhorn, aged eighty-one; John Puckett, aged seventy-six; John Bevert, aged eighty-six; and Elijah Hooten, aged ninety-three. The last-named, says John K. Bain, an old-timer, who was register of the county before the great war, lived to be one hundred and eleven years of age, and at one hundred and eight rode horseback to the Bain home, south of Smithville. James H. Burton writes: "John Smithson, who lived on Short Mountain, either in DeKalb or near the line, was a Revolutionary soldier. He was buried with the honors of war."

As Col. James Tubb made up a company for the War of 1812, no doubt a majority of his men were from this county, but it has been impossible to secure the roster. These, however, are recalled: Benjamin Garrison, of Alexandria; Mose Spencer, of Liberty; Benjamin Prichard, father of the late Brown Prichard, near Liberty; Jacob Hearn, George Thomason, Lewis Washburn, and Silas Cooper, the last four going from Alexandria. Jacob Hearn became a loved and successful Methodist itinerant, known in old age as "Uncle Jakey." James H. Burton writes that Joshua Bratten, Reuben Evans, and Archie McIntire, of Liberty, were veterans of the War of 1812, and that McIntire was possibly in the Black Hawk War. Were they members of Tubb's company? It is suggested that Benjamin Hale, the writer's paternal grandfather, was under Tubb, but that must be an error; for he is found to have been at the battle on Villere's plantation, near New Orleans, December 23, 1814, probably a member of Col. John Coffee's riflemen. A youth when he joined a company of Maryland revolutionists, Adam Dale made up a company in Smith (DeKalb) County and fought under Jackson in the War of 1812. (See the sketch of Liberty, Chapter III., as to his record.)

Colonel Tubb, grandfather of the popular Alexandria merchant, Livingston Tubb, was one of the best-known men of his county. Born March 18, 1788, he lived on Smith's Fork Creek, east of Alexandria and north of Liberty, and died July 18, 1867. He was possessed of hundreds of acres of fine land; and as he would not separate the families of his slaves, when emancipated they numbered nearly one hundred. He figured prominently in the musters which furnished so much interest to our grandfathers. From records in the State archives the following facts are gleaned: As captain of the Second Regiment of Militia his commission bears date of June 3, 1811, signed at Knoxville by Gov. Willie Blount, R. Houston, Secretary of State; as first major of the Forty-First Regiment it was signed at Nashville December 13, 1815, by Gov. Joseph McMinn, William Alexander, Secretary of State; and as colonel of the last-named regiment it is dated at Nashville February 10, 1829, bearing the signature of Gov. Sam Houston, Daniel Graham, Secretary of State.

He was captain in the Second Tennessee Regiment from September 20, 1814, to April 10, 1815, and was at Pensacola or Mobile when the battle of New Orleans was fought. On account of inadequate transportation facilities he had to pay his own expenses for baggage and transportation. Shortly after his return he filed a claim against the government (July 14, 1816). It was made out before W. Tannehill, J. P., being for four hundred pounds of baggage from Fayetteville, Tenn., where the volunteers rendezvoused, to Fort Montgomery, thence to Pensacola and back to Fort Montgomery, thence to Fayetteville from Mobile—six hundred and thirteen miles at eight cents per mile.

Colonel Tubb and his company, like other Tennesseeans, probably took up their march toward Mobile and Pensacola in response to the call of the Secretary of War in July, 1814, for 2,500 Tennessee militia, fixing September 15 for their assembling.

Was there another company from the county? Several militia officers were commissioned from 1812 to 1815. It is tradition that Col. Abraham Overall organized a company for the war. It is seen from records in the archivist's office that on May 19, 1814, he was commissioned lieutenant colonel of the Forty-First Militia. His grandson, Hon. T. W. Wood, of Bellbuckle, writes: "As to the War of 1812-15, I have often heard my mother speak, when I was a small boy, of our grandfather's being engaged under

Jackson in several battles, and particularly that of Horseshoe Bend, where he had a horse shot under him. He was major or acting lieutenant colonel. I remember now only the name of one man in the company, young Cook." H. L. Overall, a grandson, says: "I think grandfather was under Jackson, for I have heard my father, Horace A. Overall, speak of the intimate friendship existing between him and Old Hickory." Since the fact is almost wholly forgotten (except by their descendants) that Tubb and Dale had companies in the second war with Great Britain, it is possible that Colonel Overall was a veteran, and, thinking thus, it is believed that this relative to his ancestry would interest the public. In his great volume sketching the pioneers of the Shenandoah Valley, Va., Cartmell says the Overalls are in direct descent from Bishop Overall, of England, who was the author of the Convocation Book mentioned in Macaulay's "History of England." He adds: "The first settlement made [in America] by this family was in Stafford County, Va., about 1700. One member of this branch came to the Shenandoah Valley as soon as it was open for settlement. This was John Overall, who married Maria Christina Froman [granddaughter of a German who owned 100,000 acres in the valley], settled on South River, and reared seven children—viz., John, William, Nathaniel, Mary, Nancy, Robert, and Christina. John married Elizabeth Waters in 1773. She was the mother of Abraham, Isaac, and Jacob. Abraham, the oldest son, married Hannah Leath in Virginia and then moved to Tennessee in 1805. . . . Jacob, third son of John, married Nancy Lawrence and moved to Tennessee in 1805." Abraham located in what became DeKalb County and died in 1844. His wife died in 1837. Jacob settled in Smith County, but his grandsons, James H., J. W., and D. D. Overall, became citizens of DeKalb County.

DeKalb was represented in the Black Hawk and Seminole Wars. Levi Foutch, of the Alexandria neighborhood, was a soldier in the former, while Paschal M. Brien was sergeant in William B. Campbell's cavalry company in the campaign against the Seminoles. A few names of the troops are copied from Sergeant Brien's mess and guard book, still in existence. From the mess list of July 11, 1836: John Leach, G. W. Gray, W. G. Tucker, William Allison, Levi Pendleton, Hugh Reed, J. G. Shy, J. J. Reasonover, Peter Webster, John Coe, S. A. Farmer, Joseph Allison, James G. Ford, William G. Ford, Charles Wade, John Warren, James Owens, H. G. Owens, Francis Pugh, William Taylor, H. J. Cochran, William Baker, James Barrett, Alfred Womack, William Penile, William Wilson, Richard and James Booze, David Phillips, George Carmax, James Spradley, Isaac Snow, Hardy Calhoun, Richard Jones, Rufus Haynes, H. G. Maney, S. C. Beasley, Thomas Dale, T. G. Harrel, J. J. Coleman, and J. G. Debrunt. From the guard list, beginning July 11 and ending July 19: J. H. Alexander, G. G. Gray, Cyrus Hazard, Seaborn Harts, W. B. Taylor, Nathaniel Parrot, Sterling Ward, Jonah Hallum, E. W. Davis, William Hallum, Daniel Coggin, William McClanahan, William Forester, William Baker, H. B. Haney, John McFarland, John B. Claiborne, David Phillips, William Dougherty, Thomas Brooks, Elijah Hollis, Robert Hayne, Samuel Allison, Peter Webster, H. Heflin, J. G. Davenport, H. J. Warren, James Davis, James Cheek, P. Snow, William Lancaster, William Wilson, and Hugh Reed.

A number of these men were from the territory that became DeKalb. Daniel Coggin was the county's first register and first representative in the General Ascembly. Captain Campbell then lived in Smith County, removing to Lebanon later.

The first war to occur after the county came into existence was that with Mexico. Two companies were raised in DeKalb County. But few are surviving in 1914—Isaac Cooper, Alexandria; William (Cal.) Smithson, Gassaway; J. T. Finley, Celina, Tex.; House Akin, Missouri; and Wilson Bennett, Kentucky.

Capt. John F. Goodner's company, I, was made up at Alexandria. Thomas J. Finley, aged ninety-one, of Celina, Tex., has kindly sent the muster roll of these volunteers:

Officers: John F. Goodner, captain; John S. Reece, first lieutenant; W. J. Johnson, second lieutenant; W. J. Wright, third lieutenant; Thomas B. Askew, first sergeant; Isaac Belcher, second sergeant; A. N. Davis, third sergeant; William McClellan, fourth sergeant; J. W. Johnson, first corporal; Wilson Jackson, second corporal; Harrison Bennett, third corporal; John S. Gill, fourth corporal; William D. Parkerson, first bugler; William Riddle, second bugler; A. T. Jackson, forager.

Privates: J. T. Allison, W. C. Bennett, Frank Ballenger, A. J. Baker, Addison Batts, H. L. Bradley, F. L. Boyd, John Bostic, W. H. Cheek, W. R. Caskey, J. R. Cheek, Calvin Clark, J. S. Davis, J. W. Dougherty, J. H. Davis, G. W. Eastes, Amos Foutch, T. J. Finley, W. E. Foutch, Thomas Gwaltney, William Gates, Franklin Sky, R B. Kyle, T. O. Kinney, J. L. McGann, W. C. Malone, J. C. Neely, James Oakley, L. O. Patey, Moses Preston, John Patton, James W. Parker, Calvin W. Hill, B. H. Akin, Isaac Cooper.

In an interview Isaac Cooper, who is one of the survivors of Captain Goodner's company, said: "I joined Company I, First Tennessee Regiment of Mounted Infantry, for service in the Mexican War about the time I reached my majority. Our colonel was Jonas E. Thomas, while our company was organized at Alexandria and sworn in at Nashville. Our uniform was gray and was made at home. We went to Tampico and crossed the Gulf to Vera Cruz. A fourteen days' storm overtook us, and we had to throw overboard the horses of Colonel Thomas and Major Waterhouse. The other horses followed on transports. After the battle of Vera Cruz we fought at Cerro Gordo, then marched to Jalapa across the mountains, I being one of the guards of four wagonloads of gold and silver from Vera Cruz to Jalapa. On our return home we took ship at Vera Cruz for New Orleans, thence by boat to Nashville. The government bought our horses at Vera Cruz, and I received about $700 for my absence of twelve months and eight days from home."

Abram M. Savage made up Company F, Third

Regiment Tennessee Volunteer Infantry, Col. B. F. Cheatham.

Officers: A. M. Savage, captain; Reuben Simpson, first lieutenant; W. M. Bailey, second lieutenant; John W. Kennedy, third lieutenant; John England, first sergeant (appointed February 4, 1848); Benjamin Adcock, second sergeant (in hospital at Jalapa April 13, 1848); Elijah B. Hudson, third sergeant; James H. Wood, fourth sergeant; Chester F. Bethel, first corporal; Joseph Coger, second corporal; Anthony P. Adcock, third corporal; Thomas F. Kennedy, fourth corporal; Tillman Cantrell, musician; Alex Ferguson, musician.

Privates: W. D. Allen, J. W. Allen, David Adcock, William Adcock, McDonald Adcock, Perry Adcock, James Adcock, Henry Adkins, Martin Brown, James L. Blunt (died at Molino del Rey March 8, 1848), David Barrett, Eli Barrett, J. W. Barrett, Anderson Burnet (died at Rio T— June 4, 1848), Martin S. Bonham, William Ballard, Congelius Burrip, Hiram Bethel, Jim Cantrell, Ben Cantrell, Elisha and Elijah Chambers (twins), B. F. Cummings, Moses H. Cummings, Moses C. Cummings (died in Mexico City June 30, 1848), Carrol Caskey, John H. Dosier, John Atnip, Edmundson Elkins (died at Molino del Rey April 18, 1848), John A. Edwards, J. E. Edwards, Henry Edwards (died at Molino del Rey March 5, 1848), J. S. Ellige, Thomas Fisher, Thomas Fowler, Thomas Giles, James Gibson, Dillard Gannon, James R. Gapway, Moses Hutchins, William Hendrixon, William W. Harris, Hardy Johnson, Robert Jones,

HISTORY OF DEKALB COUNTY

Ed Jones, William Koger (died at Molino del Rey April 15, 1848), J. W. Lance, J. R. Looney (died at Molino del Rey July 12, 1848), James Mannon (died at Molino del Rey February 24, 1848), J. B. Mullins (died at Molino del Rey May 11, 1848), Green Melton, John Melton, Peter Maxey, Iradel March, William Markham, Ebenezer Moss, Alex Neal, W. H. Neeley, Joshua R. Neely (died at Molino del Rey April 28, 1848), Joseph Pack, Thomas Pack, James Pitman, John Barton, Abe Parton, James Pistole, W. M. Pettit (died at St. Augustine May 19, 1848), William C. Smithson, David Smithson, J. H. Sullins (died in Mexico City March 7, 1848), Joshua Simpson, Jacob Taylor, W. H. Tate (died at Molino del Rey May 5, 1848), J. A. Tate, J. B. Tate, T. G. Vance, S. Brown Whaley, William Wommack, John K. Bain (discharged at Molino del Rey February 2, 1848), E. E. Phillips and William Richard (discharged there February 2, 1848), William G. Givan (died in Mexico City February 15, 1848), John T. Hudson (died in the same city January 16, 1848), Richard Taylor (died there also January 14, 1848), Jesse W. Taylor (died there January 24, 1848), John C. Sullins (died at Molino del Rey February 7, 1848), James Young (died in Mexico City January 20, 1848.)

This company was mustered into service October 8, 1847, rendezvousing on the Nolensville Pike two and a half miles from Nashville. Taken to New Orleans by boat, it proceeded to Vera Cruz. Here a brigade was formed, but it did not reach the City of Mexico until that place was captured.

A barbecue was given the Mexican volunteers at Liberty in 1847, a heavy downpour spoiling the occasion, and a number of town cows were foundered on the damaged food. Dr. Foster writes that on this occasion "Henry Bratten, son of Isaac Bratten, was the color bearer and rode a small, prancing claybank. The cavalry presented an imposing appearance—before the rain."

Seven Adcocks from about Smithville are listed, it will be noticed. Perry Adcock, father of Hon. B. G. Adcock, a prominent lawyer of Cookeville, later raised a company of Confederates at Smithville, becoming captain.

It has been asserted that in the war with Mexico nine Americans died where one was killed. The above record is indicative. In memory of William G. Givan, who died in the City of Mexico, as seen, an empty coffin was buried in Salem Cemetery, at Liberty.

CHAPTER XV.

SECESSION—DEKALB CONFEDERATES.

UNDOUBTEDLY the stormiest period of DeKalb County's existence was the first part of the year 1861, the question before the people being separation from the Union or remaining in it. When the question was first agitated, a majority of Tennesseeans were opposed to secession. The legislature ordered an election at which the people should vote at the same time upon the subject of holding a convention and electing delegates to serve in case a convention should be held. The election came off February 9, 1861, and resulted in a vote of 57,798 for the convention and 69,675 against it; for delegates who favored secession, 24,749, and 88,803 against it. This was throughout the State. In the election DeKalb County's vote was 833 for secession and 642 against it. Thus we see the voters of the county were by a small majority (191) for withdrawing from the Union. At that time the population of the county was only 10,573.

Meantime some of the Southern States had withdrawn from the Union. On April 12, 1861, the Confederates at Charleston, S. C., fired on Fort Sumter, where a United States garrison remained, although South Carolina had voted to secede. When the news of the bombardment reached Washington, President Lincoln called for 75,000 troops to put down the "rebellion." He also declared the ports of the seceded States (South Carolina, Georgia, Alabama, Florida.

Mississippi, Louisiana, and Texas) in a state of blockade and held that all vessels acting under their authority would be guilty of piracy.

Again Tennessee became intensely excited. It was evident that the President was going to try to force the seceding States back into the Union. The orators began to harangue the people, and many of the latter, not indorsing his intention to make war on the South, changed their sentiments and clamored to withdraw from the sisterhood of States. A second election was held June 8 to get the sentiment of all Tennesseeans. The vote stood 104,913 for secession and only 47,238 against it. Isham G. Harris was at that time Governor of the State.

So Tennessee joined the Southern Confederacy. The first call was for 55,000 men; but before the close of the war the State furnished more than 115,000 Confederates. On the Union side more than 31,000 Federals were raised in the State, while Tennessee Federals who joined Kentucky organizations numbered more than 7,000. The total Tennesseeans in the two armies thus totaled 153,000.

Though about four years of age at that time, the writer recalls something of the excitement which prevailed at Liberty, and presumably the whole county was so affected. Orators for and against secession spoke at different places and made their arguments before the crowds. Former Gov. William B. Campbell, of Lebanon, was one of the speakers going over the State pleading for the Union. The cry of the Unionists was, "Hurrah for Campbell and the Union!"

and that of the secessionists, "Hurrah for Jefferson Davis and the Southern Confederacy!" What took place in Liberty, as stated before, was characteristic of other portions of the county. The Southern sympathizers believed they would triumph in a few weeks, just as the North thought the war would not last long. To illustrate, Frank Foster, an aged saddler of Liberty and an extremely small man, would when in his cups ride his big horse up and down Liberty's one street and cry, "As for Yankees, I can whip half a dozen and outrun a thousand"; while White Turney, then reading law at Smithville, declared that within six weeks he would be eating Abe Lincoln's ears with a piece of hard-tack.

At first blush it appeared that all DeKalb County was for the South. Nevertheless, there was a strong undercurrent opposed to disunion, and this manifested itself after a while. Thus William B. Stokes, who had been a popular politician, at first sided with the South, going so far as to urge the enlistment of Confederate troops; and when he changed his mind he found hundreds of men ready to follow him on the other side. Under the excitement prevailing it is not a matter for wonder that many men found it hard to come to a decision.

Some of the earliest enlistments of DeKalb County Confederates were made in a company raised at Auburn, in Cannon County; T. M. Allison, captain. This company was mustered into service at Nashville June 28, 1861. There comes back now the recollection of its advent into Liberty—musicians playing "Drive That

Black Dog Out o' the Wilderness," the lazy forenoon when, among the yard's old-fashioned roses, the bees droned slumberously, and the neighbor boys watching the troops pass in their red hunting shirts, keeping step to fife and drum. Classic music may suit the cultured, but you hear that old tune, sweet and plaintive, yet somehow moving and thrilling one impetuously; hear it under such circumstances, and it will never be forgotten.

This company consisted of eighty-two men, fully half under twenty-one years of age. Names are called that were familiar in the Liberty community: Dr. J. S. Harrison, H. L. W. (White) Turney, Bob Smith, Arch Marcum, W. A. and Pressly Adamson, Josh Jetton, and others. The company became a part of the Second Tennessee Cavalry. Bob Smith, attacked with measles at Jacksboro, East Tennessee, was discharged and later joined the Federals. White Turney became a lieutenant, was wounded twice, married in West Tennessee, practiced law in Dyersburg, and died in 1880. Dr. Harrison went through the war, removed from Liberty to Smithville, then became a citizen of McMinnville, a splendid type of the old-time Southern gentleman. He died in October, 1914. Captain Allison resigned and returned to his home, near Auburn, and was killed by Federals in his back yard August 2, 1862.

Eight Confederate companies were made up in DeKalb County, while about half of Capt. P. C. Shields's company (G) of Col. John H. Savage's regiment were from the county. The muster rolls of Confederate soldiers are in the archives at Washington. They are old, mutilated, and not easily handled. An effort was made to get the names of first enlistments, but this was hardly possible in any case. Where names were secured (photographed) they are often misspelled, as Louis for Lewis, while one name may appear in one place as "William" and in another "W. J." This has added to the problem of getting them correct. But, in spite of all, hundreds are correctly presented herein.

Capt. John F. Goodner's company was raised at Alexandria in April, 1861, and became Company A, Seventh Tennessee Infantry. When Col. Robert Hatton became brigadier general, Goodner was elected lieutenant colonel and commanded the regiment much of the time during the remainder of the war. Colonel Goodner, as shown elsewhere, commanded a company in the Mexican War. The Seventh saw much service—was in the Yorktown campaign, at Seven Pines, in the Seven Days' Battles, at Culpeper Courthouse, Bull Run, Antietam, Fredericksburg, Chancellorsville, Gettysburg, Spottsylvania, Petersburg, and Fort Archer, and surrendered at Appomattox. Colonel Goodner died at Alexandria some years after the war. The muster roll shows the following names in his company:

Officers: Captain, John F. Goodner; lieutenant, R. V. Wright. After Goodner became lieutenant colonel, R. V. Wright was elected captain, serving until Allison's squadron of cavalry was organized, when he was elected captain of Company C of that battalion. J. S. Dowell became captain of Company A, serving until the close of the war. First lieutenant, J. S.

Dowell; second, F. W. Hobson; third, Robert C. Bone; sergeants, Wilmoth Burges, James Vannata, R. D. Floyd, J. A. Donnell, J. T. Barbee; corporals, Dixon A. Foutch, James R. Newsom, A. M. C. Robinson, Bartlett Warford.

Privates: W. H. Atwell, John H. Allison, Robert Allison, William Bailiff, Joab Bailiff, William Bartlett, John Caskey, John Cheek, A. J. Cheek, V. B. Coe, J. N. Compton, G. W. Cowen, John L. Close, Hi Curtis, Chesley Chapman, G. W. Driver, Thomas Davis, Alfonse Emerique, William T. Floyd, W. J. Foster, Elijah A. Foutch, F. L. Foutch, R. D. Floyd, Levi Foutch, J. B. Garrison, G. W. Gregson, William Griffin, T. W. Goodner, Abe Hendrixon, William Hinesley, W. H. Hullet, J. R. Harris, John Johnson, L. C. Lincoln, John L. Luck, G. W. Lamberson, W. R. Lamberson, J. J. Martin, P. J. Mason, J. D. Martin, G. W. Murry, Irvin D. Murphey, L. D. McGuffey, R. Malone, Theo. Moores, J. D. Nix, T. A. Newley, R. H. Newsom, Burr F. Paty, J. W. Pendleton, Lit R. Parkinson, John Read, G. W. Reasonover, Thomas J. Sneed, C. P. Shaver, Walter Sullins, W. R. Sims, D. W. Sewell, Isaac Sanlin, Dan Snider, William Sewell, J. W. Shanks, William Terry, A. P. Tracy, W. W. Trousdale, T. D. Webb, John Williams, William Willoughby, W. C. Yeargin, O. J. Williams, T. W. Yeargin, James Winfrey, William Bartley, H. M. Wilson, Ben Hood, H. H. Hood, S. Ashby, Elijah Jones, James Risdon, Andrew Robinson, Thomas Light, Andrew Pratt, A. L. Davis, Horace Newsom, O. J. Williams.

Killed: G. W. Driver, J. B. Garrison, P. J. Mason,

James Vannata, T. W. Sewell, all at Seven Pines, May 31, 1862; G. W. Cowan, James Winfrey, J. Williams, Job Bailiff, L. R. Parkinson, Chancellorsville; Chapman Chesley, Mechanicsville. Died: J. Cheek, November 6, 1862; V. B. Coe, September 25, 1861; J. Compton, September 15, 1861; L. D. McGuffey, November 13, 1862; J. Pendleton, December 15, 1861; W. R. Sims, January 5, 1863; William Willoughby, December 5, 1863.

Capt. R. D. Allison's company (F), Twenty-Fourth Tennessee Infantry, was raised at Alexandria in 1861 and was organized with the regiment mentioned. He was elected colonel and H. P. Dowell captain. Allison resigned in 1862 and organized a cavalry battalion at Alexandria, with J. S. Reece, who had been discharged from the Twenty-Fourth because of his age. This battalion will receive further notice later on.

The Twenty-Fourth took part in the battles of Shiloh, Perryville, Murfreesboro, Chickamauga, Missionary Ridge, Franklin, and Nashville, surrendering at Greensboro, N. C.

Officers: Colonel, R. D. Allison; captain, H. P. Dowell; first lieutenant, J. F. Luckey; second, W. S. Patey; third, W. D. Fielding; sergeants, James A. Barnett, M. D. Braswell, Lewis E. Simpson, J. W. Jaques; corporals, C. Scott, G. W. Gordon, J. A. Clark, A. Rollands.

Privates: James Allison, Robert Allison, D. L. Allen, J. L. Askew, T. B. Brown, E. A. Barbee, S. Briggs, A. J. Bradford, Robert Barbee, W. P. Bennett, James

HISTORY OF DEKALB COUNTY

Barr, Tobe Briggs, J. R. Betty, T. F. Bradley, Giles Bowers, Sampson Braswell, T. Brown, L. B. Baker, G. W. Bowers, Abe Britton, Isaac Cooper, W. B. Carter, J. J. Cutter, R. D. Coffee, H. M. Coffee, Nathan Corley, W. C. Curtis, A. P. Crowder, Thomas Chandler, B. F. Cochran, M. J. Covington, W. D. G. Carnes, A. L. Cranler, Josiah Conger, N. L. Craddock, J. C. Craddock, Miles Covington, R. J. Davis, W. C. Davis, R. G. Davis, W. P. Dennie, M. F. Doss, J. D. Estes, L. H. Fite, J. C. Foutch, W. C. Fielding, C. Ferrel, J. E. Gold, J. P. Gold, J. F. Gaultney, James S. Glenn, John A. Gregory, G. W. Gordon, D. D. Hudson, Horace Hays, J. P. Hale, John R. Hale, G. W. Hale, W. H. Hays, J. W. Hubbard, A. D. Helmantaller, J. Heflin, W. T. Jones, T. L. Johnson, J. M. King, S. J. King, Robert King, John Luckey, W. H. Luckey, John Laurence, W. H. Lincoln, Sam Luckey, W. S. Lynch, Bailey Marks, J. Mooneyham, William H. Mott, J. A. Mooneyham, C. C. Martin, James Nolan, Jasper Owens, W. W. Patterson, Lewis Barrett, W. C. Preston, W. D. Prentiss, J. H. Powell, Amos Petries, J. C. Prichard, S. A. Powell, L. A. Rollands, J. S. Reece, Ed Reece, James Raney, A. J. Stephens, John Smith, J. W. Stewart, Andrew Stuart, W. H. Thomas, John Thomas, W. M. Timberlake, J. M. Shavers, N. Vantrease, J. T. Winfrey, J. W. Whitley, J. A. Winfrey, Lewis Washburn, W. E. Williams, W. H. Whittington, F. P. Lyon, J. D. Estes.

Killed: W. C. Curtis, J. F. Gaultney, F. P. Lyon, Joseph Woolen, Shiloh; J. C. Craddock, A. P. Crouch, Bailey Marks, J. A. Mooneyham, Joel Mooneyham,

Amos Petry, G. W. Hall, Perryville; J. A. King, W. J. Knight, C. Fumel, Murfreesboro; J. W. Stewart, Chickamauga. Died: James Allison, December 24, 1861; Sampson Braswell, January 4, 1862; W. B. Carter, January 10, 1862; W. H. Mott, Alexandria, after having been wounded at Murfreesboro.

Company A, Capt. L. N. Savage, was raised around Smithville in May, 1861, and mustered into the Sixteenth Tennessee Regiment June 9. Captain Savage was born in Warren County April 25, 1837, removed to Smithville in 1859, and was mortally wounded at Murfreesboro, dying March 15, 1863. The company was in the Cheat Mountain and Little Sewell Mountain campaigns and at Perryville, Murfreesboro, Chickamauga, Missionary Ridge, Kennesaw, Jonesboro, Franklin, and Nashville. It surrendered in North Carolina.

Officers: L. N. Savage, captain; I. C. Stone, first lieutenant; John K. Bain, second lieutenant; R. B. Anderson, third lieutenant; G. W. Witt, first sergeant; G. L. Talley, second sergeant; R. M. Magness, third sergeant; T. B. Potter, fourth sergeant; J. W. Harris, first corporal; L. G. Bing, second corporal; M. L. Cantrell, third corporal; S. M. Philips, fourth corporal.

Promotions: T. B. Potter, sergeant major, 1861; R. B. Anderson, first lieutenant, 1862; G. W. Witt, second lieutenant, 1862; G. L. Talley, third lieutenant, 1863; W. C. Potter, first lieutenant, 1863; J. C. Webb, second lieutenant, 1863; L. R. Witt, third lieutenant, 1863.

Privates: William Adcock, E. K. Adcock, Isaac Adcock, Benjamin Atnip, E. L. Atnip, John Atnip, Larkin Bayne, R. W. Banks, T. M. Hooper, T. A. Hooper, Dick Hooper, James Hooper, Rich Jones, J. W. Johnson, E. S. James, John James, W. L. Judkins, F. E. P. Kennedy, James Koger, Pomp Kersey, A. J. Kersey, Felix Kersey, Calvin Kersey, E. League, E. Lockhart, John Lefever, John Mason, Bud Miller, L. D. Moore, John Moore, W. C. Moore, J. A. Moore, John Martin, W. P. Martin, Thomas Martin, W. B. Martin, R. Martin, Jasper Martin, Rube Meeks, R. W. McGinnis, Elisha McGinnis, G. P. Maynard, J. M. Pertle, Charles Pullin, Robert Pullin, W. C. Potter, O. D. Potter, Thomas Potter, J. D. Philips, S. M. Philips, Dave Pittman, Robert Rowland, Jesse Redman, Ben Rowland, Rich Richardson, W. Richardson, T. J. Richardson, James Rigsby, W. G. Stevens, John Stevens, James Bing, W. H. Bing, P. Bozarth, J. H. Bozarth, James Bozarth, J. A. Briggs, W. H. Cunningham, J. H. Cantrell, U. E. Cantrell, J. R. Cantrell, James Cantrell, Jehu Cantrell, John Cantrell, M. L. Cantrell, I. D. Cantrell, W. H. Cantrell, L. D. Cantrell, B. M. Cantrell, D. W. Cantrell, Leonard Cantrell, W. C. Cantrell, Wat Cantrell, Isaac Cantrell, Peter Cantrell, P. G. Cantrell, A. M. Cantrell, G. P. Cantrell, Martin Cantrell, Thomas Cherry, Isaac Conger, J. W. Colwell, June Driver, W. L. Driver, Isaiah Driver, C. B. Davis, M. Duwese, D. C. Dollar, Thomas Dozier, Martin Delong, Wat Eastham, H. C. Eastham, J. B. Fisher, S. M. Fulton, Cal Fowler, Samuel Hathaway, Len Hathaway, W. A. Hallum, B. M. Hicks, Dallas

Hicks, William Herron, J. M. Stevens, W. B. Sweeney, A. Simpson, A. J. Smith, Burdine Smith, Noah Smith, Henry Seawells, H. C. Tate, J. R. Thompson, Fielding Turner, Garrison Taylor, Ross Unchurch, John Van Hosser, L. R. Witt, W. Walls, John Womack, P. G. Webb, I. C. Webb, D. B. Worley, W. M. Womack, W. M. Wilmoth, John E. Warren, J. B. Wilkinson, B. C. Wilkinson, Ben Judkins.

Killed: Capt. L. N. Savage, Lieut. R. B. Anderson, Lieut. W. G. Witt, Felix Kersey, E. League, W. A. Hallum, E. Lockhart, John E. Warren, Murfreesboro; W. L. Cantrell, J. H. Cantrell, James Cantrell, F. E. B. Kennedy, W. C. Moore, R. Rowland, P. G. Webb, Perryville; B. Atnip, Georgia; Wat Eastham, Thomas Dozier, S. M. Fulton, William Richardson, A. Simpson, Atlanta; W. H. Cantrell, James Driver, T. A. Hooper, A. J. Kersey, Robert Martin, Franklin; H. C. Tate, Lost Mountain. Wounded: S. G. Bing, R. M. Magness, B. M. Cantrell, S. M. Philips, R. M. Banks, D. W. Cantrell, T. M. Hooper, Rich Jones, F. Turner, John Mason, Perryville; Capt. G. L. Talley, W. C. Potter, Chickamauga; Isaac Adcock, Resaca; E. L. Atnip, J. R. Thompson, W. L. Judkins, Atlanta; Peter Cantrell, J. Lefever, G. Taylor, B. C. Wilkinson, G. W. Colwell, J. C. Webb, Murfreesboro; J. W. Johnson, Franklin. Died: William Adcock, O. D. Potter, Thomas Potter, L. R. Witt, William Walls, Camp Trousdale, 1861; William Herron, Richard Hooper, John Womack (missing), Georgia, 1864; James Bing, W. H. Bing, in prison; James Hooper, South Carolina,

1864; J. A. Moore, home, 1863; Elisha McGinnis, unknown; William Womack, Hattersville, 1861.

Capt. Robert Cantrell's company (C) recruited around Smithville, became a part of the Twenty-Third Regiment of Tennessee Confederate Infantry. Its commander was later elected lieutenant colonel. G. W. Hicks was elected colonel and later Erastus D. Foster. Other promotions were of Lieuts. W. D. Rhinehardt, Lawson W. Lee, and A. P. Cantrell. The company saw service in Virginia and at Shiloh. After fighting at Perryville, Murfreesboro, Chickamauga, and Missionary Ridge, and going through the Georgia campaign, it was at Franklin and Nashville and surrendered in North Carolina. Capt. John C. New, of Cannon County, writes: "After the Twenty-Third had served about twelve months, it was reorganized. At this time Captain Cantrell was elected lieutenant colonel, but soon resigned. Ras Foster was elected captain of the company, and after serving some time he left and carried many of his men with him. The company was consolidated with mine. Zeb Lee was a member of the company and lost a leg at Chickamauga. His brother, Lieut. Lawson Lee, was killed." Colonel Cantrell was for several years a distinguished circuit judge of Tennessee, residing at Lebanon. He was born November 9, 1823, and died February 9, 1903.

Officers: Captain, Robert Cantrell; first lieutenant, Joseph Y. Stewart; second, L. J. Magness; third, C. A. Cantrell; first sergeant, William Hi Smith; second,

A. P. Cantrell; third, L. W. Lee; fourth, A. J. Potter; corporals, E. D. Foster, P. G. Cantrell, Isaac Cantrell, A. G. Beckwith; drummer, Calvin Hendrixson; fifer, Brien Hughes.

Privates: David Adcock, Wilson Adcock, Lucian Allen, R. H. Atnip, Ben Bullard, W. G. Baker, J. C. Brock, W. M. Bryant, Asbury Barnes, S. Bradford, E. C. Barnes, D. G. Byars, John Brimer, Pleas Caldwell, H. P. Cantrell, James Cantrell, J. L. Crips, J. A. Capshaw, W. C. Cantrell, Julius Cantrell, Abe Cantrell, I. Cantrell, Jr., B. H. Cantrell, J. B. Cotton, M. Coldwell, Eliah Cantrell, W. W. Coldwell, W. Coldwell, L. L. Cantrell, W. M. Bryant, B. H. Cantrell, William Carter, Smith Cantrell, Sam Cantrell, L. D. Day, David Davis, J. H. Dodd, M. D. Davis, John Delong, Henry Frazier, Jasper Fowler, Newton Fowler, A. H. Farmer, J. L. Fuson, J. R. Fuson, J. B. Ferrell, S. M. Foster, J. H. Ford, J. D. Givan, Thomas Givan, J. W. Green, John Greer, M. Greer, J. P. Jacobs, J. C. Hodges, Isaac Hurst, Jere Hendrixon, Cal Hendrixon, Jr., Tilman Haney, William Haney, James M. Judkins, W. A. Johnson, J. P. Jacobs, P. J. Lee, Elias Lane, Jr., S. M. Liles, J. W. Lamberson, Z. P. Lee, Obe Moss, G. Lane, C. Lane, James Moor, J. Martin, R. W. Melton, J. H. Mahaffey, T. A. Mason, A. F. McDowell, Sam Mitchell, J. P. Moor, William Parsons, Oliver Parkinson, G. W. Pirtle, J. L. Pirtle, Tarleton Parrish, W. R. Parrish, Hezekiah Page, Arch Pack, Russel Rigsby, James Ridge, J. S. Ridge, J. M. Redmond, James Robinson, W. J. Rigsby, W. D. Rhinehardt, J. M. Reeves, C. C. Smith, P. G. Smith,

Bradford Sherrell, Wesley Steelmon, J. P. Stoner, A. A. Stanford, W. H. Starnes, J. S. Starnes, G. W. Taylor, L. R. Taylor, F. J. Titsworth, J. M. Vaughn, J. N. Vaughn, G. W. Warren.

Killed: A. G. Allen, Fort Munford; Lawson Lee, W. A. Carter, June 29, 1864; W. G. Warren, Chickamauga; W. L. Lawson, Bean's Station. Died: F. J. Titsworth, R. W. Melton, Chattanooga, January 24, 1863; James Ridge, July 26, 1863; Julius Cantrell, October 18, 1861; H. Page, June 1, 1862; A. H. Farmer, November 24, 1861.

Capt. Perry Adcock's company was also raised in the Smithville section. It was difficult to trace this company, but the Adjutant General of the War Department explained that Captain Adcock's company was designated as C in Colms's First Battalion of Tennessee Infantry and afterwards as Company K, Fiftieth Tennessee Confederate Infantry. The company surrendered in North Carolina in April, 1865, after having served in numerous engagements in various States, from Fort Donelson to the close of the war. Captain Adcock had served also in the war with Mexico. He was born March 4, 1829, and died January 11, 1908.

Officers: Captain, Perry Adcock; first lieutenant, J. P. Titsworth; second, C. Turner; third, W. N. Jones; adjutant, C. B. Cantrell; first sergeant, A. P. Adcock; second, David Delong; third, Henry Bain; fourth, Isaiah Bain; fifth, W. R. Dunham; corporals, Thomas Adcock, Henry Adcock, J. D. Thweat, James M. Webb.

Privates: William, J. C., John, Joseph, P. J. L., and Wesley Adcock, Rich Atnip, H. Aikens, William Allen, N. Adcock, William Bain, Isaac Bain, D. C. Bain, John K. Bain, William, John, and Wesley Blunt, Joseph Capshaw, John Capshaw, William Capshaw, William J. U., Richard, and Jason Certain, T. Cantrell, Giles Driver, Jr., Noah Deboard, Watson Delong, James Delong, John Davis, John Fisher, Joseph and William Fisher, Daniel Fowler, Charles Ferrell, A. Goodson, O. D. Goodson, Webb and L. Hutchins, Andrew Jackson, H. G. and Grundy Kirby, C. Lack, David Looney, William Love, T. J. Lewis, J. P. Jones, Alfred Lewis, John McFall, Vincent Manor, Abijah Martin, D. W. Marsh, Ben Pinegar, Ben Pollard, Henry Pitts, G. W. Pollard, John Pinegar, Bart Pack, N. B. Parker, Ben Roland, James Ray, James Rigsby, Dr. J. D. Rigsby, Sam Roberts, E. C. Roland, L. P. Rigsby, S. Slaten, O. and William Sullivan, Wilson Taylor, G. W. and William Turner, James Webb, Jackson West, Alex Walker, F. M. Wilkinson, Isaac, Pleasant, and Thomas Young, J. M. Stephens, D. W. Marsh, John McAfee, I. P., Jasper, and Alfred Lewis, J. K. Delong, William Certain, W. D. Jones, William Lane, W. Z. Pollard, Francis, David, J. P., and Thomas Lewis, G. W. Pollard, J. G. Rankhorn, W. R. Dunham, John Fuller, A. B. Cheatham, R. Presnel, Sam Roberts, Joshua Seal, J. A. Walker, Ainsley Stephens, Canada Rigsby, George Stidman, John Corley, D. C. Delong, A. B. Cheatham, J. W. Green, G. A. Neal, Henry Pitts, Claiborn Edwards, Elijah Quillen, J. M. Webb.

Died: James Webb, Memphis, October 6, 1862; S.

D. Lane, Tappan, Miss., November 16, 1862; W. Z. Pollard, Clinton, La.; John Castel, Brookhaven, Miss.; G. W. Turner, Lauderdale Springs, Miss.; Isaiah Bain, Alton (Ill.) Prison.

Allison's Battalion of Cavalry, raised by Col. R. D. Allison, John S. Reece, and Robert V. Wright at Alexandria, consisted of three companies and was, besides taking part in a number of the most important battles of the war, very active in DeKalb County during Morgan's occupation and afterwards. It was with Wheeler on his last raid through East Tennessee in the summer of 1864; but it seems from Du Bose's "Life of Wheeler" that it was, with other companies, sent under Gen "Cerro Gordo" Williams to attack a Federal garrison at Strawberry Plains. Finding the garrison too strong, it marched to overtake Wheeler, but did not succeed. It followed close on his heels through Sparta, Liberty, and Alexandria, and went into camp near Murfreesboro, soon, however, taking the Woodbury Pike and returning south across the mountains, engaging in considerable fighting on the way.

After the war Colonel Allison removed to Texas, where he thrice represented his county in the State legislature, and died at an advanced age. Captain Reece removed to Nashville, becoming prominently identified with the city's interests, though his sight was greatly impaired before the close of the war. As Colonel Allison was old and Captain Reece with impaired sight, Captain Wright commanded the DeKalb

Countians, who had been consolidated with Shaw's Battalion after Missionary Ridge, in the later months. Captain Reece was born in Virginia in 1814, and died in February, 1868, only fifty-four, but a veteran of the war with the Seminoles, the Mexican War, and the War between the States. Captain Wright also located in Nashville, where he won splendid business success. He was living in 1914, somewhat more than eighty years of age.

This from Lieut. B. L. Ridley's published diary gives in a small way an idea of the horrors of war. It is dated Smithville, N. C., March 27, 1865: "This afternoon went with General Stewart to the depot, where we found Colonel Allison, a Tennessee cavalryman, on his way westward with the body of his son, who was killed a day or two ago near Goldsboro trying to rescue some ladies from the clutches of the enemy." By the way, still as illustrative, General Forrest and his escort were on a road three miles from Selma, Ala., one night after the retreat from Nashville. Suddenly the cries of women in distress reached them. "Guided by the sounds," to quote the diary of Ben Hancock, of the Second Regiment of Cavalry, "Forrest and some of his men dashed thither, to find a neighboring house in the possession of four Federal bummers who, having rifled it, were engaged in the effort to outrage the women who lived there. Summary was the fate of these wretches. The escort was now getting excited, . . . and, meeting a number of these fellows loaded, down with plunder, they did not hesitate to slay them on the spot. Hearing the sounds of what was happening ahead, Forrest, to check it, took the conduct of the advance upon himself." It is not believed that any DeKalb soldiers on either side were ever charged with assaulting women.

Allison's squadron, when it surrendered with General Shaw in North Carolina in 1865, numbered only about thirty men, according to Lieut. Ed Reece.

The writer has been able to secure from the mutilated records in the archives at Washington the following names only of the troops of Allison's Battalion. They cover various periods of the war:

Company A, officers: Senior captain, R. D. Allison; captain, John H. Allison; first lieutenant, James A. Nesmith; second, James N. Eaton; third, James W. Foutch; sergeants, J. A. Atwell, J. L. Reasonover, J. E. Robinson, J. W. Boyd; corporals, James B. Gregston, Ab Drury, W. J. Eaton.

Privates: R. D. Allison, J. W. Allen, William Allen, George Ashe, William Ashe, William Eskew, J. A. Boyd, William Corley, David Crook, Robert Caskey, John Cartwright, William Carr, Daniel Driver, A. Davis, Hardin Denny, J. H. Foutch, J. W. Floyd, E. and Joseph Gann, Freeling H. Hayes, J. A. Higdon, Horace M. Hale, Leander B. Hale, F. W. Hobson, John Johnson, Gus H. Johnson, James W. Keaton, R. W. Keaton, Jake H. King, R. A. King, W. R. King, H. D. Lester, S. M. Leftwick, L. C. Lincoln, James C. Malone, N. J. Petty, W. F. Powell, Irving Parsley, Ben Robinson, James M. Turney, H. J. Wills, Pleas C. Adams, C. A. Bailiff, G. W. Adkins, M. Byford, Monroe Bailiff, P. Dedman, M. L. Dedman, J. H.

Gann, N. Gann, Thomas Malone, R. W. Tubb, W. S. Webster, W. M. Walker, J. D. Wheeler, James Mullinax, D. L. Braswell, James Rigdon, H. J. Wills, Newton Petty, Shade L. Davis, Patterson Dedman, John H. Gann, Michael Gann, W. H. Gann, Nathan Gann, Denham Bethel, D. L. Russell.

Killed: Edward Gann, Chickamauga, September 19, 1863. Died: Joseph Gann, Tunnel Hill, Ga., January 5, 1864.

Company B, officers: Captain, J. S. Reece; first lieutenant, D. Brien; second, J. M. Floyd; third, L. P. Rutland; sergeants, T. W. Yeargin, T. R. Foster, James Jones, Britton Odum, Ed Reece; corporal, J. J. Cutler.

Privates: W. W. Adams, N. B. Bradley, W. C. Craddick, David Curtis, J. P. Doss, M. B. Dunn, Pack W. Florida, Tilman H. Foster, J. Ervin Foster, T. J. Finley, R. B. Floyd, L. H. Fite, Sam George, C. A. Hollinsworth, D. H. Hale (teamster), W. H. Jackson, Wiley Jones, W. H. Luckey (bugler), W. C. McGann, George Neal, Robert Neal, Ervin Newsom, L. F. Porterfield, Oliver W. Roberts, William Shanks, J. C. Trammel, J. B. Tarpley, J. B. Thompson, G. W. Vantrease, Thomas Warren, Newt Warren, David Wallace, Isaiah White, J. R. Witt, Columbus Yeargin, G. W. Lanier, Henry Lanier, James Pope, G. H. McGann, T. J. Coleman, I. C. Stone, William Hullet, James Jones, R. H. Newsom, Sim Adamson, Henry Bell, William Adamson, J. H. Burton, Hiram Carter,

W. J. Covington, J. C. Estes, William Foster, James S. Foutch, Bartley L. James, A. A. J. Jennings, J. M. Jones, Thomas King, Calaway Neal, J. R. Newsom, J. B. Pendleton, J. J. Rich, Presley Stroud, O. B. Staley, Jacob Vantrease, Jackson Vantrease, J. Willoby, J. Washer, Nathan Walden, G. Hutchinson, Fayette Henley, Nelson Bryant, J. W. Buckner, B. J. Bethel, Henry George, Sam Huggins, A. J. Lanier, J. T. Lawrence, Dan McKee, Monroe Malone, John Marks, S. T. Porterfield, J. J. Porterfield, S. A. Rickett, Lander Jackson, Thomas Estes, John Shores, J. R. Smith, Ed Winn, Henry Bell, G. C. McGann, Hiram Curtis.

Killed: William Hullet, James Jones, R. A. Newsom, Chickamauga, September 19, 1863.

Company C, officers: Captain, R. V. Wright; first lieutenant, A. W. O. Baker; second, Orson B. Wright; third, W. V. Harrel; sergeants, John A. Jones, W. A. Yeargin, John Heflin; corporals, William Hubbard, John A. Mooneyham.

Privates: L. J. Allison, William C. Bradford, J. C. Bailey, A. M. Cantrell, C. F. Cantrell, G. C. Flippin, John Gilly, James Hawkins, William Mooneyham, James Jones, James Hines, J. D. Martin, W. S. Patey, J. B. Palmer, W. B. Price, Thomas Spears, George Springfield, Sam Hooper, Jonas Whitley, C. M. Thompson, J. T. Thompson, Z. U. Thompson, J. S. Thompson, Garrett Clay, B. F. Batts, W. D. Yeargin, Bethel Batts, John A. Farmer, Thomas Howard, William Harper, Charles Harris, W. W. Minton, George

Nichols, P. Simpson, C. Vanderpool, Jeff Braswell, John A. Mooneyham, J. H. Baird, A. M. Carter, H. D. B. Anderson, T. C. Bradford, R. Barbee, C. Barbee.

Killed: Garrett Clay, Chickamauga, September 19, 1863.

The above are from Captain Wright's rolls from December 31, 1863, to February 29, 1864; from February 29, 1864, to April 30, 1864; from April 30, 1864, to June 30, 1864; and from June 30, 1864, to December 31, 1864. Under the first date A. W. O. Baker was first lieutenant; second, O. B. Wright; third, W. V. Harrel. Under the second date W. V. Harrel is third lieutenant. Under the third date no lieutenants are mentioned, nor are there any for June 30, 1864, to December 31, 1864. These are the latest existing records. But two or three living members of the squadron have sent in the names of a few other troops, though it is not known to what companies they belonged. Lieut. Ed Reece's list is: John Bowman, John Batts, J. T. Quarels, Isaac Cooper, and Jerome Barton. James H. Burton contributes this list: Bill Bone, Cain Adams, John Parkerson, Lito Hullet, Alex Stanley, John Reeves, George Beckwith, Mose Blythe, and Dr. Fayette Knight.

Of course during the war there were many changes in subordinate officers not mentioned here—promotions, resignations, and here and there a desertion. The desertions in both Federal and Confederate companies from the county were considerable, and now and then we find men, as Lowell's bashful beau "stood awhile on one foot fust an' then awhile on t'other," who fought in the cause of both South and North, at first with one side and then with the other.

DeKalb County officers in P. C. Shields's company (G) of Col. J. H. Savage's regiment: A. T. Fisher, first lieutenant; James K. Fisher, third. A. T. Fisher was promoted to captain in 1862.

Privates: Jasper Adcock, H. P. Adcock, William Allen, A. J. Allen, Ben Atnip, John Atnip, Alfred Bain, Peter Bain, Josiah Bain, John Bain, Peter Bain (second), Henry Bain, C. Bain, J. L. Britton, M. Blount, Joseph Cantrell, C. W. Cantrell, W. L. Cantrell, H. B. Cope, W. A. Cotton, Ben Capshaw, T. A. Cotten, John Denton, D. L. Dunham, L. R. Dunham, John Donnell, Gabriel Elkins, John Fisher, L. B. Fisher J. P. Fisher, Lawson Fisher, M. L. Fisher, G. W. Gilbert, L. W. Gilbert, William Goodson, Thomas Hodges, Robert Love, Joseph Ray, C. G. Rankhorn, Levi Lassiter, H. L. P. Sanders, Wiley Sanders, Isaiah Lassiter, F. M. Wright, S. L. Walker, John Meggerson, O. D. Walker, Alex Walker, Seth F. Wright, D. W. Worst, James Wright, and Deskin Wright.

Killed: Isaiah Bain, C. Bain, W. L. Cantrell, H. B. Cope, Lawson Fisher, F. M. Wright, S. L. Walker, Perryville; J. L. Britton, Thomas Hodges, John Fisher, Murfreesboro. Wounded: W. A. Cotton, Perryville; C. G. Rankhorn, Kennesaw Mountain. Died in service: D. L. Dunham, in prison; C. A. Cantrell, Georgia; A. J. Allen, Kentucky.

Horace McGuire gives this memory list of DeKalb County Confederates living in 1914: B. M. Cantrell,

Horace McGuire, Thomas Hooper, Sam Hooper, R. W. McGinnis, B. N. Hicky, John Vanhouser, Hans Merritt, John D. Johnson, Dick Moore, J. M. Redmon, Jim Fuson, W. T. Wall, Mose Rankhorn, T. C. Allen, Jim Wilkins, Watt Cantrell, W. C. Gilbert, Louis Bing, A. P. Cantrell, Hes Cantrell, Joe Cantrell, John Givan, Polk Johnson, J. H. Mahaffy, Luke Simpson, J. W. Watson, Jesse Redman, Madison Pass, Newt Avery, John K. Bain, Ed Reece, Bob King, William Lucky, R. V. Wright, Isaiah White, Thomas Givan, Roland Foster, and Horace M. Hale.

CHAPTER XVI.

STOKES'S CAVALRY.

The Fifth (Union) Regiment of Tennessee Cavalry, sometimes called the First Middle Tennessee Cavalry, was organized at Nashville, Murfreesboro, and Carthage, from July 15, 1862, to March 26, 1864, to serve three years, and was mustered out of service August 14, 1865. The regiment consisted of twelve companies and was recruited by Col. William B. Stokes, acting under authority from Military Governor Andrew Johnson. The regiment was in various battles and skirmishes during the latter part of 1862 and was in the battle of Murfreesboro, or Stone's River. From that battle till the close of the war the regiment was employed mainly in detachments in the eastern part of Middle Tennessee. One battalion was stationed at Shelbyville for some time and was in several skirmishes there. The other portion of the regiment was stationed at Carthage and was kept busy also, as, among other duties, it was required to carry the mail from that point to Gallatin. A portion of Stokes's command, under Captain Cain and Lieutenant Carter, was in the battle of Lookout Mountain. A part was also at Chickamauga and Chattanooga under Lieuts. Wingate T. Robinson and Nelson. Subsequently the regiment was ordered to Sparta, Tenn., to break up the guerrilla bands under Ferguson, Hughes, and Bledsoe, a contest in which no quarter was given.

History of DeKalb County

After this it was ordered to Nashville, where, under Lieut. Col. W. J. Clift, it participated in the battle in front of that city. Upon the removal of the command to Nashville, Colonel Stokes was assigned to command the forces at Carthage.

Three of Stokes's regiments—Company A, J. H. Blackburn, captain; Company B, Shelah Waters, captain; and Company K, E. W. Bass, captain—were made up of DeKalb County men.

There were some resignations from this regiment in 1864, and a new regiment was formed by J. H. Blackburn. Colonel Stokes resigned March 10, 1865, but was breveted brigadier general by President Andrew Johnson. Other resignations from Stokes's original regiment were: Maj. Shelah Waters, January 24, 1865; Capt. John T. Armstrong, April 7, 1865; Capt. J. H. Blackburn, June 5, 1864; Capt. James T. Exum, March 10, 1865; Capt. Monroe Floyd (who married Captain Blackburn's sister), May 11, 1865; Capt. Robert E. Cain, July 13, 1865. First lieutenants resigned: W. M. Beasley, October 16, 1862; James Worthan, March 21, 1863; H. L. Newberry, April 8, 1863; William L. Hathaway, April 10, 1864; Sylvanus Puckett, September 1, 1864; Thomas A. Beaton, January 6, 1862; A. A. Carter, February 21, 1865; James L. Hix, May 12, 1865; J. T. McIntyre, July 2, 1865; L. L. Faulkner, July 16, 1865. Second lieutenants resigned: J. M. Phillips, Marshall B. Truax, C. T. Martin, E. H. Stone, W. J. Bryson.

Those discharged were: Second Lieuts. James H. Gossett, March 3, 1863, R. C. Couch, April 25, 1863 (but recommissioned first lieutenant September 4, 1863), and Charles T. Martin, May 20, 1863 (but recommissioned second lieutenant September 4, 1863).

Those killed were: Capt. A. T. Julian, near Hillsboro, Tenn., March 18, 1863, and Surgeon J. B. Moore, killed by guerrillas September 5, 1864.

Dismissals were: Capt. E. W. Bass, December 4, 1864; First Lieuts. R. H. Sivley, January 10, 1864, John T. Van Keren, December 14, 1864, and E. Chastaine, September 25, 1864.

First Lieut. Robert A. Shepard was cashiered in January, 1863.

Maj. John Murphey on May 15, 1864, was promoted to lieutenant colonel of the Second Regiment of Mounted Infantry, and on February 7, 1865, Capt. Thomas Waters was promoted to major of the Fourth Regiment (Blackburn's) of Tennessee Infantry.

William J. Clift was appointed lieutenant colonel June 30, 1864.

John Wortham on July 1, 1864, and Faver Cason on June 24, 1865, were appointed majors.

The following captains were appointed some months after the regiment was organized: W. O. Rickman, April 22, 1863; R. C. Couch, September 10, 1863; James Clift, March 26, 1864; H. N. T. Ship, July 1, 1864.

W. P. Hough was made first lieutenant November 11, 1862; W. B. Pickering, adjutant, June 9, 1863. Second lieutenants: W. H. Nelson, August 6, 1863; Wingate T. Robinson, August 9, 1863; J. B. Raulston, September 10, 1863; W. G. Davis, July 10, 1864; E.

H. Gowen, December 14, 1864; C. W. Stewart, regimental quartermaster, February 8, 1865.

Later appointments of second lieutenants were: Elisha P. Reynolds, January 23, 1863; John B. Turner, August 9, 1863; J. W. Mallard, November 4, 1863; Henry H. Morris, January 1, 1864; H. M. Marshall, February 28, 1864; John J. White, July 10, 1864; J. W. Bryan, February 7, 1865; G. B. Johnson, February 22, 1865.

Four of Stokes's officers were marked missing on the rolls: Capt. T. C. Davis, since October, 1862; Capt. E. G. Fleming, since December, 1862; Second Lieut. A. C. Denson, since October, 1862; Second Lieut. Carl D. Brien, since June, 1863.

General Stokes was born in Chatham County, N. C., September 9, 1814, and died at Alexandria, Tenn., March 20, 1897. As shown in the sketch of Temperance Hall, his widowed mother located on her husband's land near that village, where she remained until her death, in 1853. This section was attached to DeKalb County in 1850, so that the county claims William B., Jordan, and Thomas Stokes among its pioneer citizens. In 1832 General Stokes married Paralee, daughter of Col. Abraham Overall. Farming for several years, he began his political career in 1849 as Representative of DeKalb County. He was twice elected to the House and twice to the Senate, and, defeating John A. Savage for Congress in 1859, was reëlected. He served in Congress two years after the war, and he was the nominee of his party for the governorship in 1870. Until 1868 he resided three miles north of Liberty,

HISTORY OF DEKALB COUNTY

when he removed to Alexandria, where he devoted himself to the practice of law.

In the memoranda of the volume by Adjutant General J. B. Brownlow giving the rolls of Tennessee Federals for 1861-65 it is said of Stokes's Regiment that it was in the routing of Colonels Bennett and Ward on the Dickerson Pike in September, 1862; in the defeat of Colonel Dibrell, driving him out of Neely's Bend, in October, 1862; in the battle with Forrest on the Franklin Pike, and drove him from the field at Lavergne. It was in numerous skirmishes around Nashville and on Big Harpeth in the same year; fought at Triune December 27, 1862, and was in the battle of Murfreesboro from first to last; a part, under Colonel Murphey, was at Bradyville; and, under Colonel Blackburn, a part was in the battle of Milton and in numerous engagements around Liberty and Snow's Hill. The muster rolls of his three DeKalb County companies are given below:

Company A, officers: Lieutenants, W. G. Davis, John J. White; sergeants, J. B. Allison, Robert A. Smith, F. M. Close, Hamp Woodside, Thomas E. Bratten, J. W. Thomas, Riley Dale, Lee Lafever; corporals, John Neal, W. R. Bratten, W. J. Watson, J. W. Jones, John Garrison.

Privates: W. D. Davis, J. White, J. A. Allen, R. A. Smith, T. E. Bratten, J. W. Thomas, Riley Dale, Lee Lafever, John Neal, W. R. Bratten, W. J. Watson, J. W. Jones, John Garrison, Sol A. Neal, Thomas Kirby, E. C. Edwards, J. M. Allen, W. G. Allison, William Arnold, Lige Bryant, James Blythe, Calvin Blythe,

P. Bozarth, Pete Brazwell, J. M. Brazwell, N. H. Craddock, J. W. Crook, J. R. Corder, Jim Carney, Thomas Cripps, Fred Chest, Joseph Davis, Reuben Davis, William Davis, D. D. Driver, J. Estes, W. R. Farler, Jap Fitts, W. J. Givan, Jonathan Griffith, J. M. Hays, Jasper Hays, Joe Hendrixon, James Hollandsworth, H. N. Hill, C. D. Hutchens, J. H. Hendrixon, Wilson Hendrixon, William Hill, H. James, M. F. Jones, W. H. Jackson, John Keef, John Lynch, J. B. McGee, James McGee, J. A. Mahan, William Manared, Elisha Morris, Mon Malone, W. S. Parker, A. W. Patterson, D. C. Patten, W. J. Pugh, Hiser Richardson, B. F. Read, A. A. Robinson, Thomas Self, J. S. Shehane, Peter Starnes, James Smithson, Monroe Spencer, J. J. Smith, W. G. Smiley, Wilson Taylor, J. C. Vickers, Thomas Vinson, William Warford, G. P. W. Williams, J. W. Wooden, Oscar A. Woodworth, W. H. Word, J. B. Yeargin, J. H. Blackburn, Monroe Floyd, W. L. Hathaway, J. J. Evans, J. H. Gossett, J. T. Exum, A. J. Garrison, L. N. Woodside, Martin E. Quinn, E. H. Stone, James H. Blackburn, George Adamson, C. M. Brown, W. W. Govern, R. M. Hawkins, Henry Malone, Ed Pennington, Josiah Youngblood, Elijah Yeargin, J. Murphy, P. M. Radford, James H. Bratten, William A. Dale, D. A. Davis, Joseph Adamson, David Barr, Hiram Barret, William Bullard, J. M. Campbell, T. J. Chapman, A. G. Davis, R. H. Green, G. H. Leaver, S. J. McCalib, R. S. Neely, G. W. Robinson, J. B. Scott, J. M. Smith, A. M. Stone, W. J. Vickers, S. M. Williams, Joseph Wilcher, A. Yeargin, James Garrett, Elisha Kerly, F C. Overcast.

Killed: J. B. Moore, by guerrillas, 1864; W. J. Vickers, by guerrillas, 1863. Died: Joseph Adamson, David Barr, Joseph Bryant, April, 1863; Andrew George, 1861.

Company B, officers: Lieutenants, E. H. Gowan, J. W. Bryan; sergeants, T. W. Kenner, J. W. McDonald, W. Wood, Ralph Compton, J. W. Saulmon, W. F. Turner; corporals, J. W. Brown, H. McClure, P. Horley, T. A. Morris, J. Cothran; bugler, J. C. Haley.

Privates: M. A. Alder, W. H. Anderson, S. P. Burchett, I. W. Baker, D. H. Brewer, Thomas Borum, R. I. Bell, J. T. Ballance, E. Burnett, T. B. Brown, J. H. Brockett, L. W. Cherry, J. W. B. Davis, Zach Davis, Arch Davis, Anderson Davis, T. M. D. Earhart, Horace Francis, S. L. George, I. T. Goodson, L. M. Green, Jerome E. Goodner, J. Hale, Eli Herron, Wilson Herron, J. G. Jennings, Frank Johnson, Thomas Ketchum, J. K. C. Lance, E. H. Linton, John Morris, A. J. Merrill, A. C. Mayer, S. McDermot, W. Melvin, James Manus, John Oakley, Thomas Rogers, M. Rohelia, G. M. Robertson, John Robinson, David Redd, James Sands, Elgin Sands, W. Singleton, James Strauther, G. W. Tuck, James Talley, B. C. Vinson, J. Waggoner, J. W. Westfall, Taylor Warren, N. Winnett, C. T. Winnett, James Winnett, John Williams, T. A. Welland, M. F. Young, J. Nems, Henderson Smith, Thomas Davis, H. L. Newbury, W. W. Barker, Alex Davis, T. H. Berry, J. T. Thompson, S. B. Whitlock, W. G. Davis, A. Ham, T. B. Oakley, James Oakley, J. P. Paty, Thomas Reeves, John Simpson, R. Wadkins, Shelah Waters, Thomas Waters, John Everett, J. M.

Hutsell, R. P. Mayer, E. H. Gowan, J. E. Pendergrass, W. H. C. Young, B. F. Bowar, J. A. Ellis, Cass Goad, M. F. Hale, J. L. Laurance, J. M. Shairts, W. L. Thompson, H. B. Thomas, F. M. Ensory, P. Giller, A. J. Hesson, Joseph Hester, J. C. Yell, P. M. Gascock, J. M. Groop.

Killed: J. E. Pendergrass, Murfreesboro, 1863; J. L. Laurance, in Lookout Valley. Died: W. H. C. Young, in prison January 12, 1863; B. F. Bowar, May 23, 1863; J. A. Ellis, M. V. Hale, J. M. Shairts, November 14, 1862; W. L. Thompson, December 29, 1863; Cyrus Y. Goad.

Company K, officers: Captain, E. W. Bass; lieutenants, W. T. Robinson, John B. Turner, J. H. Smith; sergeants, J. L. Rollins, W. R. Lewis, Marion Cubbins, John A. Bass, W. H. Trammel, James H. Overall, R. M. Johnson; corporals, William Davis, Wells Barrett, G. B. Pedigo, T. N. Close, Alex Petty, John Tarpley, W. R. Caplinger; bugler, John C. Bennett.

Privates: J. B. Turney, Harvey Smith, J. L. Robinson, W. R. Lewis, Marion Cubbins, John A. Bass, W. H. Trammel, J. H. Overall, R. M. Johnson, William Davis, J. T. Meares, Wells Barrett, G. B. Pedigo, T. N. Close, Alex Petty, John Tarpley, W. R. Caplinger, J. C. Bennett, T. D. Oakley, B. J. Holloman, H. Y. Yeargin, Chris E. Adamson, John Adamson, W. T. Alexander, H. C. Alexander, Thomas Alexander, F. M. Allen, James Brent, Nathan Blythe, W. C. Bennett, John Case, J. G. Close, John Caplinger, John Coley, T. J. Davis, James Davis, Elam Edge, Denton

Griffith, George Henley, George Hickman, W. L. Hail, W. H. Hays, Charles Hill, Reuben Hail, Thomas Hendrixson, R. Hinesly, J. H. Hicks, W. P. Hawker, J. M. Jones, Wesley Jennings, W. J. Jones, James A. Jones, W. H. Jones, James Lee, J. R. League, J. B. Lemmons, Blueford Mathis, Alex Manners, J. Mullican, L. H. McGinnis, G. B. Mahan, W. H. Pedigo, T. J. Perkins, James Petty, Joseph Pistole, William Patterson, John Parker, Travis Tarpley, A. J. Pugh, Matlock Roberts, W. A. Sullivan, Anthony Stanley, Noah Smith, John Taylor, J. P. Tomlinson, William Trusty, R. B. Waller, E. B. Watson, J. B. Wilson, E. W. Bass, Hinton A. Hill, James McMillin, J. J. Ross, Wiley Snow, James Williams, A. C. Rogers, R. H. Ponder, David Grandstaff, George C. Turney, W. C. Crossland, N. Alexander, James Baugh, W. H. Christian, David A. Farmer, James Gibson, James Hail, Jonathan Jones, T. J. Pistole, H. C. Richards, Alex Stanley, R. Pendergrass, Henry Stayner, Emanuel Williams.

Killed: David Grandstaff, G. C. (Kit) Turney, James Baugh, D. A. Farmer, Joseph Hail, Jonathan Jones, T. J. Pistole, James Fuston, Alex Stanley, Calf Killer battle, February 22, 1864; H. C. Richards, by accident, Carthage, 1864. Died: William Crossland, of wounds at Carthage, 1864; W. H. Christian, of wounds, 1864.

CHAPTER XVII.

BLACKBURN'S AND GARRISON'S FEDERALS.

LIEUT. COL. JOSEPH H. BLACKBURN'S Fourth (Union) Regiment of Mounted Infantry, with the exception of Company B, was recruited at Liberty, Carthage, Alexandria, Pulaski, Livingston, Shelbyville, and Nashville from September 1, 1864, to April 22, 1865, to serve one year. Company B was made up of Memphis home guards and was mustered out of service June 1, 1865; the other companies were mustered out August 25, 1865. Colonel Blackburn was appointed lieutenant colonel November 26, 1864, at the age of twenty-two years. Thomas Waters was appointed major February 7, 1865.

Appointments of captains: Norton E. Quinn, October 27, 1864; William L. Hathaway, October 29, 1864; Macadoo Vannata, December 11, 1864; A. C. Card, January 10, 1865; J. P. Patey, February 2, 1865; John Simpson, March 11, 1865; Rufus Dowdy, May 5, 1865; G. W. Gray, June 14, 1865.

Appointments of first lieutenants in Blackburn's Regiment: James H. Blackburn, October 27, 1864; James H. (Pet) White, October 29, 1864; William J. Stokes, adjutant (son of Colonel Stokes), December 8, 1864; Marcellus C. Vick, December 11, 1864; W. B. Overcast, January 10, 1864; H. C. Sanders, February 1, 1865; S. B. Whitelock, February 4, 1865; J. T. Thompson, February 4, 1865; H. T. Smallage, February 28, 1865; C. W. Meeker, June 28, 1865.

Second lieutenants: T. G. Bratten, October 27, 1864; Elijah Robinson, October 29, 1864; James Williams, December 9, 1864; R. Wiley, January 11, 1865; James H. Kitching, February 2, 1865; T. H. Berry, February 2, 1865; W. H. Wilhite, April 24, 1865; C. M. Pitts, June 30, 1865; A. J. Miller, July 3, 1865.

Those who died among the officers appointed from time to time were: Capt. George Oakley, July, 1865, of disease; First Lieut. James Oakley, February 4, 1865, of wounds; First Lieut. William McDowell, lost off the steamer Sultana April 27, 1865.

Colonel Blackburn was born in Wilson County, near Cottage Home, in 1842, his father having come from North Carolina. He married Miss Jennie Barger, of Liberty, in 1861. His company (A), of Stokes's Regiment, elected him captain at the age of eighteen. As shown, he raised a regiment after resigning from the Fifth Cavalry. He was in quite a number of battles and skirmishes, receiving one wound—probably made by Oscar Woodworth, a Federal—while a battle was on with Morgan's men at Liberty. After the war he was a delegate to the Constitutional Convention at Nashville, but refused to sign the schedule because of the poll tax provision as a qualification for voters. He was also United States marshal for the middle district of the State. Shortly after the war he, with others, created a sensation in Nashville by attacking and wounding Gen. Joseph Wheeler. Colonel Blackburn died in May, 1913.

In Goodspeed's history of the State (biographical section) this statement is made: "Colonel Blackburn was in several battles, the most important of which were Nashville, Chattanooga, Snow's Hill, and Milton. . . . He also cleared of guerrillas White, Putnam, DeKalb, and Jackson Counties by capturing Champe Ferguson, after which even Rebel sympathizers felt more secure. He is said to have been in two hundred and seventeen engagements, in all of which he was successful. He was wounded at Liberty." In the same history it is stated that in 1864 R. B. Blackwell's guerrillas made a raid into Shelbyville, Tenn. The depot was guarded by twelve of Blackburn's troops, who were captured, escorted into the country, and shot. Were these members of Company A? Blackburn's companies were:

Company A, officers: Captain, James Wortham; lieutenants, C. W. Meeker, G. W. Gray, William McDowell, William Smith, A. J. Miller; sergeants, J. S. Ray, W. L. Jackson, J. M. Jarrell, T. V. Jones; corporals, W. G. Reavis, W. W. Harrian, J. Williams, W. C. Dickens, J. A. Holcomb, J. A. Brooks, C. M. Clark.

Privates: J. F. Ray, W. L. Jackson, J. M. Jarrell, T. V. Jones, A. J. Jarrell, W. G. Reavis, W. W. Harman, I. Williams, W. C. Dickens, J. A. Holcomb, J. A. Brooks, C. M. Clark, Tom Anderson, W. Blacker, A. J. Cleck, W. J. Clark, J. W. Cunningham, E. G. Davis, G. B. Dawson, Linsley Evins, R. C. Eaton, T. J. Fisher, J. H. Griffin, W. J. Gordon, J. N. Gibson, J. L. Hill, J. T. Harris, G. Ivy, James and John Jones, T. J. Little, W. S. Lacey, E. Lockhart, G. Little, M.D., J. H. Moon, J. P. Mankin, J. C. McMinn, L. Moore, J. C. Matthews, I. Norvill, G. Primrose, R. J. Patton,

J. A. Rollins, C. S. Richard, S. J. Riner, M. Shoffner, J. D. Sanders, James C. Turner, R. F. and W. W. Tindell, J. H. Webster, W. W. Waide, V. H. Wright, H. P. Watkins, Joseph A. White, P. M. Melton, Berry Bruton, S. J. Cheek, M. C. Davis, J. Hashaw, John Hyde, H. J. Johnson, George Ross, W. J. Shaw, H. F. Sutton, W. McMurry, J. M. Bearden, R. Brown, R. M. Dromgoole, A. R. Hashaw, P. M. Odum, J. B. Summers, H. V. Stahum, A. D. Hopkins, Robert F. Smith, J. W. Tredinger, John Williams, N. S. Brownsheres, W. Davis, W. H. Johnson, J. W. Smith, A. J. J. Horton.

Killed: P. M. Melton, Berry Bruton, S. J. Cheek, M. C. Davis, James Hashaw, John Hyde, H. J. Johnson, George Ross, W. J. Shaw, all at Wells Hill September 28, 1864. Died: William McMurry, May 21, 1866; M. Bearden, April 7, 1865; R. Baugh, January 10, 1865; R. M. Dromgoole, lost on the steamer Sultana.

Company B, officers: First sergeant, J. M. Whitten; second sergeant, W. T. Hopper; corporals, E. J. Spencer, L. W. Dawson, B. F. Parlon.

Privates: J. Austin, G. W. Anglin, M. M. Brison, J. Black, John Burks, J. M. Chapman, J. R. Chapman, W. Cheek, H. J. Crow, W. A. Cooper, H. T. Forbes, H. Gorman, R. Holliday, W. H. Harland, R. Howard, M. L. Inge, A. F. Ingle, T. Johnson, James Keyton, J. Louden, J. H. Moore, T. Martingale, C. Newland, J. Prime, R. J. Rankin, W. W. Robinson, H. Riner, J. A. Robinson, J. K. Stone, M. Spencer, J. Shelton, D.

D. Sanders, A. Tibbets, P. Trease, M. A. Thompson, W. W. Whitby, W. M. Whitehorn, J. Weaver, N. A. Whitehorn, M. P. Henry, D. S. Ingle, J. W. Whitehorn, J. A. Griffin, J. Golden, I. Trotter, John Pierce.

Died: J. A. Griffin, April 15, 1865; J. Golden, 1865; I. Trotter, May 18, 1865.

Company C, officers: Captain, A. C. Card; lieutenants, W. B. Overcast, R. Wiley; sergeants, E. D. Jones, J. E. Austin, W. N. Austin, James Greer, L. T. Larue; corporals, M. D. Smith, W. H. Stephenson, J. B. Cherry, J. S. Reese, Thomas Gore, J. S. Gibson, W. S. Cavett, John Armstrong, G. B. Baker.

Privates: W. H. Stephenson, J. B. Cherry, J. S. Reese, T. G. Gee, J. E. Gibson, W. S. Cavett, John Armstrong, G. B. Baker, W. Baldwin, H. Bledsoe, J. Barron, L. F. Cain, H. Clark, G. W. Clark, W. H. Clark, W. J. Cochran, Peter Cochran, J. E. Cooper, A. Crane, N. B. Daniel, E. P. Estes, L. C. C. Estes, P. T. Fisher, J. L. Foster, J. E. Fox, J. Freeman, F. E. Glasscock, G. Glasscock, T. H. Grey, J. Hall, J. P. Hoskins, W. D. Hill, T. Johnson, W. Johnson, W. H. Kiser, J. O. Cumpie, A. Lamb, T. H. Lamb, G. W. Lock, David Lynch, W. G. Lynch, W. Malone, J. W. Mallard, H. E. McGowan, W. Melton, J. Moore, J. H. Neely, J. M. Orr, C. Overcast, A. Perryman, W. R. Posey, J. J. Reeves, G. W. Reece, J. W. Reed, S. A Rundle, A. Shaw, Joab Slawtre, Hiram, J. A., and J. G. Smith, J. L. Stallings, J. Stone, C. Tarwater, J. H. Tucker, N. Walker, S. Williams, J. T. Glasscock, T. J. Hopper, I. D. Smith, Henry Thomas, Robert Wiley,

T. F. Logsten, W. W. Waide, J. M. Austin, H. Holmes, Jonathan Johnson, H. L. McConnell, C. Mitchell, H. C. Moore, J. W. Prince, E. Seatons, W. H. Wright.

Died: J. T. Glasscock, January 10, 1865; T. J. Hopper, February 5, 1865; I. D. Smith, Andersonville Prison, March 10, 1865; Henry Thomas, of gunshot wounds in Bedford County.

Company D, officers: Captain, Norton E. Quinn; lieutenants, J. Henry Blackburn, T. G. Bratten; sergeants, W. W. Colwell, J. B. Taylor, D. L. Floyd, J. W. Atwood, N. Hodges; corporals, J. A. Colwell, William Batts, John W. Vandergrift, W. Lawson, N. E. Brandy, J. McAlexander, William Coffee, H. C. Jenkins.

Privates: P. Atkins, G. B. Anderson, J. A. Barnes, W. A. Barren, W. Bain, W. T. Blackburn, M. Bradley, A. J. Bennett, J. J. Bennett, W. Bullard, A. Certui, L. D. Colwell, Andrew Chumley, J. C. Clemmons, T. Davis, D. H. Davis, W. H. Fann, Joe B. Gilbert, C. W. Hollandsworth, J. D. Hall, T. J. Hays, Lawson Hall, T. J. Hale, John Herriman, Stephen Herriman, Sam P. Herriman, J. C. Hiddon, J. L. Jenkins, J. B. Kyle, J. Kenton, M. J. Luck, Jesse Lafever, C. Lawson, A. H. Leack, Bunk Malone, S. B. Morris, C. Mosby, T. Davis, W. Phillips, H. P. Pass, A. Ready, J. W. Reynolds, J. O. Rich, John Robertson, G. Stevens, J. E. Tedder, A. H. Thomason, J. Tuggle, H. M. Tuggle, P. N. Turner, George Turner, Henry Vandergriff, John Vandergriff, William Vandergriff, W. and

Thomas Veri, Sam Vannata, G. A. Vansell, O. D. Williams, M. Wilson, T. L. Ray, J. F. Yeargin, O. D. Goodson, G. M. Jennings, W. A. Morgan, W. Benson, Irving Driver, W. L. Hathaway, T. Brennan, Thomas Hays, John Hollandsworth, C. Peterson, A. Smithland.

Killed: O. D. Goodson, Cannon County, March 15, 1865, probably by guerrillas; J. M. Jennings, same; W. A. Morgan, battle of Nashville, December 17, 1864. Died: W. Benson, May 10, 1865; Irving Driver, May 10, 1865.

Company E, officers: Captain, Macadoo Vannata; first lieutenant, M. C. Vick; second lieutenant, James Williams; first sergeant, Bove Oakley; second sergeant, W. J. Crook; third sergeant, J. M. Johnson; fourth sergeant, George Turner; fifth sergeant, G. W. Martin; corporals, C. Booker, A. C. Cox, Virgil Ray, J. Ricketts, H. McCork, A. Blythe, C. Manners, F. A. Right; bugler, Len R. Scott; smith, G. W. Lanier.

Privates: J. N. Alexander, H. C. Bennett, J. Y. Bennett, T. Beadle, J. Crook, Tilman Crook, S. M. Christian, Leonard Cantrell, J. Capshaw, William Conley, F. Culwell, J. W. Carroll, W. F. Craven, Berry Driver, H. H. Eskin, H. M. Fite, S. L. Gay, Leman Hale, J. Hickman, J. C. Huchens, Thomas Hass, T. Harris, J. Harden, A. Harris, W. R. Hill, J. Hill, J. Hodges, Francis Hollandsworth, S. Hughes, B. Hill, W. Jenkins, T. P. James, James Keaton, William King, J. L. Kenard, J. Lawson, A. Lack, J. Manners, J. Maxfield, W. F. Metcalf, H. W. McGuire, Dous, John, James, and Joseph Oakley, A. Pack, Barn Page, W. R. Parris, S. H. Patterson, P. Roberts, J. H. Rany, J. F. Scott, R. Stewart, J. P. Smith, Manson Scott, Isaac Turner, J. Thomas, John M. Trammel, T. W. Trammel, Thomas W. Turner, William I. Turner, Barney Taylor, T. I. Vance, E. Williams, B. G. Warren, Leonard F. Woodside, E. C. Walker, W. J. Stokes, D. F. Floyd, Dallas Adkins.

Company F, officers: Captain, William L. Hathaway; first lieutenant, James H. White; second lieutenant, Elijah Robinson; first sergeant, Ben Hall; second sergeant, Tom Curtis; third sergeant, James Robinson; fourth sergeant, Seaborn Page; fifth sergeant, W. B. Corley; corporals, John Hendrixon, Jesse Farler, Ike Gibbs, Daniel Hale, W. M. Moore, S. M. Pirtle, William Adamson, W. M. Short.

Privates: L. J. Allison, Joe M. Banks, Thomas Biford, J. R. Cantrell, J. B. Carter, Asa Driver, J. M. Dunlap, Sim Estes, Isom Etheridge, Eli Evans, E. D. Fish, William Fitts, James Ford, Erastus D. Foster, Jonathan R. Fuson, James H. Fuson, J. M. Gilbert, Len Hathaway, J. B. Hardinlay, Smith Hendrixon, James R. Hicks, R. Hill, E. D. Hutchens, H. and I. C. Johnson, Tilman Joins, John Lasiter, Thomas Leadbetter, L. B. Linsey, J. Linsey, Giles, R. E., and W. J. Martin, J. J. Maxwell, V. McIntire, S. Neal, J. M., A., John, and Jacob Pack, Allen Page, Erwin Page, Wash Parsley, J. A. Parsley, J. F. Petit, J. E., Levi D., and C. H. Robinson, Ike Shehane, W. Snyder, E. Snow, John Smithson, E., J. T., Chesley, Bailey, and

Henry Taylor, W. Thomas, Joseph Turner, R. Woodward, G. B. Woodward, J. M. Pack, A. L. Cummings, J. B. Edney, F. P. Kephart.

Died: G. B. Woodward, J. M. Pack, April 8, 1865; A. L. Cummings, April 8, 1865.

Company G, officers: Captain, James P. Patey; first lieutenant, S. B. Whitlock; second lieutenant, James A. Kitchings; first sergeant, G. E. Coatney; second sergeant, H. C. Barry; third sergeant, J. M. Enoch; fourth sergeant, A. Gwaltney; fifth sergeant, J. B. Barber; corporals, T. H. Campbell, W. T. Allen, F. C. Allen, I. Manning.

Privates: Henry H. Jones, D. B. Gwaltney, W. Beasly, J. T. Highers, Jere Agee, J. D. Agee, W. B. Agee, F. Adcock, Benjamin Allen, G. K. Baker, A. J. Baker, Turner Barrett, N. B. Boulton, J. Bray, P. J. Baker, Ben Bradley, F. E. Buckner, L. Chandler, G. P. Campbell, A. H. Cowen, W. H. Corley, M. F. Coatney, Wamon Capshaw, William Cheek, Thomas Clark, Sam Denny, D. R. Enoch, T. F. Estes, W. Fuller, J. B. Farmer, J. Frederick, A. B. Fuller, A. Girins, John Gregory, C. G. Caskey, R. F. Hale, A. D. Helmantaler, W. D. Hudson, T. H. Hughes, J. Hunt, J. A. Hunt, Simeon Highers, B. A. James, G. D. King, B. F. Kidwell, E. H. Liggin, W. J. Lance, J. W. Merritt, D. A. Macon, Burrel Manning, T. B. Mathis, S. B. McDowel, S. W. Macon, William Moss, A. C., J., J. N., and T. Nolan, John Ogle, J. G. Parton, James Preston, Moses Preston, James Pritchett, John Prentice, W. T. Stalings, J. B. Smart, B. F., J. M., and W. J. Thomas, J. M. Watts, Dock Wilkerson, J. N. Webb, G. Williams, Sam Winfrey, G. B. Boulton.

Company H, officers: First lieutenant, J. T. Thompson; second lieutenant, T. H. Berry; sergeants, T. D. Sutney, James Weaver, J. R. Word, T. H. Lanham, J. W. Fisher; corporals, Paris Campbell, J. Campbell, D. S. Holt, W. N. Ricks, D. T. Thomison, W. S. Stuart, E. A. Barbee, W. A. Jacobs.

Privates: T. M. Allen, S. H. Alexander, A. H. Ashworth, W. E. Bond, J. W. Berry, T. J., J. F., and James F. Bell, W. Ball, G. and W. L. Biss, J. Berry, J. Bond, B. Craig, J. R. Cummings, J. H. Cunningham, B. Climer, Jim W. Carney, A. N. Cummings, J. A. Cunningham, J. C. Edwards, Ben Elkins, L. A. Farmer, J. Griffin, W. H. Gill, C. B. Griffin, J. Harrison, J. W. Herron, J. P. Henderson, L. F. Holland, J. W. James, William Kelly, H. B. Gurnan, J. M. Gurnan, H. A. Midgit, Presley Merritt, R. M. Porterfield, S. T. Porterfield, G. W. Patterson, W. L. Singleton, William Springs, G. Springs, E. Shadwick, S. Spears, Z. F. Spears, M. H. Thompson, J. R. Thompson, J. L., J. M., and A. Tanner, Thomas Tuggle, R. F. Thomas, W. Thompson, E. P. Tracy, I. N. Vaught, W. J. Vaught, M. A. Wallace, R. H. Walker, M. Wintherly, G. W., A. P., Ben, and William Williams, C. C. Wood, C. H. Young, William Younger, George Oakley, James Oakley, James Yates.

Died: James Oakley, of wounds, February 4, 1865.

History of DeKalb County

Company I, officers; Captain, John Simpson; first lieutenant, H. C. Sanders; second lieutenant, C. W. Meeker (later C. M. Pitts); first sergeant, G. W. Dimean; second sergeant, J. W. Fleman; third sergeant, C. A. Bailiff; fourth sergeant, T. J. Wilburn; fifth sergeant, Joel Dodson; corporals, T. W. Johnson, J. T. White, J. M. Haney, J. F. S. Hardaway, W. P. Conner, J. F. Rombo, J. C. Chambers, J. Walker.

Privates: R. M. Adams, W. S. Ashen, James Allen, A. G. Barnes, N. F. Bishop, J. M. Bankston, Bird L. Bates, F. M. Barnett, D. O. Brown, F. M. Cassell, S. D. Eddie, D. C. Fleeman, D. G. Greer, C. G. Head, J. Head, J. Heath, W. W. Heath, M. Hart, R. Harrington, S. House, C. Jones, N. F. Jones, C. Jordan, O. Jordon, Thomas Keath, John Kirby, F. M. Keath, J. D. Lossen, James Laurence, Miles Leary, T. J. Lewis, R. J. Maxwell, A. Medley, L. McGinnis, Alfred Morris, Thomas Malone, T. M. McCormack, J. A. Manley, J. F. and G. W. Majors, W. P. Maxwell, J. Mitchell, Isham A. Morris, S. McCroy, H. Nolly, J. Penny, A. L. Perryman, D. E. Perryman, W. Pearce, J. Reaves, D. R. Roberts, T. J. Riggs, T. L. Richardson, A. Riley, Ben Scaggs, J. H. Sandusky, W. F. Sandusky, J. J. Spray, P. Seay, T. Smith, L. D. Smith, J. G. Smithson, J. T. Tanner, R. A. Thatch, J. R. Tubb, W. L. Todd, J. Wiley, J. Watson, L. D., W. H., and R. P. Williams, J. W. Todd, J. Tolman, John C. Conner, T. J. Hart, W. H. McClaffity, F. Spurlock, T. J. Welch, J. W. Armstrong, S. M. Baker, Eli Barnett, J. Baker, J. H. Crane, A. Gibbs, W. H. Gillan, W. J. Hollis, J. E. Sweeler, G. W. Smith, J. W. Worley.

Died: John C. Conner, January 26, 1865; T. J. Hart, January 16, 1865; W. H. McClaffity, February 16, 1865; F. Spurlock, February 8, 1865; T. J. Welch, February 8, 1865.

Company K, officers: Captain, Rufus Dowdy; first lieutenant, H. T. Smallage; second lieutenant, W. H. Wilhite; first sergeant, John Parker; second sergeant, James Wilhite; third sergeant, E. M. Long; fourth sergeant, J. F. Deck; fifth sergeant, F. Coatney; corporals, J. A. Hill, J. F. Mulligan, J. F. Koger, William Frederick, J. Cooper, D. Godsey, J. Stover, J. R. Grimes.

Privates: H. Armis, John, W., and Van Allen, J. M. Boyle, L. P. Baker, M. M. Bryan, B. H. Bracher, E. Bird, J. Bohanan, J. H. Briant, W. T. Curnley, John Courlington, E. Cash, H. Clark, D. C. Clark, Green P. Cantrell, H. I. Cooper, W. H. Capshaw, J. Cargill, H. L. Dox, William Duese, J. Dickson, C. C. Fowler, F. M. Ferguson, William Flowers, G. Goodman, William Green, J. Godsey, W. B. Hill, R. Highers, G. W. Hendrixson, D. H. Hall, W. B. Hoyder, J. N. Johnson, R. M. Johnson, E. Jackson, L. Jackson, W. E. Jones, W. S. Kirby, L. Liles, J. F. Martin, Thomas Mason, J. H. Moore, John Maries, James Maires, R. L. Newman, J. Prater, G. W. Plumlee, A. Parker, R. Poe, J. S. Prater, G. W. Roberts, Jeff Reynolds, J. S., F., and A. Sliger, Asbury Scott, W. J. Smith, G. Stephens, S. Settle, R. Savage, J. R. Sisson, D. M. Southerland, William H. Southerland, A. J. Sells, J. H. Smith, J. A. Stone, G. A. Finch, A. J. Tucker, J. Whitaker, A.

J. Williams, Marshall Walker, W. B. Davis, J. P. Hill, W. L. Hunter, T. McNair, J. E. Pritchard, W. A. Pritchard.

A. J. Garrison made up a company (G) which became a part of the First Federal Regiment of Mounted Infantry, Col. A. E. Garrett. The regiment served mainly in the northeastern part of Middle Tennessee, having frequent encounters with guerrillas. Captain Garrison was born in DeKalb County of a pioneer family. He probably died in Arkansas, to which State he removed after the war.

Company G, officers: Captain, Andrew J. Garrison; lieutenants, L. N. Woodside, appointed March 21, 1864; Elijah Bratten, appointed December 5, 1864.

Privates: Stephen Barnes, C. A. Coe, John Conley, H. M. Crook, M. Harris, Amos Gilly, John Hill, Joe Herryman (1), Joe Herryman (2), B. Herrington, A. J. Hullet, William Jones, B. F. Jones, W. W. Jackson, Morris Marcum, G. W. Norton, I. N. Fite, James Waford, Francis Hall, Jo and John Parkerson, John Merritt, Mickeral Manners, John Rodgers, John Reynolds, R. Sullens, J. A. Taylor, M. A. Thomason, H. Vanover, S. O. Williams, Lem Barger, John Martin, William Scott, Newton Brown, Brax Malone, Thomas Bates, James Allen, W. B. Bates, N. Bradley, J. H. Bradley, G. Chatham, R. S. Dale, John G. Dale, O. P. Durham, W. B. Farmer, H. L. Farmer, J. H. Fite, Jason Foutch, W. J. Foutch, Josiah Hicks, John W. Hass, Joe Hullet, H. C. Hardcastle, Ainberson Corley,

John Jones, W. W. Jackson, J. B. Lewis, J. B. Malone, Daniel Mathis, Jo Neal, Levi Neal, William Pogue, Lem Parker, Oliver Patterson, Shadrack Robertson, William Reasonover, William Sewell, J. Scudder, George Thomason, James Woodside, Henry Wooden, O. Parkerson, Memphis Goodson, W. Midigett, W. H. Adams.

Died: W. H. Adams, Ainberson Corley, Memphis Goodson, and W. Midigett, 1864; Oliver Patterson, 1865.

CHAPTER XVIII.

Progress of the Big War.

In Gen. M. J. Wright's volume, "Tennessee in the War," are listed the following fights which took place on DeKalb County soil from 1861 to the close of the War between the States:

Alexandria, February 3-5, 1863; Smithville, June 4, 5, 1863; Snow's Hill, April 2, 6, June 4, 1863; Liberty, January 21, 22, February 3-5, 17-20, March 19, April 1-8, May 12, 16, June 4, 1863; Salem, March 21, May 20, 1863; Salem Pike, June 12, 1863.*

Some of these skirmishes were long-drawn-out, and of course they do not include occasional uncontested entrances of one side or the other into the county, such as the passing of Wheeler's Cavalry in 1864.

It is seen in the list that almost every section of DeKalb had some knowledge of war's alarms. Stokes's, Blackburn's, or Garrison's men frequently camped on their old Liberty stamping grounds. At this place there was for a while a negro company, maybe more, the headquarters being the Methodist church. The DeKalb County Federals built the stockade on the hill just west of Liberty, and while at Alexandria they occupied the fair grounds. Occasionally they were at Smithville, but only for short periods. Troops under

---

*The number of battles and skirmishes in the entire State is given in Volume XII. of the "Confederate Military History," and each is pointed out by date and location. The number was seven hundred and seventy-four.

Gen. J. T. Wilder or one or more of his colonels and other Federal officers made frequent forays from Murfreesboro and Nashville via Auburn and Alexandria.

While the writer was on the editorial staff of the Knoxville *Evening Sentinel* in 1898 General Wilder made occasional visits to the office, and when compiling the "History of Tennessee and Tennesseeans" in 1913 he requested the General to write of his experiences in Middle Tennessee. This was graciously agreed to, but later the General found it impossible to comply. However, there is an interesting biography of him in the history mentioned. He had the Liberty steam mill* burned and also William Vick's vacant storehouse. The latter was destroyed because the Confederates had wheat stored in it. In the biography it is said: "He [Wilder] took a specially active part in the operations through Central Tennessee. At one time Rosecrans had ordered him to burn all the mills in this region of the State; but instead of destroying them he broke the principal gear, so that they could not be operated. When he reported to Rosecrans what he had done, the general told him he had disobeyed orders, but would excuse him that time."

From the occupation of the county by Gen. John H. Morgan's forces date the series of skirmishes which took place therein. In the history of Morgan's Cavalry Gen. B. W. Duke declares that the object was to defend Bragg's right wing after the latter had re-

---

*After the destruction of the mill the citizens had to depend upon Crips's Mill, on Dry Creek, and that of William Bate, on Helton Creek.

treated following the battle of Murfreesboro, December 3, 1862, to January 1, 1863. This wing extended from Woodbury, Tenn., into Wayne County, Ky., a distance of one hundred and twenty miles. Liberty being the most important point on the line, strategically considered, the main force was established there. Duke says also that they kept within safety of Snow's Hill; but he finally decided that this place of retreat, when the command was closely pursued, was not as safe as it had been regarded.

Morgan's command reached Smithville January 4, 1863. It remained there and at Sligo ten days. Then it marched to McMinnville, where the commander made his headquarters. On January 23 Col. John C. Breckinridge was ordered to move to Liberty with three regiments—the Third Kentucky, Lieutenant Colonel Hutchinson; the Ninth Kentucky, Lieutenant Colonel Stoner; and the Ninth Tennessee, Colonel Ward. Col. A. R. Johnson was already in the vicinity of Liberty with the Tenth Kentucky.

Capt. Thomas Quirk was sent ahead of the three regiments. He was an Irishman commanding sixty scouts. Before he could be supported, he was driven from the village by Federals, however. This must have been about January 21 or 22.

When Colonel Breckinridge arrived he occupied the country immediately in front of Liberty, picketing all the roads. Shortly afterwards Colonel Stoner, with several companies, was ordered to Kentucky, leaving the Confederate force about one thousand effective men. There was a similar force in the neighborhood of McMinnville and Woodbury. During January, February, and March the Confederates were kept constantly scouting and making expeditions. Fights were of almost daily occurrence somewhere near the line they were defending. "Perhaps no period in the history of Morgan's Cavalry can be cited in which more exciting service was performed," avers General Duke.

General Stokes's troops, or a portion of them, were frequently with General Wilder's in making these forays into the county. The Stokes home was three miles down Smith Fork Creek, north of Liberty, and the Confederates had a great desire to capture its owner. One of the Kentucky soldiers, writing to the *Confederate Veteran* for September, 1898, says: "Liberty is a village situated at the base of Snow's Hill, fifty miles due east from Nashville. Rome would have been a better name for the town, as it seemed that all the pikes and dirt roads in Tennessee led to Liberty. . . . Somewhere on the road between Liberty and Cumberland [Caney Fork] River there lived at that time a Col. Bill Stokes, an officer of some note, of whom we heard a good deal in time of the war. It was Colonel Ward's ambition, as well as that of his men, who were Tennesseeans, to capture Colonel Stokes, and they made diligent search for him and at the same time guarded his house closely with the expectation of finding Colonel Stokes at home."

While Lieut. G. C. Ridley was with Morgan's force at Liberty in 1863 he received an order to select ten picked men to go by way of Alexandria, Lebanon, and Goodlettsville and send a messenger on the quiet to

Nashville to ascertain the location of the Federals and their approaches. Near Payne's Ferry, on the Cumberland River, they found a young lady willing to make the secret trip into Nashville. In twelve hours she was back with a complete diagram. Receiving it, Lieutenant Ridley started back posthaste, but soon learned that General Wilder with a large force had marched from Murfreesboro by way of Lebanon and Alexandria to attack Liberty. Ridley changed his course for Columbia, going by Peytonville, Williamson County. Near the latter place he was chased by Cross' Southern guerrillas, who thought he was a Federal. Lieutenant Ridley and squad finally reached General Forrest at Columbia.

Speaking of General Wilder, he was once assisted into DeKalb County by a Union girl. She was Miss Mary, daughter of Dr. J. W. Bowen, of Gordonsville. He had started out from Nashville with seven scouts. These scouts were captured by Confederates, all wounded, five dying from their wounds. General Wilder reached Gordonsville after dark. Dr. Bowen being absent, Miss Bowen volunteered to act as his guide to Smithville. It was dark and rainy, but the trip was successfully made. Miss Bowen became Mrs. Aust, mother of John R. Aust, a prominent lawyer at Nashville.

On January 29, 1863, General Morgan, with Major Steele, Captain Carroll, and a few men, came to Liberty from McMinnville and selected fifty men to enter Nashville stealthily, burn the commissary stores, and in the confusion of the fire make their escape. Among these intrepid scouts was Captain Quirk. But at Stewart's Ferry, on Stone's River, they met the captain of a Michigan regiment with twenty men. For a while the enemy conversed, Morgan claiming to be Captain Johnson, of the Fifth Kentucky Regiment of Federals. Presently the Federals saw under their overcoats the Confederates' gray pants. This spoiled the raid; for while fifteen of the Federals were captured, the others reached Nashville and gave the alarm.

Before Mr. B. L. Ridley, of Murfreesboro, became a lieutenant on the staff of Lieut. Gen. A. P. Stewart he was a private in Colonel Ward's regiment, camped at Liberty. In a letter dated March 23, 1914, he writes:

I was a boy then—had been in the war a good while before, but had never regularly enlisted until Morgan settled down in Liberty. Our quarters for the winter were near where the pike runs through between the creek and the hillside, forming a covered road [Allen's Bluff]. We were just north of the road that runs toward Woodbury, and my regiment guarded that road. We also scouted toward Auburn and Alexandria; and on one occasion Colonel Ward took us over to near Carthage, where we captured a big wagon train and a large escort of guards. All the prisoners we marched through Liberty to the rear.

Rosecrans was stationed at Murfreesboro, and General Wilder was one of our adversaries. With him was Stokes's regiment. The latter, with Wilder's support, made frequent raids upon us. They came out on foraging expeditions and a number of times drove us back to Snow's Hill. Sometimes Federal parties would go out on the Woodbury Pike to McMinnville. Then we would intercept the raiders by marching out from Liberty and threatening the rear, when they would get back toward Murfreesboro. My company was often made to picket the Woodbury [Clear Fork] Road. One day our base was near the house of a man who seemed to have two hundred chickens. He looked as surly as a snarling cur. His folks were in the Yankee army, and he was no doubt a home guard. We tried to buy some of his chickens, but he would not sell. Anyhow, the boys captured twenty-five and hid them. The officers found it out, and we had to carry them back. He refused even to give us one or two!

We got the wife of one of Stokes's cavalry to wash our clothes and cook our rations. We made a contract with her that if we captured her husband we would treat him kindly if she promised she would make him be kind if he captured us. She agreed. But after the war Favor Cason told me it was fortunate that we did not fall into that fellow's hands, as he was a cutthroat. I have forgotten his name.

Together with my brother, I called on Mrs. W. B. Stokes, and she treated us kindly.

All of these raids were made by General Wilder, but Stokes's cavalry was usually with him.

While at Liberty the battle of Milton came off, Captain Cossett, of my company, being killed by my side. *He was under arrest for writing a letter to President Davis asking for a pass to slip into the Federal lines and kill Abe Lincoln,* but, securing weapons, went into the fight.*

The battle of Milton took place March 20, 1863. Early that morning Morgan's men at Liberty were notified to hasten toward Milton and attack Colonel Hall, who had already driven the Confederate outposts to within a few miles of Liberty. All was excitement. The pike from the village was crowded with horsemen,

---

*All Americans have heard of the assassination of President Lincoln by John Wilkes Booth, the actor. Few have heard that it was meditated two years previously by a soldier in camp at Liberty. Were Booth and Captain Cossett rendered insane by brooding over the war and its havoc?

first in a gallop, then in a wild dash toward Auburn. Many horses fell, but the Confederates passed through Auburn amid cheers and waving of handkerchiefs by the citizens. Colonel Hall retreated, but was overtaken and forced to fight; then came the pop of small arms, the roar of cannon, and the yells of the contestants. The battle was stubborn and long. It lasted three hours, the Confederate loss being about three hundred. Morgan's ammunition gave out, and he had to withdraw. The Federals went back to Murfreesboro, the Confederates to Liberty. Captains Cossett, Cooper, Sale, and Marr were killed.

When Morgan reached Liberty with his two thousand cavalry the citizens looked on a sight they would always remember—the dead cavalrymen tied on horses and the dead artillerymen strapped on the caisson and gun carriages.

The St. Louis writer to the *Confederate Veteran*, R. L. Thompson, mentioned a while ago, was a soldier at Liberty at this time. In his article he says of the battle of Milton: "While in camp at Liberty I remember one morning about two o'clock, while the cold rain was pouring down, Cooper the bugler gave the boots and saddle call quick and lively. At the same time Johnson's pickets were hotly engaged on the Murfreesboro Pike. We went briskly toward the sounds of the guns and continued to go until we reached the town of Milton. There we found General Morgan with a part of his force in battle with Federal infantry. Two batteries were engaged in a duel when we arrived. As soon as our regiment put in its appearance the Federal battery began firing on our column. . . . One shell stopped at our feet, and Comrade Judge emptied his canteen of water on it, extinguishing the fuse. We dismounted and entered a large cedar thicket, the ground being covered with large rock which sheltered us from bullets. When the battle ceased we withdrew, bringing the dead and wounded away, all that we could find, on our horses, the dead tied on. The battery removed its killed and wounded in the same way, the dead strapped on the caisson and gun carriages."

The writer recalls this scene of the dead soldiers. The day was cool and cloudy. The main street was then about where W. L. Vick's business house stood in 1814. At this point the command halted. Some of the wagons with the dead were near the yard fence of the writer's home.

A former DeKalb Countian and a gentleman of veracity writes: "An incident of the Milton fight I remember very distinctly. I was then at Sligo Ferry, a small boy. My father had been paroled and had taken his family to Sligo. Captain Ragen, of Morgan's command, was sick at our house. Learning of the probable fighting at Milton, he went to his command against my mother's protest. Leaving one day, he was killed the next. I presume he was one of the dead men brought through Liberty tied on horses. Another incident: The Kentuckians at one time were camped in the woods on our place at Sligo. They had no tents. One mess, sleeping behind a log, were, with the exception of one man, killed by a falling tree. All were buried at Sligo. My mother took their trinkets and forwarded the same to their relatives. Afterwards their remains were removed, I think, to Versailles, Ky. About eight years ago I was on a train going from Louisville to Chicago and met a very handsome gentleman, finely dressed and prosperous-looking. I cannot now recall his name, but in the course of conversation I learned that he was the soldier who escaped death from the falling tree. He had been hurt, but not seriously."

CHAPTER XIX.

Personal Experiences.

During the winter and spring of 1863 the Federals advanced three times in heavy force against Liberty—cavalry, infantry, and artillery. On these occasions the noncombatants went in droves to the hills northwest of town for protection, stopping either at the home of John Bethel or that of Thomas Richardson. From Bethel's the movements of the troops could be seen. If the Confederates were beaten and pushed back on Snow's Hill, they often followed the pursuers when the latter retired.

While all this was occurring Allison's Squadron frequently took part. Not infrequently it was engaged alone with the enemy. James H. Burton, of the squadron, relates this experience: "On one occasion a part of the battalion was camped in the beech grove near Daniel Smith's, just north of Liberty—about seventy-five men, portions of the three companies. Lieut. D. Brien was in command of the picket guard of ten men. He placed a vidette at the corner of the two streets, where stood the storehouse of William Vick that was burned. The picket guard were all the troops whose horses were saddled, when a stranger came along with a wounded horse and told us that a large force of Federals had fired on him at the forks of the pike, two miles west of Liberty. The guard went to meet them and did meet them not far from Salem Church. We fired a volley, and then the race back through the village and toward Snow's Hill began. All the guard had an even start, but by the time I reached Leonard Moore's (about the center of Liberty) I was at least seventy-five yards ahead and constantly gaining. I soon made the turn down the main street and heard no more bullets. When the Yankees began shooting down the main street I had made the turn for the bridge. Keeping the advantage to the end, I beat the other guards about one hundred yards. The boys guyed me for leaving them. I resented this, when Colonel Allison said he saw the race from start to finish and that I came out ahead only because I had the best horse."

Mr. Burton adds: "When the picket guard reached the command north of Daniel Smith's, the boys were mounted, and a running fight occurred to Dry Creek bridge. Here Company C, under Capt. R. V. Wright, stopped and waited for the Federals, then fired when they came up, checking them for a short time. At the Stanford home Company B, under Captain Reece, was left on the south side of the pike. His men, when the Federals approached, fired again, checking them the second time. Company A was left behind Asbury Church, and it held the enemy back till our company wagons, loaded with bacon, got well up Snow's Hill. The bacon was what we were fighting for. One of our men, Tom Coleman, was slightly wounded in the foot by a spent ball. In the skirmish at Dry Creek bridge Lieut. D. Brien's horse got away from him. He could not be caught, and, seeing the Federals would get the animal, Brien ordered the men to shoot him. At Stanford's place a good roan horse came into our lines, and Lieutenant Brien got him. He had blood on the saddle and a Spencer rifle and belt of cartridges on the saddle horn. There were seventy-five men all told on our side, and fifteen hundred Federals. They thought we were the advance guard of Morgan's Cavalry. If they had known our real strength, they would have made short work of us. I never knew till I came to Arkansas that we hit any of the enemy, when Frank Dowell told me they used his barn for a hospital; that four died, and he thought four more died later. Dowell lived near the Dry Creek bridge."

A considerable fight came off near the intersection of the Murfreesboro and Lebanon roads, or the forks of the pikes. Lieut. Ed Reece, who took part, tells this incident in connection with the affair: Capt. Jack Reece's company of Allison's Squadron, which usually camped near Alexandria, left the camps on Helton Creek, going west toward Wilson County. They were scouting for Yankees. None being discovered, they made a fierce attack on John Barleycorn, intrenched at Isaac Smith's stillhouse, on the road leading north from the present store or post office called Mahone. Turning back toward Alexandria directly, they learned of an engagement going on near the forks of the pike and galloped in that direction. Reaching the scene of battle, Captain Reece and his troopers took a position in the woods and awaited orders. While there Colonel Allison and the remainder of the squadron arrived.

"Captain Reece," said Allison, "you have no business here. Withdraw your company." "Colonel Allison," was the reply [Captain Reece feeling the stimulus yet over the victory of John Barleycorn], "Company B will remain where it is." "Captain Reece, you are drunk," asserted Allison. "Colonel Allison," snapped Reece, "you're a damned liar."

At this the two urged their horses nearer each other and on horseback engaged in a savage fist-and-skull battle. When both were nearly out of breath, and it was forced upon all that their energies were needed against the common enemy, comrades interfered.

Isaiah White was in this skirmish, and he says the Federals and Confederates were so near each other that he recognized acquaintances on the Federal side—Captain Hathaway, Colonel Blackburn, and others. H. L. Hale, recalling boyish memories of these occasions, says that there were times, as the Confederates were pushed back stubbornly through Liberty and north toward Snow's Hill, when the opposing forces were only a few hundred yards apart. Part of Stokes's Regiment was advancing one day, and he saw Miss Mattie Hathaway run out to the front gate and speak a few words to her sweetheart, Capt. W. L. Hathaway, while bullets were whizzing around them.

Skirmishes were so frequent that comparatively slight disturbances would put the citizens and soldiers in commotion. About sunset on one occasion a tremendous roar, somewhat resembling the roll of thunder, was heard westward. Confederates at supper in the writer's home hastened to the street. The sound grew louder as the moments passed. The mystery was soon solved. A Federal wagon train had been captured, and the captors were forcing the teamsters to drive their fastest. This may have been the train mentioned elsewhere by Lieutenant Ridley. It proved a rich haul. That evening boxes were opened and the Confederates' hosts and hostesses given many fine presents.

The following notes may be of interest, some of them being illuminative of village life during war times:

In January, 1863, Maj. J. P. Austin and Capt. William Roberts, Confederates, with fifty men, left Liberty for the Andrew Jackson home to capture a squad of Federal couriers stationed there. Passing through Alexandria, then between Lebanon and Baird's Mills, they reached the Hermitage by midnight. The couriers having left, Morgan's men repaired to Lavergne, where, finding the enemy barricaded in a log house, they captured the latter, thirteen in number, and carried them to Liberty. By the way, during the time Morgan's men were in the county, says General Duke, they captured more Federals than there were effective men in Morgan's command.

In a sharp fight at Lavergne between DeKalb Federals and a force of Confederates Charley Blackburn, brother of Col. Joe Blackburn, was killed.

There were a number of tragedies in the county. Sim Adamson, who had been in the Confederate army, was killed near Alexandria. Mon Adkins, a Union soldier, was killed by Capt. Jack Garrison, at the latter's home, near Forks-of-the-Pike, at the close of the war. James Hays, a young man, and Mr. Bullard, an aged citizen, were brought to Liberty by Federals, tried by court-martial, and shot. A Confederate soldier was killed in a field near Salem Church. The killing of several Union soldiers at Smithville by Pomp Kersey's raiders is mentioned in this work. A Confederate prisoner named Parrish was killed one night in Alexandria by the Federal soldier guarding him. While conscripting to recruit Allison's Squadron at Alexandria John Bowman was slain.

Sometimes when the Confederates would chase the Federals out of Liberty it was a good opportunity for the wives of secessionists to get together and rejoice in secret. There was one lady, Polly Hayes Knight, who lived three or four miles away, truly a feminine fire-eater, and who frequently came to the writer's home with no other object, as she said, than to "indulge in a big laugh over some unhappy defeat of the Yanks." The stories she told and the laughter she and her listeners indulged in were really refreshing. One day while there Mrs. "Puss" Turner, the wife of a Unionist and one of the sweetest of the neighbor women, came in.

"I was passing the house of Spicy Combs just now," she said. [Spicy was the wife of a rather sorry Federal soldier named Bill Holly, but was always called by her former husband's name.] "She called me in to taste some sweet cakes she had just baked." "And you found them very crisp and nice?" she was asked. "I will let you say," said she, "when I tell you that I could have put my toe on the edge of one of those cakes and stretched the other side to the overhead ceiling."*

During the stay of Morgan's men at Liberty, Quirk's Scouts especially made friends with both Union and Confederate sympathizers. While snow was on the ground the soldiers would encourage the village lads to engage in cob battles and greatly enjoyed them. With Morgan's troops was a seventeen-year-old youth named John A. Wyeth. He is to-day one of the leading physicians and surgeons of New York and author of the finest life yet written of General Forrest. The writer of these annals recalls one Federal soldier whom the three boys in his home learned to love—Joe Baker, probably with a regiment of Kentuckians. He was kind-hearted and loved nothing better than to romp with the children. A well-remembered Kentucky Confederate trooper of Morgan's command was Jeff Citizen, who was bibulous. When drinking he disported on his calico mule and sang continuously and unmusically:

---

*Was there at any time during the war a United States, Confederate States, or Tennessee statute or license providing for something in the nature of trial or special marriages for the soldiers? As a small lad the writer heard such a thing discussed at Liberty, and there was a mutual-consent contract of the kind there between a soldier from another State and a widow. They cohabited about six months, when the soldier was called to some other section. The marriage thus annulled by mutual consent, the woman some months later married another man according to the conventional law. This is not a dream; others remember the facts.

> I lay ten dollars down,
>   And bet them every one,
> That every time we have a fight
> The Yankees they will run.

Mr. B. G. Slaughter, formerly of Quirk's Confederate scouts, but after the war editor of the Winchester (Tenn.) *Home Journal,* wrote W. L. Vick in 1902, something of the scouts' stay in Liberty. He says that Captain Quirk had headquarters in the Methodist church, and his men were quartered near, taking meals with the villagers, Union and secession.* He recalled his own host's family, "a gentle wife and daughter and peaceful-faced old gentleman, who had a son-in-law in Stokes's Cavalry." Mr. Slaughter adds: "On one occasion we were on scout toward Murfreesboro—I think to a point about three miles from Liberty. We had just gone down a long slant through a wooded country to a branch emptying into Smith Fork (which flowed parallel with the pike). The bridge over the branch had been washed out, or else the floor had been removed by the Federals that morning as a trap should they force us to retreat. The place was a deep gulch. We had to take a stock path above the bridge to cross and get back to the pike. We had not gone far—little more than a mile—when we reached a glade to our right, where a dirt road intersected the pike at right angles, though pointing from us. Just beyond this

---

*The writer of this history remembers having been often aroused from slumber by the songs of the scouts—Jim McGowdy, Bill McCreary, and others—singing "Lorena" or "Tenting on the Old Camp Ground." They were a jovial set.

Captain Quirk called a consultation. It was decided that the Yankees were 'laying' for us, a larger force than ours. He called me by my camp name, 'Squirrel,' and ordered me to go back to camp and bring all our men fit for duty, cautioning me that the Yankees might cut me off just ahead. With a dash I began the daring ride. At the intersection of the dirt road and pike I saw two bluecoats under spur to cut me off. They commanded me to halt, but I went down the pike, the enemy in pursuit. They were no doubt confident of capturing me at the floorless bridge. They were gaining ground; but with a firm, steady pull old sorrel Charley cleared the breach, a distance of nearly twenty feet and deep enough to have killed rider and horse. The animal did not make a check on the other side. With a loud cheer and a parting shot I soon left the pursuers."

The bridge mentioned was probably near the present residence of Grant Roy, the county surveyor.

Alexandria did not escape the excitement of the times. Besides the encampment of local soldiers, General Wheeler, General Wharton, Colonel Smith, and Colonel Harrison (of the Eighth Texas) were familiar in that and the surrounding communities. They were camped on the various roads—Carthage, Statesville, Lebanon, and Murfreesboro. It was from Alexandria that General Morgan started on his famous raid through Ohio and Indiana.

Sometime during the war an old Scotch word "skedaddle," which was applied to milk spilt over the pail in carrying it, was made to take on a new meaning.

The Northern papers said the Southern forces were skedaddled by the Federals. The word soon became common. Many rich stories were told of how the DeKalb County noncombatants would flee from their homes when the enemy dashed suddenly into a community. Perhaps one of the best is that in which Hon. Horace A. Overall figured. A number of skedaddlers on a very cold night were sleeping in a barn at the head of one of the Clear Fork hollows, among them a rather simple-minded man. This man about midnight awoke his comrades with the startling news that the Yankees were coming. "How do you know its Yankees?" he was asked. "Because I hear Patsy Spurlock's dogs barkin' down the branch," was the reply. "But before I take the bitter cold," said Overall, crawling back into the hay, "you'll have to convince me that Patsy Spurlock's dogs won't bark at anything but Yankees."

The following, contributed to a newspaper some years ago by the writer, has to do with a very small lad's memories of the time that tried the soul:

It does not appear now that war times in our village were so unpleasant. But at moments the childish heart must have been filled with fear. I remember the sudden dash of soldiers into the village now and then, the popping reports, the scampering to a hiding place by noncombatants. One late afternoon some Confederates took the village, but all I remember of that occasion is that one of the men entered Joe Blackburn's stable and took out a fine stallion. On another afternoon old Mr. Bullard was executed east of the steam mill, and four Federals, ahold of his hands and feet, brought him up the street. I noted that his hair hung down and his coat tail dragged on the ground. There was a night when we were awakened by excited citizens on the street. Some one explained that "Uncle Ben Blades has been killed in his own house and is swelling badly." My mother told the informant to put a small bag of salt on his stomach, and it would prevent swelling. Jim Clark, a youth, had been killed on another occasion by Pomp Kersey's men. Often that day I looked across the fields toward his home, saw the crowd of sympathizing friends gathered before his burial, and wondered how he looked and how his father comported himself. General Wilder's men burned a storehouse in the village. Doubtless there was fear in many hearts, but I only noticed how black the smoke was that bulged out of the chimney. Then when he burned the big mill, and I stood looking out the south window, again I was attracted mainly to the black volume rolling up from the smokestack. I marveled greatly when I saw on the ruins of the store molten glass; that it could be melted was something I had not known. One late summer afternoon an ox team toiled up the village street, stopping in front of the John Hays storehouse, which, like all others, was vacant. Seven or eight dead bodies, piled on the cart like rails, were carried in and laid on the floor—all that was left of Kersey's guerrillas. In one room in our home there were two beds, my father occupying one with the youngest child, Bruce, and my mother the other with two children. Suddenly one midnight the hysterical wife of a Union soldier in night clothes rapped at the door, imploring us to admit her quickly. My mother opened the door, when the woman, in the darkness and while in terror crying that the Rebels had entered the town, jumped into the wrong bed!

CHAPTER XX.

REGULAR AND GUERRILLA WARFARE.

The most important battle in the county took place in the spring of 1863. It seems to have been expected by Morgan's command at Liberty, for the scouts—the eyes of an army—were out all night in the direction of both Auburn and Alexandria.

Burns's Confederate Battery was posted on one of the hillsides east or northeast of the village, where it could be trained on the bridge and turnpike at the northern extremity of the town. At various distances on the turnpike between Liberty and Snow's Hill were stationed forces of Confederates. Allison's Squadron was engaged in this affair, as well as Morgan's command.

After daylight the Federals appeared in force some distance west of the village. They were met by the Second Kentucky and Quirk's Scouts. Charged upon vigorously, the Confederates retreated. It was a miracle that they were able to pass through the covered bridge. It was here that Burns's artillery did good work. As the Confederates choked the bridge, the battery opened up on the Federals swarming out the north end of the village, checking them sufficiently to allow the Confederates to pass through the bridge.

By this time the Federals had from the northwest trained their cannon on their foes, and soon Burns's Battery started for Snow's Hill.

There was a stubborn fight all along the road, and

at last Snow's Hill was reached, where the Confederates made a stand, though not for long. It was soon ascertained that a column of Federals had gone up Dry Creek and out the Manhill road to strike them in the rear and cut them off completely from escape. This road passes by the farm of the widow George Turner, through the Farler hollow, gradually climbs the southern side of Snow's Hill, and intersects with the stage road near the Atwell schoolhouse, east of where the Confederates made their stand.

Discovering the intention of the enemy, Colonel Huffman, with the Third Kentucky Confederates, was sent to check them, but did not reach the gap in time. However, he delayed the advance guard until the troops of Colonel Breckinridge (now retreating) had passed the point where the Union cavalry might have cut them off from Smithville seven miles east.

Lieutenant Ridley, already quoted, says further in his letter: "I recollect well that Snow's Hill fight. General Morgan was at McMinnville that day. The enemy commenced pushing us back about daybreak from the intersection of the Auburn and Alexandria Pike, gradually driving us to Snow's Hill. Our regiment was on the hill, and our troops formed all the way from the hill to the rear of about where Colonel Stokes's residence was. Our artillery was planted on the pike approaching the hill (I believe it was Burns's Battery), and we had an artillery duel for several hours. After a while we were ordered to form a line of battle in the rear of Snow's Hill, on the Dry Creek road. Quirk's Scouts, it seems, were fighting Captain Blackburn, of

Stokes's Cavalry, on that road and falling back on us. The Dry Creek road at that point flanked the hill. As we lay there, two or three other regiments formed behind us, and our orders were, if too heavily pressed, to fire and fall back on these regiments.

"Suddenly we saw the Yankees coming around the hill on the Dry Creek road. Some of the men said it was Joe Blackburn in lead of the cavalry. We fell back on Duke's Regiment, while they fell back on another regiment, so that we were all jumbled up together. Then our stampede began. It was said that some of Stokes's cavalry recognized Captain Petticord in our retreating troops. They had gotten out of ammunition, but we were stampeded like cattle on the prairie, and they dashed along behind us, calling: 'Halt there, Petticord! Halt!' About this time I, with my little pony that couldn't run, and Captain Sisson were about to be captured, when the pony ran into a mudhole. It fell over two or three other horses that had likewise floundered. My mouth was soon full of mud. Captain Sisson had two loads in his navy and fired them at our pursuers, who were also out of ammunition. These were the last shots of the famous stampede, and they stopped the pursuers. Our command moved on to Smithville and from there to McMinnville. All scattered and broken up, we met Duke and Morgan, who rallied us and took us back. The difficulty with us was that Morgan had not been married long and was with that good wife at McMinnville, and our organization was bad.

"We 'seesawed' after this, fought the battle of

Greasy Creek, Ky., and went back to Liberty. It was at Liberty that I got my commission as additional aid to General Stewart."

Several men were killed in this fight and were buried near the old Atwell schoolhouse, on Snow's Hill. Dr. J. A. Fuson, of Dry Creek, turned his dwelling into a hospital and treated the wounded free of charge.

According to General Duke, the Confederates returned to Liberty on April 7, 1863, in obedience to orders from General Wheeler, who had reached Alexandria with Wharton's Division. Two or three days later Wheeler, with a small force, proceeded to Lebanon, where he remained three days. "During that time," to quote Duke, "the enemy advanced once more from Murfreesboro, but retreated before reaching our pickets. Upon our return from Lebanon only a portion of the forces were sent to Alexandria; more than half, under command of General Wheeler, passed through Rome to the immediate vicinity of Carthage. Remaining there during the night, General Wheeler fell back toward Alexandria, reaching that place about 1 or 2 P.M. Wharton's Division was again encamped here, and Morgan's Division, under my command, was sent to Liberty, except Smith's Regiment, which was stationed near Alexandria."

In the latter part of April the First Brigade made headquarters at Alexandria, encamping on the Lebanon Pike and the roads to Carthage and Statesville. The country around Alexandria, Auburn, and Statesville was scouted in every direction, for Federal spies were numerous. On June 10 General Morgan himself arrived at Alexandria, and orders were issued to march the next day. The great raider was about to start from DeKalb County on his expedition into Indiana and Ohio. His fighting in Middle Tennessee was over.

It should be added that while raiding in Indiana and Ohio he was captured. Escaping from prison, he was soon in East Tennessee, reaching Greeneville on September 3, 1864, and making his headquarters at the residence of a Mrs. Williams. About daylight on the 4th some Union soldiers, dashing into town, surprised and killed him. Duke seems to think he was betrayed by Mrs. Williams's daughter-in-law; but Scott and Angel, authors of a history of the Thirteenth East Tennessee Regiment of Union Cavalry, say that a twelve- or thirteen-year-old boy, James Leady, went to Bull's Gap and informed General Gillem of the presence of the Confederates in Greeneville.

Of course the county was still to suffer from the presence of soldiers. In less than a year from the departure of Morgan's Cavalry a corpse was brought to Liberty from White County which told of a disaster to DeKalb Federals. It was that of George C. (Kit) Turney, a very popular young man of the Clear Fork country, who had been serving under Stokes. He was killed February 22, 1864, in the battle of the Calf Killer by White County Confederates.

That battle was really a massacre. Stokes was stationed at Sparta. It is said he had raised the black flag. No quarter was to be given to such men as Champe Ferguson, George Carter, John M. Hughes, W. S.

Bledsoe, Gatewood, and other guerrillas. In February, 1864, he sent out a company to hunt down the guerrillas. Hughes heard of it and mustered a force to attack the Federals, who were commanded by Capt. E. W. Bass. The guerrillas, about forty, hid in ambush in Dry Valley, on the headwaters of the Calf Killer, and fired into Bass's unsuspecting company, killing forty or fifty. The remainder fled to Sparta, probably without firing a shot. One White County gentleman who saw the dead Federals after they were brought in says that thirty-eight were shot through the head and three had been killed with stones. Among the names of the slain, besides Kit Turney, were Ben Fuston, Jim Fuston, Henry Hendrixon, Jerry Hendrixon, David Grandstaff, J. B. Moore, David A. Farmer, Joseph Hail, Jonathan Jones, T. J. Pistole, and Alex Stanley, all of DeKalb County. So, unaware, these men had ridden into the jaws of death, into the mouth of hell. The roadside blazed, there was a deafening volley, and men in blue began tumbling from their horses. The scene in that wild region must have been strikingly weird. The sharp, cruel cracks of pistols and their infinitely multiplied reverberations from mountain to valley (the cries of the dying blended with the metallic clanging of the hoofs of scampering and riderless horses) could never have passed out of the memory of the survivors. James H. Overall stated to the writer that one Federal, Russel Gan, fell on the field, and, playing dead, afterwards hid in a hollow log and escaped after nightfall.

In the autumn of 1864 Gen. Joseph Wheeler, returning southward from his raid into East Tennessee, passed through Liberty and Alexandria and on toward Nashville. He had started from Georgia with four thousand cavalry and four cannons. While in East Tennessee he sent Gen. "Cerro Gordo" Williams, with two thousand men and two cannons, to capture the Federal garrison at Strawberry Plains. With General Williams was Allison's squadron of DeKalb Countians. Williams found the garrison too strong to attack and attempted to overtake Wheeler, but failed. Wheeler came to Sparta, having General Dibrell's regiment with him. Dibrell was left at Sparta two days, while Wheeler took McMinnville and, reaching Liberty, captured the stockade, which had been deserted on his approach. Reaching Nashville, he kept the Federals uneasy for some days, then marched south. In his report he said he did not have a man or any material captured. It is alleged that Wiley Odum, of Cherry Valley, was the first of Wheeler's men to enter Liberty on that raid.

Two or three days after General Wheeler passed Gen. "Cerro Gordo" Williams, Dibrell's cavalry, and Champe Ferguson's guerrillas came through, Ferguson bringing up the rear. The inhabitants along the turnpike dreaded Ferguson, especially the Liberty people. This town was the home of Stokes, Blackburn, Hathaway, and Garrison. He burned James Lamberson's barn and thresher at Liberty for some cause. On the pike west of the village he met W. G. Evans, C. W. L. Hale, William Vick, and William Ford, who had been to bury a neighbor, Mrs. John Bratten. The guerrillas asked where they had been. The reply would have been satisfactory if Mr. Evans had not added: "We also buried an unknown Confederate soldier in Lamberson's field, where he had been shot by two DeKalb County Federals." The guerrillas then asked if there was a Union man in the crowd; if so, he should be killed in retaliation. Mr. Ford, a man of the highest character and most harmless disposition, was the only one; but his neighbors pleaded so earnestly for him that he was spared.

James H. Fite, formerly a trustee of DeKalb County, but now residing in Anthony, Kans., was a sixteen-year-old private in Capt. Jack Garrison's company of Federals. His home was on the pike a mile and a half west of Liberty. Of some of his experiences, he writes:

Our regiment, the First Tennessee Mounted Infantry, was mustered in at Carthage early in 1864. About May the different companies were sent to various portions of the State for garrison duty and scouting after Champe Ferguson and other guerrillas. A good part of my company (G) was from Liberty and vicinity, the officers having been a part of Stokes's regiment. We were first sent to Granville, above Carthage, on the river, to build a stockade, and then to Liberty to build another, our force numbering seventy-five or one hundred men. The latter was well started when about the first of September, late in the afternoon, Wheeler's cavalry took us by surprise, and like a covey of birds we were scattered.

A week or so prior to this Gen. H. P. Van Cleve, at Murfreesboro, sent word to our officers that Wheeler was reported coming through Sequatchie Valley and suggested to them to scout in that direction and see if the news was correct. Instead of doing that they selected about twenty of us and went through Lebanon and by Cedar Glade and Cainsville. We returned to Liberty about two hours before Wheeler came upon us from the direction of Smithville. It was a complete surprise, and the result was a route. There was considerable firing; and, while nobody was killed, they captured something like a dozen of our boys.

My horse had given out on the expedition into Wilson County, and I was riding one belonging to a member of Stokes's regiment. In returning to Liberty I stopped at my mother's, just west of that village, to get supper. She prepared a sort of feast, setting the table on the front porch. I recall the big peach cobbler. I had finished supper when T. G. Bratten stopped at the gate and told me that they were fighting in town and suggested that we ride down and take part. As I had no horse, he went alone. He returned in a gallop shortly, calling to me that the Confederates were coming. I watched for the advance guard, soon seeing four about three hundred yards away, and retreated in fairly good order to a plum thicket back of the house. The Johnnies rode into the yard. Having brother to hold their horses, they ate supper. Mother said one of them, finishing first, walked to the back door, and she expected every moment that I would shoot him, though I would never have killed one from the bushes. I am glad to this day I did not, for that Confederate too had a mother somewhere waiting for his return.

About sunset quite a bunch came by and stopped. Their officer proved to be a relative of ours. He asked for a pillow for a wounded man, mother taking it to the gate. They had already taken a buggy from a neighbor. When asked who was in command, the officer said, "Wheeler," adding that the force was ten thousand strong and would be a week in passing. In the night I went to the house; and, learning that the Confederates were under Wheeler, I was relieved. The impression was that they were Ferguson's guerillas, and I knew I would be murdered if caught by them.

The next day I found a hiding place, a thicket back of the

field, and had a narrow escape. Some Confederates came down to the creek very close to me, and a number went swimming. Others were as thick as blackbirds in Eli Vick's cornfield, just across the creek. While some were at the house eating, a soldier went up and said that they had killed a Yankee back of the field. It was supposed that some one in the neighborhood told him to say that before mother, believing that she in her emotion would give me away. My little brother, Robert, whispered to her to be quiet, and he would go and see if anybody was killed. When within thirty yards of me a Confederate asked where he was going. His reply was that he was hunting where the hogs had been getting into the field. My brother soon found me and reassured mother. Truly the mothers, daughters, sisters, and sweethearts deserve as much honor as any of the soldiers.

After Wheeler passed through, our men got together again and finished the stockade. I think we could have kept off quite a force now, unless the attacking party had had cannon. We were at the stockade when the battle of Nashville took place between Hood and Thomas. We expected an attack from Forrest, but I'm thankful he never came. Only sixteen, I did not have sense enough at that age to be scared. I have seen older men have ague when they expected an attack.

Stragglers from Wheeler's command depredated on the farms near the turnpike. In this way Thomas Givan, on Clear Fork, lost five fine mares. All the horses on Eli Vick's farm were carried off. Many other citizens suffered losses.

General Williams, as remarked, never overtook Wheeler. On the way he camped at Alexandria, where the troops of Allison's Squadron had an opportunity to meet their families and friends. Reaching a point in Rutherford County, he went eastward on the Woodbury Pike, where he had a considerable fight with the Federals. Later on he reached Saltville, Va., where the guerrilla, Capt. George Carter, a leading spirit of the battle of the Calf Killer some months previous, was killed October 2, 1864. Carter's slayer was recognized and his body riddled with balls.

The war had demoralized both Federals and Confederates. Many young men of excellent families throughout the South and Tennessee became enamored of the spirit of adventure, as shown in the daring and reckless exploits of cavalry raiders. This is how, perhaps, Pomp Kersey's small company came into existence.

Kersey had been a private in Capt. L. N. Savage's DeKalb County company of the Sixteenth Confederate Regiment. Returning home, he for some reason did not go back to his command, but remained on Short Mountain, where he collected a band of ten or fifteen fellow adventurers. Some of them had not reached their majority. A leading business man of Nashville writes: "Those men were run from home by Stokes's troops, some of them being no more than sixteen years of age. I knew several of Kersey's men. One of them was between fifteen or sixteen. He afterwards got into the regular Confederate army and died about 1910, a prominent and respected citizen of White County."

The writer was very young when the band made raids into Liberty, and he regarded its members with prejudice from the fact that they took valuables from William Vick and James Fuston. But another business man of Nashville, who was reared in Smithville, writes: "If they robbed anybody, it was because they thought he was a Union sympathizer, and pillaging the enemy was not regarded as robbery. Regular Federals and Confederates did that."

This same gentleman relates an incident that took place in Smithville during the war. "One day," he says, "there gathered in the northern part of the town a squad of men belonging to Company F, Blackburn's Regiment, to secure Federal recruits—Ras Foster, 'Black Bill' Foster, Jim Eastham, Pal Rigsby, John Colwell, and others. Suddenly Kersey's men dashed into town, stampeding the recruiters. Eastham killed a horse trying to get away, while eight of the Federals were killed, among them Rigsby and Colwell." Another DeKalb Countian says: "The Rebel citizens of Smithville were pleased over this raid, for they had much to bear. I recall how a Federal was pursuing a citizen through mischief, shooting and pretending to want to kill him, when the man's little son at the window suggested a new sort of military tactics, for he cried out: 'Run crooked, pap, run crooked, an' maybe the bullets will miss you!'"

As indicated, the Short Mountain men often entered Liberty at night. On one of their raids they surrounded the home of Squire Ben Blades, a pioneer and good citizen of Union sympathies, about midnight. He tried to escape out a back door, but a shot fired through the door killed him almost instantly. After this the citizens armed themselves, resolved on defense; but the raiders did not appear while they were on watch.

On the evening of July 23, 1864, there was a dance

on Canal Creek at the home of Mr. Dennis. A number of Federals were attending—Captain Hathaway, Lieut. Thomas G. Bratten, Henry Blackburn, and a man named Parrish. Dr. Shields, of Smithville, was also there. Later in the night Louis Lyles and James Clarke made their appearance. Clarke, a mere youth, had on a Federal uniform, but was not a soldier.

None seemed to apprehend danger. The fiddlers played and "called the figures," and the house rocked to the rough dances of the time.

Kersey's men got word of the ball and the Federals' presence and, about fifteen in all, came from Short Mountain to exterminate the men in blue. It appears that when Lyles and Clarke arrived with shouting and shooting from down the creek the band, who were near, withdrew, thereby putting off the attack.

Tired out at last, Hathaway had gone to sleep in a room adjoining that of the merry-makers. Bratten was sitting with a young lady on the stairway. It was far in the night, but the buzz of conversation went on. Two or three soldiers were preparing to mount their horses when suddenly the hills resounded to the reports of guns and the wild shouts of Kersey's men. Bratten and Lyles reached their horses, but the former had forgotten his gun. As he rushed back for it he discovered the enemy in the yard, shooting. As they passed the door he fired, somewhat checking them. The girls were trying to awaken Hathaway; and, calling out that the bushwhackers were on them, Bratten got on his horse and dashed away.

The scene was now one of confusion. Hathaway

had mounted his horse, Blackhawk, a fine animal that could pace a mile in 2:30, but not before the assailants had started in pursuit of his comrades. Nevertheless, he resolved to overtake and pass the pursuers. Clarke had been overtaken. Seeing that he could not escape, he dismounted and from a sheltering tree trunk emptied his pistols at the enemy. He was soon killed. While this was going on Hathaway swept by. "I've just come through hell!" he said.

The Federals were pursued no farther after the killing of Clarke. Hastening to Liberty, they later in the day, with twelve men, set out to overtake Kersey and his band. Stealthily approaching a thicket half a mile south of Half Acre, they found Kersey's horses haltered and a part of his men asleep. A volley was poured into the slumberers. One of them, untouched, ran down the mountain and escaped. Pomp Kersey was also unhurt and mounted his horse, but could not untie the halter. Bratten put his gun against him, but it only snapped; whereupon Kersey dismounted, but in trying to get away he was killed by Bratten and Hathaway. Another man, perhaps twenty years of age, tried to escape, but was slain by Hathaway and Dan Gan. Five had been killed at the first volley.

Among the slain were Pomp Kersey, Jack Neely, two Arnold brothers from Murfreesboro, a man named Seats, Benton, Kelly, and one other. It seems that two who slept some distance from the others escaped— Ike Gleason, later of White County, and a man of the name of Hawkins, who was some years later a citizen of Oklahoma.

The seven bodies were hauled to Liberty on an ox wagon, reaching the village about sunset on July 24. Thrown into a vacant storeroom, they were the next day buried on the Daniel Smith farm, about one hundred yards from the town bridge. Their remains were exhumed after the war by friends and relatives and carried to their respective neighborhoods and buried. The Arnold brothers, who were regular soldiers, but cut off from their command, were reinterred in the Confederate Cemetery at Murfreesboro.

By and by fighting ceased throughout the county, though the Federal blue was still in evidence. That period in the writer's memory is blurred and hazy. But one scene stands out clearly—that of his father, C. W. L. Hale, who was an excellent reader, standing in the midst of a group of villagers, Union and Southern in their sympathies, with a Nashville newspaper in his hand. It must have been April 16 or 17, 1865. The late afternoon was cool and damp, but not gloomier than the upturned faces. The Southern sympathizers were filled with dread; the others with sorrow. They were listening to the earliest news they could get of the assassination of Lincoln.

CHAPTER XXI.

PEACE AND THE AFTERMATH.

WHEN peace came in April, 1865, there was a feeling of relief to the people at home, not entirely unmixed, however, with dread. It was not supposable that neighbors who had been at war so long would dwell together without friction. War makes us brutal in action, while as it continues morality retrogresses. In a measure the people who sympathized with the South in the great struggle expected the triumphant Unionists to be overbearing, and this was the case in a few instances. It is to the credit of the Northern sympathizers that hundreds of them seemed ready to encourage peace and amity. Not only was there a conservative faction with the successful side which did everything possible to restore good will, but it was not long before ex-Federal soldiers became the most loyal patrons of those merchants who had been loyal to the Confederacy. Such men as Joseph Clarke—there were a number in the county—often risked life that the returned ex-Confederates might have justice.

There were here and there a few men who, having become desperate through war's carnage, were slow to yield to the influences of peace. When inflamed by strong drink they were especially hostile. So it was that, following the war, there was here and there a killing, while some feuds developed. It is possible, human nature being the same, that there would have been among the Southern sympathizers an element just as lawless and overbearing had the cause of the South succeeded.

It would have been wonderful had the noncombatants living in the villages shown no antagonism toward each other occasionally while the war was going on. Even the women now and then took sides. One day the children of two ladies of opposite sentiments were scrapping. The parents of each passed a few words. Said the one of less refinement: "The children of no old 'secesh' can run over mine." "And who are *you?*" asked the "secesh" with some scorn. The answer was long-drawn-out and smacked of much pride: "I'm a U-U-U-Union woman."

As a rule, however, neighbors got along well. The Southern "skedaddlers" frequently found a safe refuge in the homes of Unionists in the country. The writer takes this opportunity to say that, though his parents were Southern in sympathy, they were never molested by Stokes, Blackburn, or Hathaway; but, on the other hand, were treated with great respect. Colonel Blackburn one night was seen passing through the yard spying while the village was filled with Confederates. He was not reported—he was "a neighbor's boy"—and went his way safely, as he knew he would.

Peace brought with it a new aspect to occasions like elections. The freed negroes gathered by hundreds in the towns. In vividness the scenes return to-day—old blacks like Ike Lamberson, with competitors, selling cider and ginger cake, others vending melons, and all noisy and happy over their liberation. If there was any violence on their part, it is not recalled. There was a kindly feeling on the part of ex-slaves for their "white folks," and numerous families did not leave their old quarters for some years.

As the soldiers swore mightily in Flanders, so there was in DeKalb much drinking and fighting, particularly on Saturdays and on election days. When the Loyal League, an order composed mainly of negroes, was formed, it was regarded as a menace to the safety of society, and many whites began to view the freedman with disfavor. The Ku-Klux Klan was organized, and it soon had the blacks terrorized. No member of the order was ever convicted in Tennessee. One indictment at least was found in DeKalb County, and two cases of whippings occurred. There were at one time half a million members in the South. The order was formed in Pulaski, Tenn., in the summer of 1866 and was disbanded in March, 1869. Its name continued to be used by unknown organizations, and alleged "Ku-Klux outrages" were reported as late as 1872. Governor Brownlow in 1868 called out the militia to suppress the order, many DeKalb Countians becoming militiamen.

Tennessee was readmitted to the Union in July, 1865. Prior to that (April 5) William G. Brownlow was inaugurated Governor of the State. The legislature, in session that month, practically disfranchised all those voters who had not been Union men. In 1866 the negroes were given the right to vote by the Brownlow legislature, made up of Radicals and Conservatives, the former in favor of very harsh laws toward the ex-Rebels, the latter (who had always been

Union men) in favor of milder treatment. There was a "split," and the two wings, or factions, became very bitter toward each other. In February, 1869, Governor Brownlow was elected to the United States Senate, the Speaker of the State Senate, D. W. C. Senter, becoming Governor. In the same year Governor Senter was a candidate for election, nominated by the Conservatives. William B. Stokes was nominated by the Radicals.

There was an exciting joint canvass. Both candidates were excellent speakers, Stokes, the "Bald Eagle," being the better under normal conditions. They spoke in DeKalb County in their itinerary. Reaching Liberty, Stokes had luncheon at the home of his brother-in-law, C. W. L. Hale, a Southern sympathizer. In the afternoon the contestants held forth in a grove near where the Murfreesboro road intersects the Lebanon and Sparta Turnpike. The audience was large and somewhat boisterous, but order was good.

Meantime plans had been put on foot to insure the "Bald Eagle's" defeat. At the time of the contest the Confederate element was led by Gen. John C. Brown. His followers offered to support Senter if the latter should allow them to vote. He agreed. The vote on election day stood: For Senter, 120,234; for Stokes, only 55,046.

The legislature was Democratic in both branches and met October 4, 1869. Thus the Democratic party regained ascendancy in about four years after the close of the war.

Then came the convention, in 1870, to form a new

Constitution—the one which exists at present. The delegate from DeKalb County was Col. J. H. Blackburn, as previously stated.

The people by a four years' war were placed as the pioneers were—they had to begin over to establish themselves socially and materially. In depicting their makeshifts and customs one but depicts the makeshifts and customs of the grandparents to a large extent, and it is profitable and illuminative to sketch these rather in detail.

Boots were almost wholly worn by men. The custom prolonged the life of the serviceable bootjack, once familiar in all homes. There were no screened windows. Wherefore the house fly was a greater nuisance than now—that is, if he was as prone to load himself down with disease germs as he is to-day. The foreparents knew a thing or two, however, and used a "fly broom" in the dining room. Some of these brooms were things of beauty. An elderly lady named Grandstaff lived on Dismal Creek, and her handiwork was so artistic as to give local prestige to a stream even so wretchedly named as that. The brush of her fly brooms was made of the tail feathers of peacocks; while the handle, some four feet long, was covered with the plaited white quills of the same bird. It was gorgeous and must have cost several dollars.

In the village and country back yards the homely ash hopper was a familiar object—made usually of a barrel, each end knocked out, and set on a slightly inclined platform. It was filled with wood ashes, through which a few bucketfuls of water were allowed to seep. The product was lye, and the product of lye and meat rinds and bones boiled together was an excellent quality of soft soap. By the way, the ash hopper was the *bete noir* of the head of the house. The springtime was not a sweet time to him until the ash hopper had been made and filled. Somehow he dreaded the task, and it is little wonder that a member of his tribe perpetrated this: "The hardest things that come up in a man's life are building the spring ash hopper and cutting summer stove wood."

Another feature of the back yard was the dye pot. The foremothers made much—almost all—of the family's wearing apparel, as well as their carpets, necessitating the cards for carding wool, the spinning wheel, the reel, the winding blades, and the loom. All of these, excepting the hand cards, were homemade. To give the cloth, or thread, or "chain," for the carpet the desired color, it was put into the dye pot. Dyeing materials were logwood, cochineal, indigo, madder, and copperas. Blue-mixed jeans was regarded the most suitable for men's suits. A kind of jeans was woven especially for vests, or "weskets," with red or yellow stripes, and sometimes red, yellow, and blue stripes occurred in the same piece. The writer during the post-bellum period saw his mother make a "pattern" for the sort of cotton dress goods she desired, the weaver following it faithfully. Threads of different colors were wrapped around a bit of cardboard or a flat piece of wood, the stripes—red, yellow, black, or blue—being of uniform width or varying to suit the fancy. When woven the cloth would indeed "fairly hurt the eyes."

Tin molds for making candles were used some years after the war. They were made in sizes to suit—to mold a half dozen or a dozen tallow candles at a time. A wick was run through each mold and fastened at both ends. At the top all were attached, so that every candle could be drawn out at once. The molten tallow would then be poured in, forming around the wicks. When the tallow had become hard the molds were heated slightly, when the candles could be pulled out easily.

Bread trays, bee gums of hollow logs, ax handles, ox yokes and bows, rolling pins, chairs, chests (makeshifts for trunks), water buckets, tubs, and churns were handmade of buckeye, cedar, hickory, and other woods. No doubt there are still hickory chairs in Tennessee made more than a century ago. Gourds sufficed for dippers, while a larger variety were used in the kitchen for holding salt, soft soap, brown sugar, and the like.

A relic of the old times was the horse block near the front gate of village or farmhouses. It was constructed for the ladies, who seldom rode in a carriage and never dreamed of an automobile. They would mount the horse from it if going visiting, while visiting guests would dismount upon it. Horseback-riding was popular as well as necessary if one were "going abroad," as even neighborhood visiting was spoken of. Riding man fashion was not in vogue even by the most hoidenish girl. Ladies were, as may be imagined, accomplished equestrians. Moreover, a country girl prized a new sidesaddle and riding skirt as much as a city girl would now prize a piano. Those of well-to-do parents were often provided with a good mount, usually a pacer. It was a delightful experience to see some village belle and her beau taking a ride, the former, adorable in her riding habit, putting her pacer to the limit, her escort keeping alongside on a galloping animal.

Other "luxuries," necessities, and fashions of "auld lang syne" were: Candle snuffers, casters, accordeons, picture albums, paper collars, dickeys (false shirt fronts), reticules, hoops, petticoats, bustles, chignons, sunbonnets with pasteboard stiffening, snuff boxes and hickory or althea toothbrushes, home remedies like horehound sirup and vermifuge made of boiled pink-root, knitting needles, yarn socks, breakfast shawls, nubias, comforts, hair nets, and hair oil for men.

But the old order has passed away. Not only buggies and carriages are common, but the automobile is no longer amazing. In town and hamlet the girl who "sets out" makes her début; "infairs" are receptions; "going abroad" is spending the week-end; the "party" or "frolic" has been turned into a function, and reference to color schemes, linen or kitchen showers, and progressive luncheons does not send the latter-day rural belle to the dictionary for light.

While from 1900 to 1910 the county lost 1,026 of its population, it has made remarkable progress. In 1914 it was out of debt, with a comfortable surplus ($6,000) in the hands of the trustee. Every part shows this substantial progress. In the Highlands old agricultural methods have given way to new, and thrift followed in spite of the inferiority of the soil compared with that in the Basin. Better homes and more comfortable living are decidedly apparent. A feature of that section is the great number of nurseries. It is estimated that the income from them will reach a quarter of a million dollars yearly.

In the Basin live stock and grain—"hog and hominy"—still hold the closest attention of the farmers. There are quite a number of fine farms with progressive owners. United States Marshal John W. Overall possesses about nine hundred acres, raising cattle on a large scale. Ed Simpson, near Alexandria, is widely known among breeders for his registered Hereford cattle.* Dr. T. J. Jackson, with about five hundred acres, devotes much time to cattle. Herschel Overall, with six hundred acres, sells annually a large number of mules, cattle, and hogs. There are stockmen who buy as many as two thousand suckling mules and raise them to maturity with profitable results. J. I. Banks, of Dry Creek, is regarded as one of the best beekeepers of the State. He makes a specialty of queens and has patrons throughout the Union. Rev. O. P. Barry, of Alexandria, besides doing a produce business of $200,000 annually, is a successful breeder of

---

*It may be remarked that Mr. Simpson served in Company H, Twelfth Regiment United States Volunteers, in the Philippines. Other young men from the county who took part in the war there were Gray Davis, Frank Colvert, George Bratten, Lewis Smith, Robert Givan, and Herbert L. Hale.

pure-bred hogs. The smaller farmers are touched with the spirit of progress also and contribute largely to the volume of business done by the six local banks. Under such conditions it is not to be wondered at that merchandising and other businesses succeed as never before.

The redemption of Pea Ridge strikingly illustrates the spirit of progress. Twenty-five years ago the wonder was if anything good could come out of this Nazareth. The years have replied. Pea Ridge is a long ridge extending from Clear Fork to Dry Creek eastward and to Short Mountain on the south, covering a territory from two to seven miles in width. It is level and ten or twelve miles in length. The land was covered with scrub oak, blackjack, and pine. For years the inhabitants made a scant living by selling rails, boards, hoop poles, baskets, charcoal, tar, whortleberries, chestnuts, and service berries. Here and there one made whisky. Tom Anderson, a Pea Ridge citizen of some humor, once observed that the people were "only a tribe of board makers." But after the timber showed indication of giving out the inhabitants began to till the soil in earnest. To their surprise, it proved quite productive. Orchards were planted, yielding abundantly. No finer vegetables can be grown anywhere. Large crops of corn meet the eyes of the traveler in season. It is really one of the best country sections in the county. The moral tone has been elevated also. There are schoolhouses, two churches, and a well-patronized general store kept by M. D. Herman.

The circulation of agricultural and other journals

has increased a thousandfold since the war. With the telephone (it is in the homes of even small farmers), better roads, lighter vehicles, good churches and schools, and the rural service, the isolation which was once noticeable is now negligible. The split-oak chair, corded bedstead, and homemade clothing are rarely seen. The fiddle and dulcimer have been banished for the phonograph and piano. These material means influence the mental life, and both material and mental changes act and react on the spiritual life for the better. But it will be well if the swing toward the commercial side does not go too far, allowing manhood to decay while wealth accumulates.

www.ingramcontent.com/pod-product-compliance
Lightning Source LLC
Chambersburg PA
CBHW020645300426
44112CB00007B/243